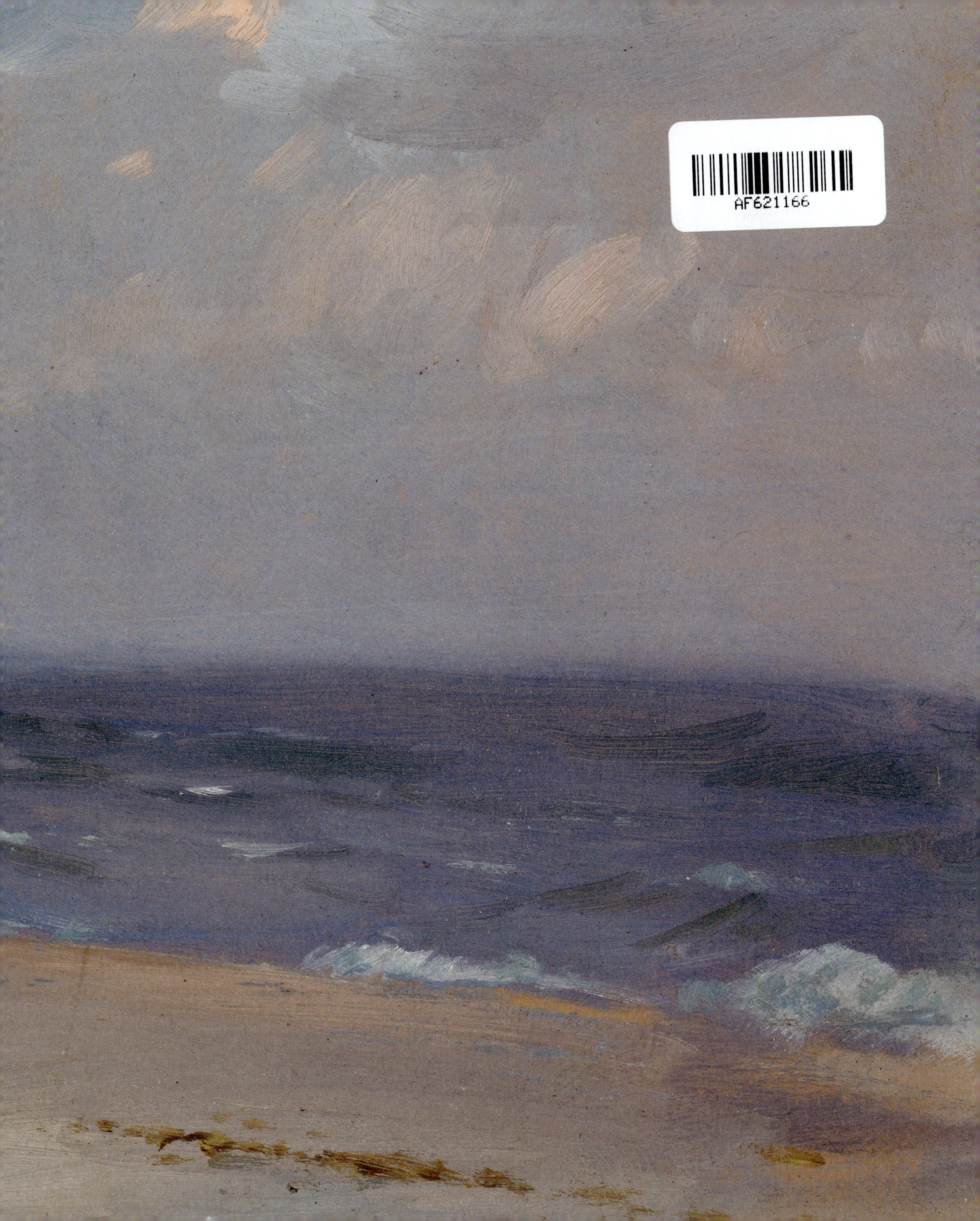

ANNA ANCHER

PAINTING LIGHT

DULWICH
PICTURE
GALLERY

First published in Great Britain
in 2025 by Dulwich Picture Gallery
on the occasion of the exhibition
Anna Ancher: Painting Light,
4 November 2025–8 March 2026.

This exhibition is created in special partnership with Skagens Museum. Our thanks to the staff of the Museum, especially Lisette Vind Ebbesen, Mette Harbo Lehmann and Mette Bøgh Jensen. Thank you also to Her Excellency Kristina Miskowiak Beckvard Danish Ambassador to the United Kingdom, and Lone Britt Christensen.

THE GENEROUS LENDERS
Skagens Museum
SMK, National Gallery of Denmark
The Hirschsprung Collection
Sandi Toksvig

IN PARTNERSHIP WITH
Skagens Museum

SKAGENS MUSEUM

SUPPORTERS

Exhibition Catalogue

The Elizabeth Cayzer Charitable Trust

NY CARLSBERG FONDET
NEW CARLSBERG FOUNDATION

Exhibition

The Hoffmann and Husman Foundation

The Topinambour Trust

MINISTRY OF FOREIGN AFFAIRS OF DENMARK

Kultur MINISTERIET

BECKETT-FONDEN

JORCK's FOND
Konsul George Jorck og Hustru Emma Jorck's Fond

KNUD HØJGAARDS FOND
– GRUNDLAGT 1944 –

VisitDenmark

Digital Exhibition Guide

Bloomberg Connects

In Partnership with

Embassy of Denmark in the United Kingdom

EMBASSY OF DENMARK
London

This exhibition has been made possible by the provision of Government Indemnity. Dulwich Picture Gallery would like to thank HM Government for providing Government Indemnity and the Department for Culture, Media and Sport and Arts Council England for arranging the indemnity.

Department for Culture, Media & Sport

With thanks to all members of the Patrons and Friends of Dulwich Picture Gallery

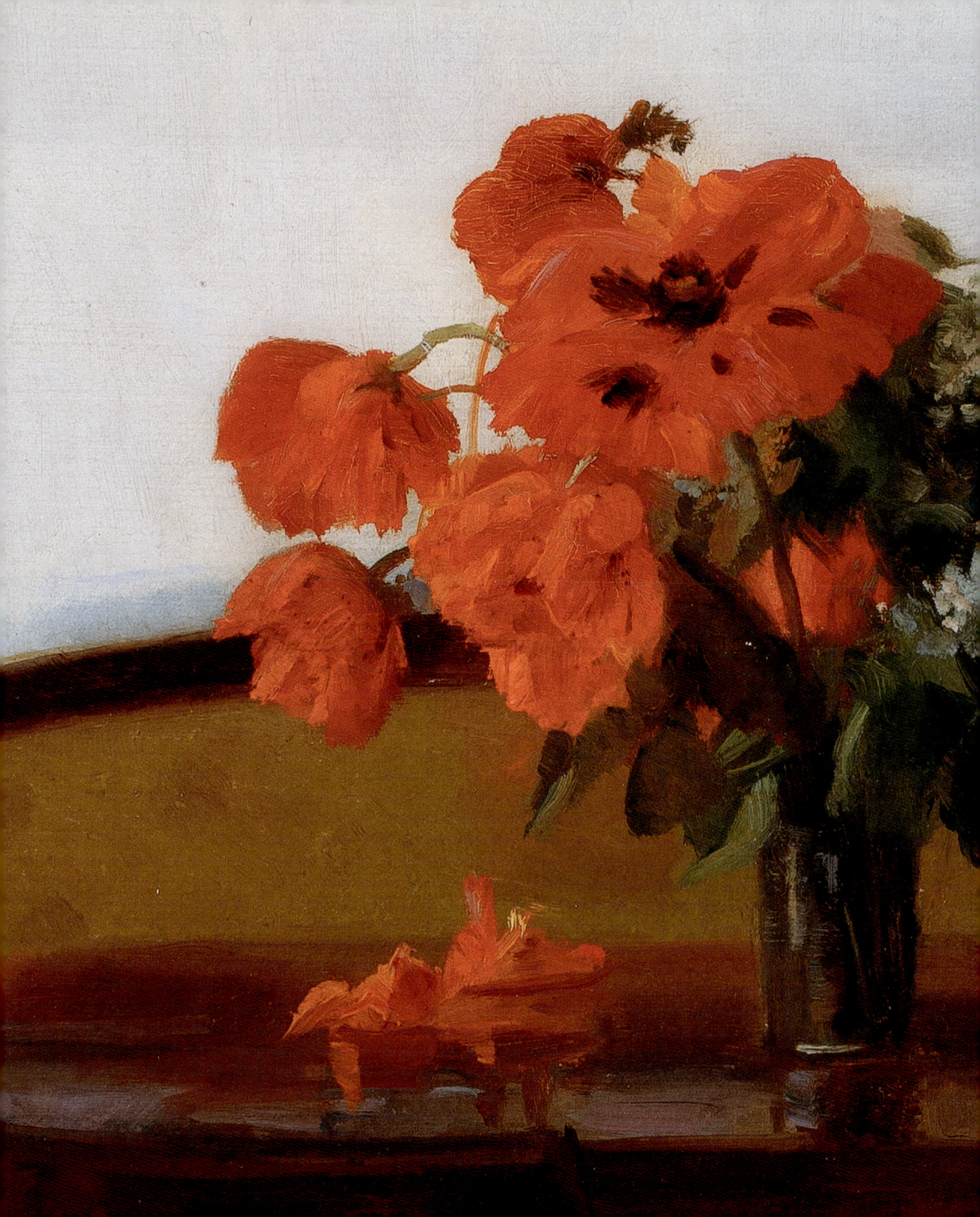

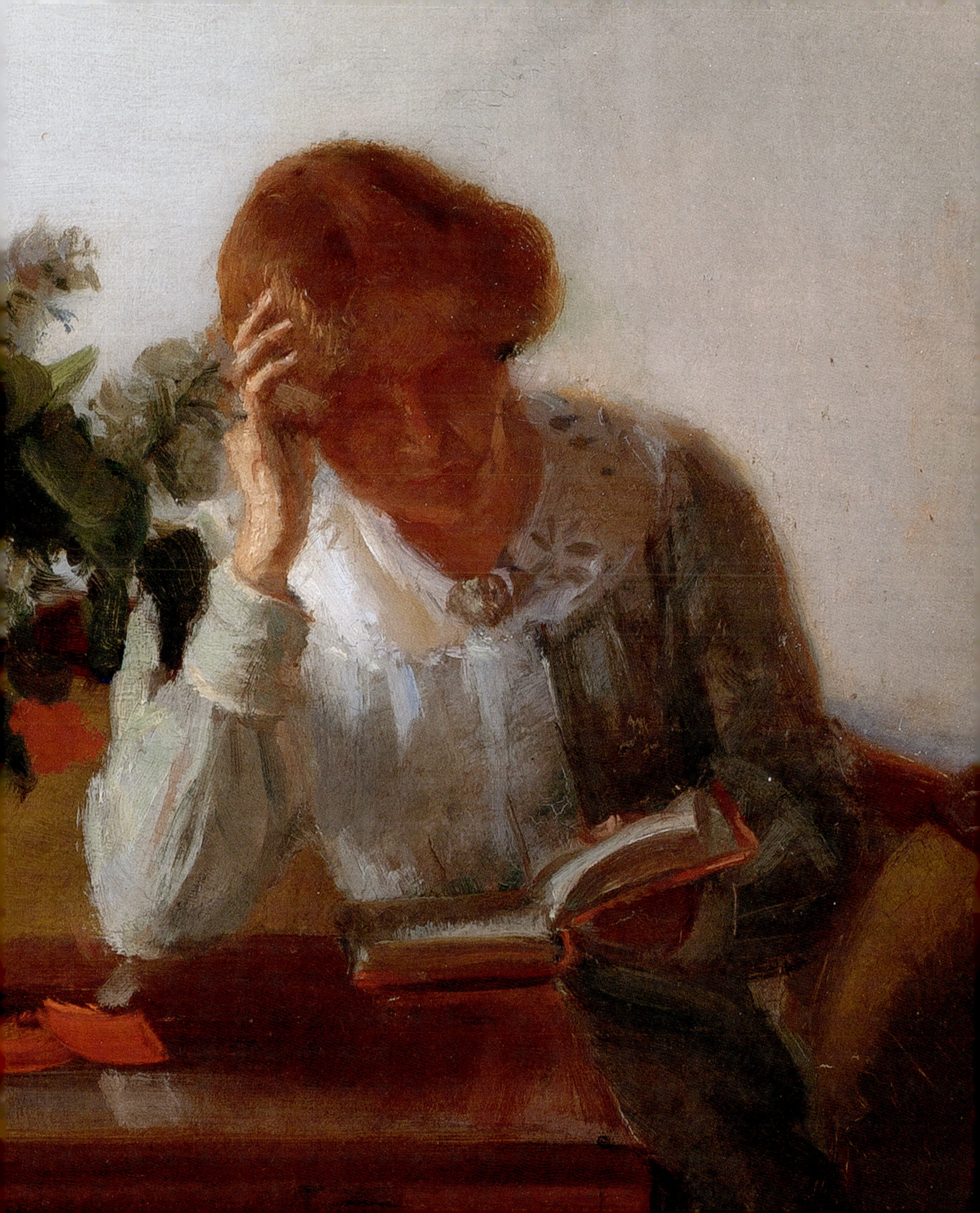

Foreword

"The sea will drum in my ears. The white petals will be darkened with sea water. They will float for a moment and then sink. Rolling me over the waves will shoulder me under. Everything falls in a tremendous shower, dissolving me."

Virginia Woolf, *The Waves*, 1931

Anna Ancher's work anchors her in the land of her roots: Skagen, where two seas collide, a place to awaken creativity. By engaging, through dreamlike colours, with the rhythm and repetition of human experience, Ancher reminds us how time continually ebbs and flows, rolling us over like the sea.

Anna Ancher: Painting Light has been a joyful endeavour thanks to the exceptional support of many people. Our partners, Skagens Museum have shown unmitigated enthusiasm and unparalleled generosity in sharing their masterpieces. Institutional friendships such as these are precious. We are indebted to Lisette Vind Ebbesen for her inspiring leadership and to Mette Harbo Lehmann and Mette Bøgh Jensen for their profound knowledge.

Our gratitude also to the SMK, National Gallery of Denmark and The Hirschsprung Collection for lending their artworks. Particular thanks to Astrid La Cour, Karoline Hvalsøe, Camilla Klitgaard Laursen and Karina Lykke Grand.

Helen Hillyard devised this project and has curated it with characteristic passion, skill and care. Helen and Mette's exquisite words in this book capture Anna Ancher's world. Helen extends her thanks to Mads Neumann and Lars Neumann for fact checking, proof-reading and translating, and to MaryAnne Stevens for her advice. Sandra Zellmer's design for this book, and Annabel Dalziel's exhibition design, mirror the elegance of their subject. Thanks also to acapmedia, Nicole Ryder, Patina Art Collection Care Ltd, Constantine Ltd, Andy Grant, David Arkell and Susan Ghosh. The Dulwich Picture Gallery team consistently delivers creative projects of the highest quality. Particular thanks to Imogen Lyons, Alexander Moore, Bryony Haffner, Sophie James, Jane Findlay, Felicity Sutherland, Lucy West, Alice Carr-Archer, Sara Juel Andersen and Yayra Dziworshie Soda.

We are honoured that Her Excellency Kristina Miskowiak Beckvard, Danish Ambassador to the United Kingdom, officially opened this exhibition. Thanks to the Embassy of Denmark, The Danish Ministry of Foreign Affairs and The Danish Ministry of Culture for their support, and to Lone Britt Christensen, Cultural Attaché, for being our guiding light throughout the planning and delivery of this project.

The Elizabeth Cayzer Charitable Trust has supported this beautiful publication. Special thanks to Elizabeth Cayzer for her invaluable academic insights, impeccable discernment and dedicated patronage. This publication is also supported by the New Carlsberg Foundation with thanks to Michael Thouber and colleagues.

Heartfelt thanks also to The Hoffmann and Husman Foundation, Beckett-Fonden, Jorck's Fond, Knud Højgaards Fond, Visit Denmark, and Glenn and Barbara Wellman.

A few years ago, I was fortunate to hear a powerful speech by Sandi Toksvig OBE. Afterwards, I thanked her for her call-to-action to get female artists 'out of museum basements'. She complimented Dulwich Picture Gallery's track record of putting trailblazing women in the spotlight with shows from Tove Jansson to Berthe Morisot. Huge thanks to Sandi and Debbie Toksvig for helping us to shape this initiative and for sharing works from their own collection of hitherto overlooked women artists.

As Sandi Toksvig says on the Bloomberg Connects App that accompanies this exhibition: "Skagen... is the northernmost tip of the Danish mainland and the light is magnificent. It is as if everything in the world comes into sharper focus and briefly we might all long to paint." Fortunately for us all, Anna Ancher did just that.

Jennifer Scott
Director, Dulwich Picture Gallery, London

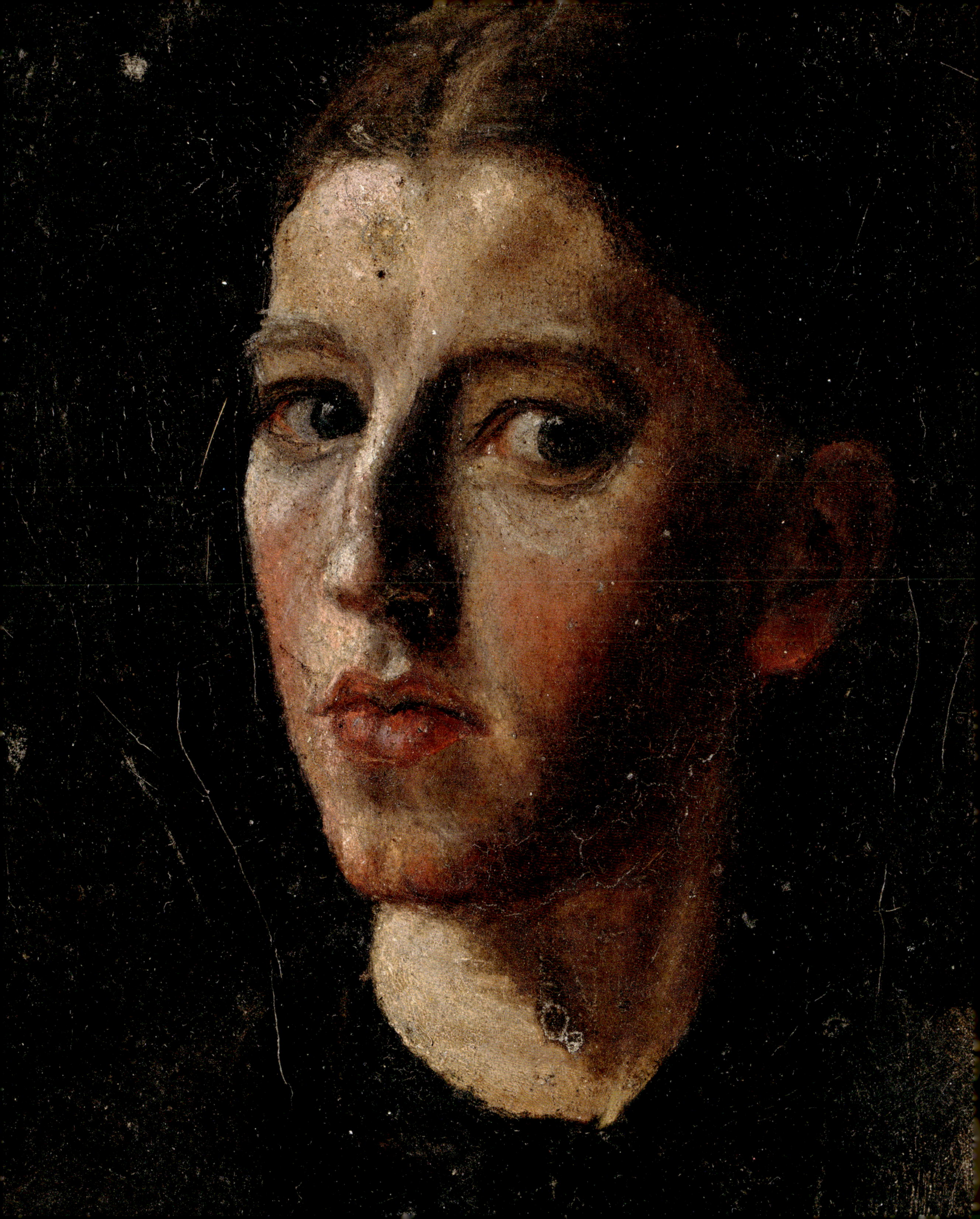

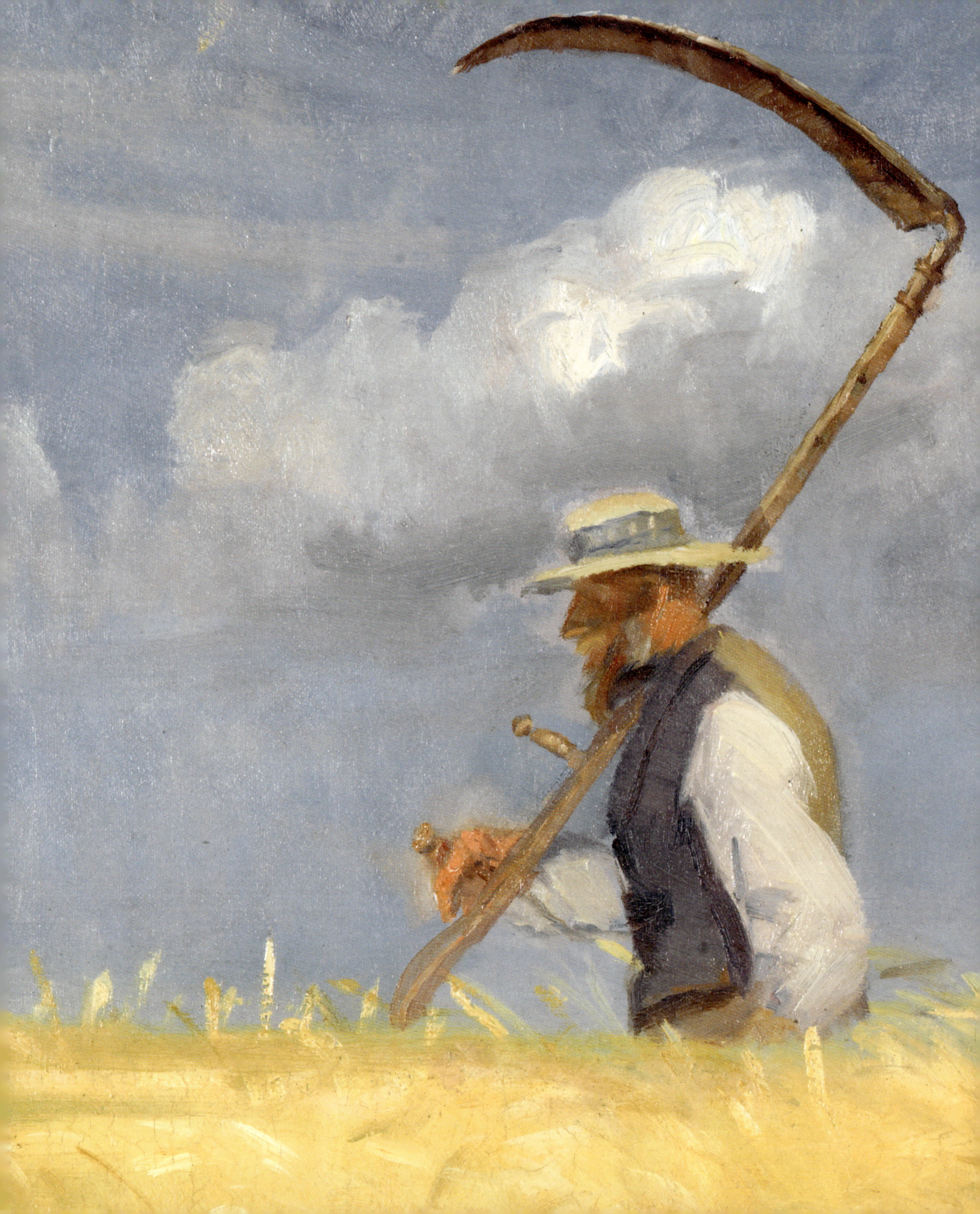

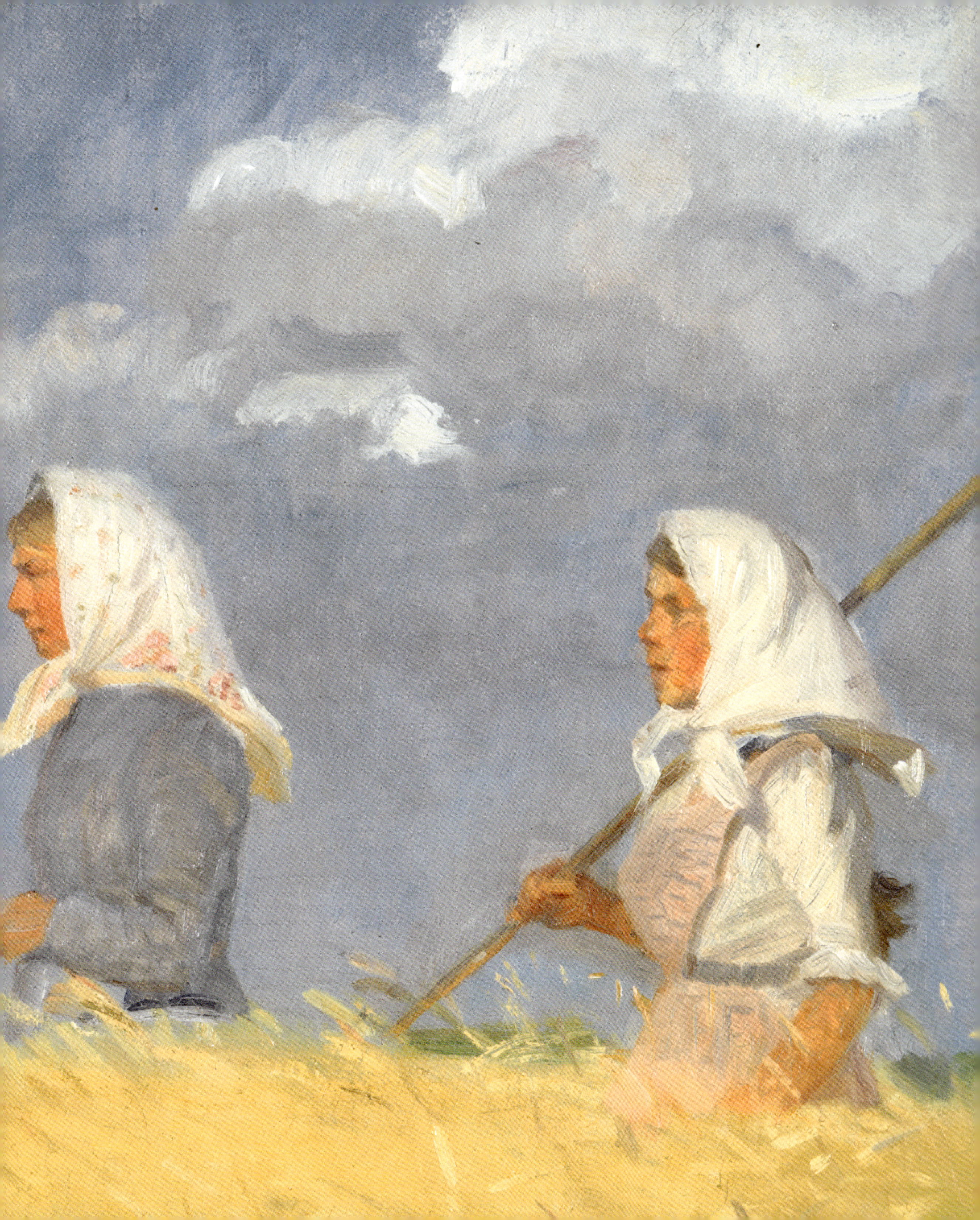

Timeline

ANNA ANCHER

1859
Born Anna Kirstine Brøndum, in Skagen, a seaside town at the northernmost point of Denmark.

1874
Meets the artist Michael Ancher (1849–1927), her future husband, for the first time when he travels to Skagen to seek inspiration and new subjects for his art.

1875
Enrols in Vilhelm Kyhn's (1819–1903) drawing and painting school for women in Copenhagen. Ancher takes classes at the school for three winters.

1880
Marries Michael in Skagen Church.

Formally debuts as an artist, exhibiting at the Charlottenborg salon in Copenhagen, where she presents *Old Man Whittling Sticks* [cat. 2]. Ancher exhibits every year at the salon from 1880 to 1935, except 1908 and 1928.

1882
The artist and her husband travel to Berlin, Dresden, Vienna and Munich, where they spend time visiting museums and seeing art.

1883
The couple's only child, Helga Ancher (1883–1964), is born. She later becomes an artist, like her parents.

1885
Travels to Paris with Michael for the first time to experience the Salon of contemporary art and the international exhibition at Galerie Georges Petit.

SKAGEN, DENMARK AND BEYOND

1859
Danish author Hans Christian Andersen (1805–1875) travels to Skagen, where he stays at Brøndum's Hotel, which is owned by Anna Ancher's parents. His visit inspires him to write a travelogue about the town, as well as *A Story from the Dunes* (1860).

1862
The Swedish brig *Daphne* is wrecked off Skagen north beach. Eight Skagen fishermen drown attempting to save the crew.

1864
Second Schleswig War commences when Prussian and Austrian forces cross the border into the Danish territory of Schleswig. The war ends after nearly nine months with a Prussian-Austrian victory and significant territorial losses for Denmark at its southern border.

1872
Two key artists of what would later become the Skagen artist colony, Frits Thaulow (1847–1906) and Holger Drachmann (1846–1908), visit Skagen for the first time.

1874
The first impressionist exhibition opens at the studio of the photographer Nadar on the Boulevard des Capucines, Paris, showing works by Claude Monet (1840–1926), Pierre-Auguste Renoir (1841–1919), Edgar Degas (1834–1917), Berthe Morisot (1841–95) and Paul Cezanne (1839–1906).

1879
The brewer and art collector Carl Jacobsen (1842–1914) shows his collection of French art at the spring exhibition at Charlottenborg in Copenhagen.

1883
Artists visiting Skagen start to decorate the dining room of Brøndum's Hotel with portraits of each other, as well as scenes of Skagen life. This practice was influenced by other artist colonies in Europe.

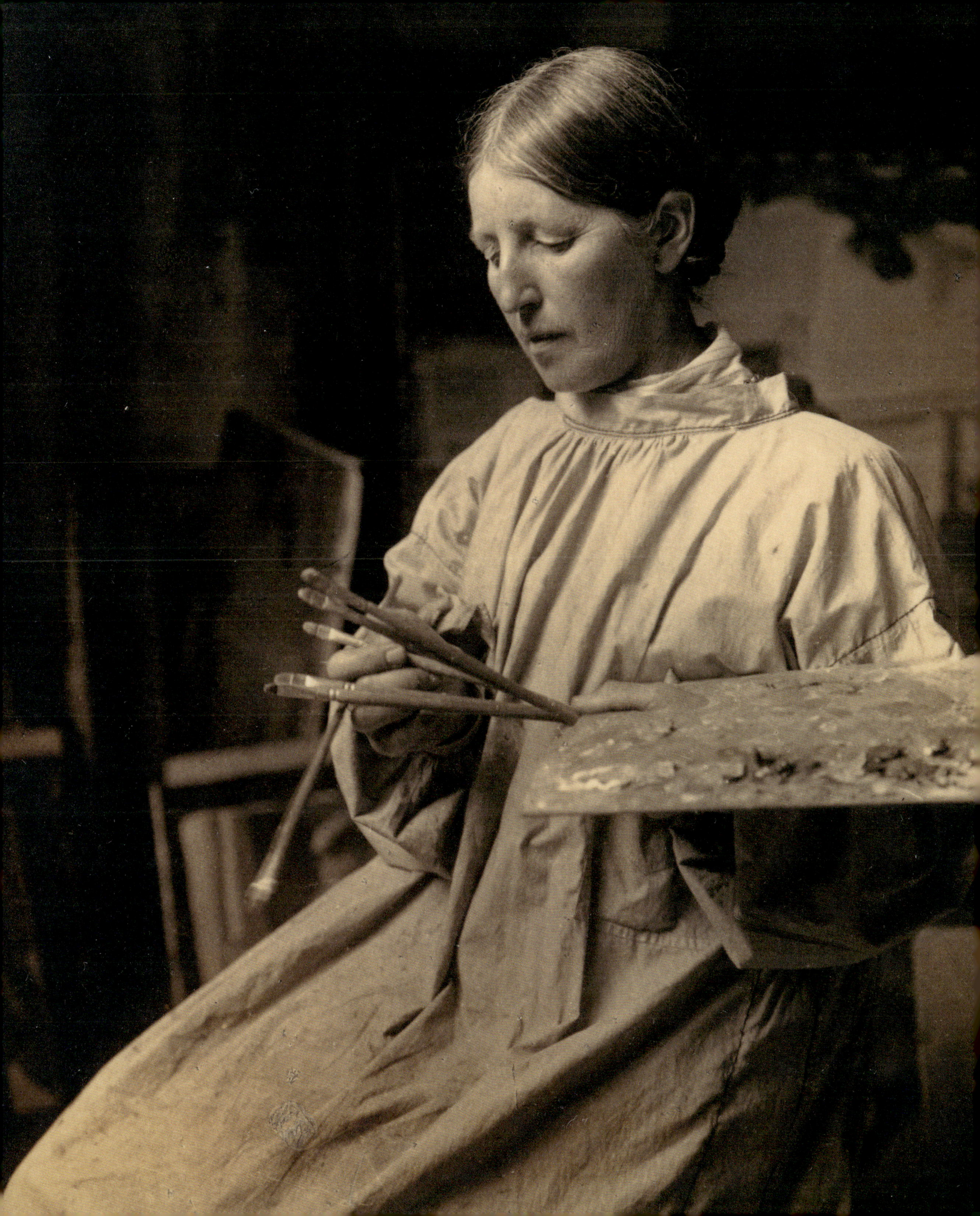

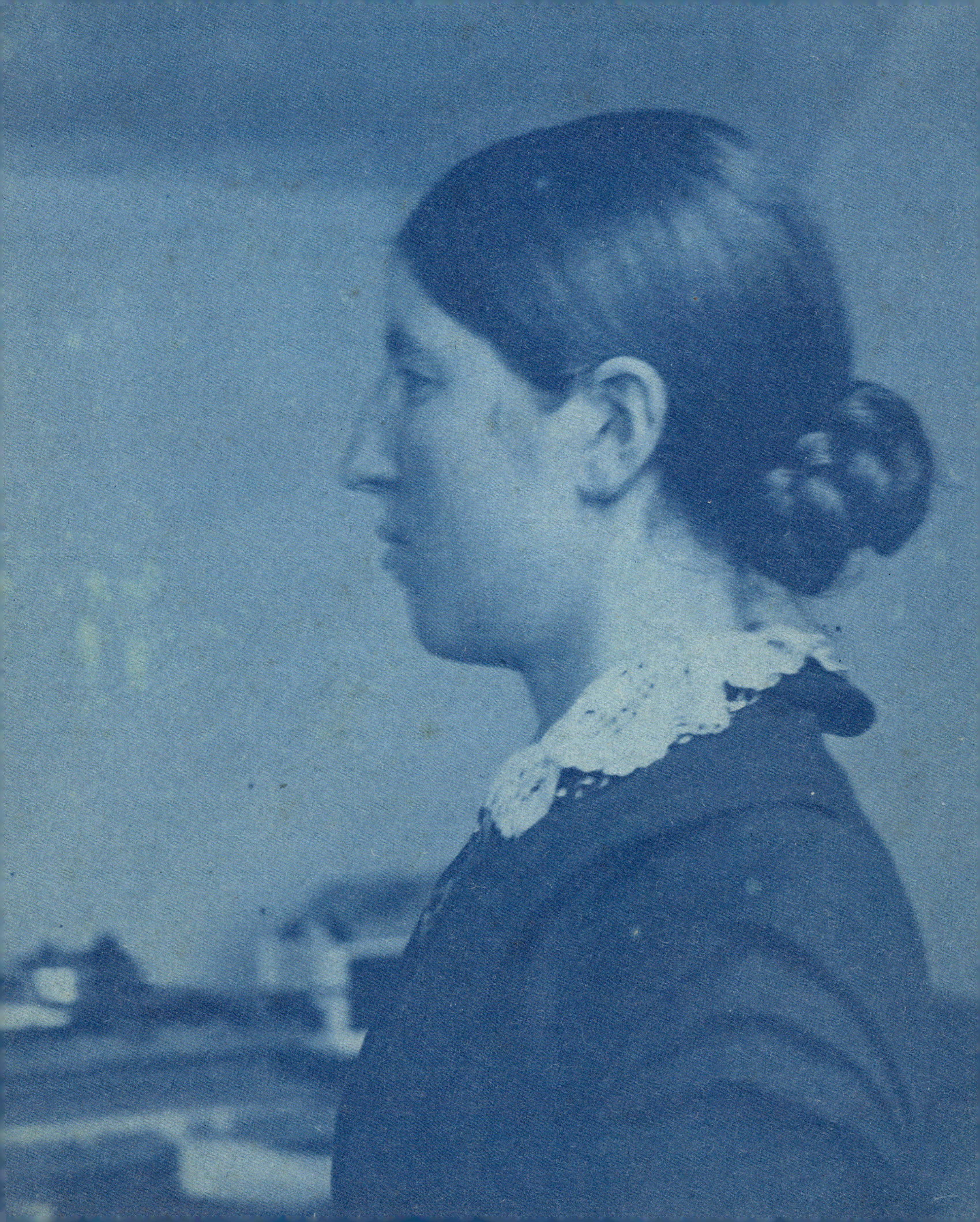

1889
The couple return to Paris for a longer period, settling there for six months. There they participate in the Exposition Universelle and visit various exhibitions in the city. Ancher enrols in the art school of Alfred Philippe Roll (1846–1919) under Pierre Puvis de Chavannes (1824–98).

1891
The Royal Picture Gallery in Copenhagen (now SMK, National Gallery of Denmark) buys Ancher's painting *A Funeral*.

1895
The Women's Exhibition in Copenhagen opens, inspired by an exhibition held at the World's Fair in Chicago in 1893. Ancher contributes works and sits on the committee for visual arts for the Women's Exhibition.

1907
Travels to London for an exhibition of works by Danish painters at the Guildhall Art Gallery, where *The Maid in the Kitchen* [cat. 4] is exhibited.

1916
Ancher's mother, Ane Brøndum, dies. She depicts her mother on her deathbed [cat. 32].

1927
Michael dies in Skagen.

1928
Skagens Museum opens at its present site, Ancher holds a board position.

1935
Anna Ancher dies in Skagen.

1888
The Royal Danish Academy of Fine Art opens a school for women at a separate premises and admits female artists for the first time. The women's school was not fully incorporated into the Royal Academy until 1908.

1889
The artist and art historian Karl Madsen (1855–1938), a friend of the Anchers, organises an exhibition of French and Nordic art in Copenhagen. The exhibition includes Paul Gauguin's (1848–1943) collection of impressionist art, which had been left to his Danish wife, Mette (1850–1920).

Exposition Universelle opens in Paris. The Eiffel Tower is erected for the Exposition.

The Volpini exhibition, showing works by Paul Gauguin, is held at the Café des Arts on the Champ de Mars, Paris.

1890
Skagen railway line opens, connecting Skagen with Frederikshavn and so providing transport links to the rest of Denmark. Before the Skagen railway line, the journey from Frederikshavn was usually made by horse-drawn carriage along the shore. Tourism to Skagen increases throughout the 1890s.

1908
Skagens Museum is founded at the initiative of the Skagen artists. Works are initially exhibited in the late Peder Severin Krøyer's house from 1911. Later, a museum building is constructed, opening in 1928.

1914
First World War commences, Denmark remains neutral.

1915
Danish women gain the right to vote. Due to World War I, this does not come into effect until the 1918 election.

1920
Following the end of First World War, and according to the terms of the Treaty of Versailles, plebiscites are held to determine the allegiance of Schleswig, and northern Schleswig is reunified with Denmark.

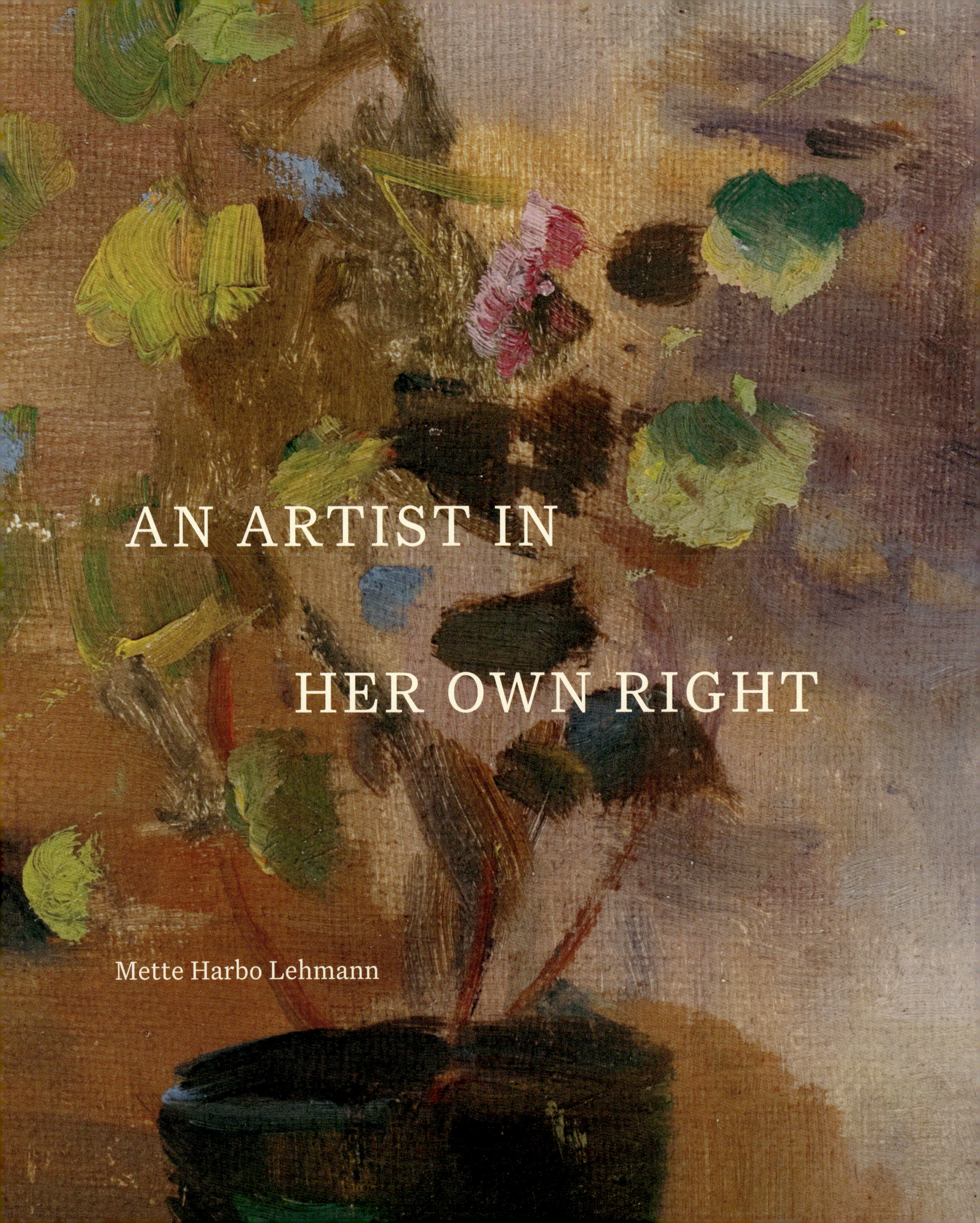

AN ARTIST IN HER OWN RIGHT

Mette Harbo Lehmann

Among the international painters who flocked to the art colony in Skagen during the 1880s and 1890s, Anna Ancher was the only one not only from Denmark but actually born in this small, remote fishing village. She was a painter of the Danish 'Modern Breakthrough' and even though she did not have the same access to education as her male peers, she achieved almost instant success, and maintained it throughout her career. One wonders if her success would have been possible without the help and support of the male painters in the artist colony, including her husband, or whether she could have achieved it independently of – or without being associated with – the label of this group of artists. The situation for female artists at the turn of the nineteenth century is a factor to consider, but so is artistic quality, talent and self-confidence.

Cat. 1
Anna Ancher
Self-Portrait, c. 1879
Oil on canvas,
18.8 × 11.6 cm
Skagens Museum

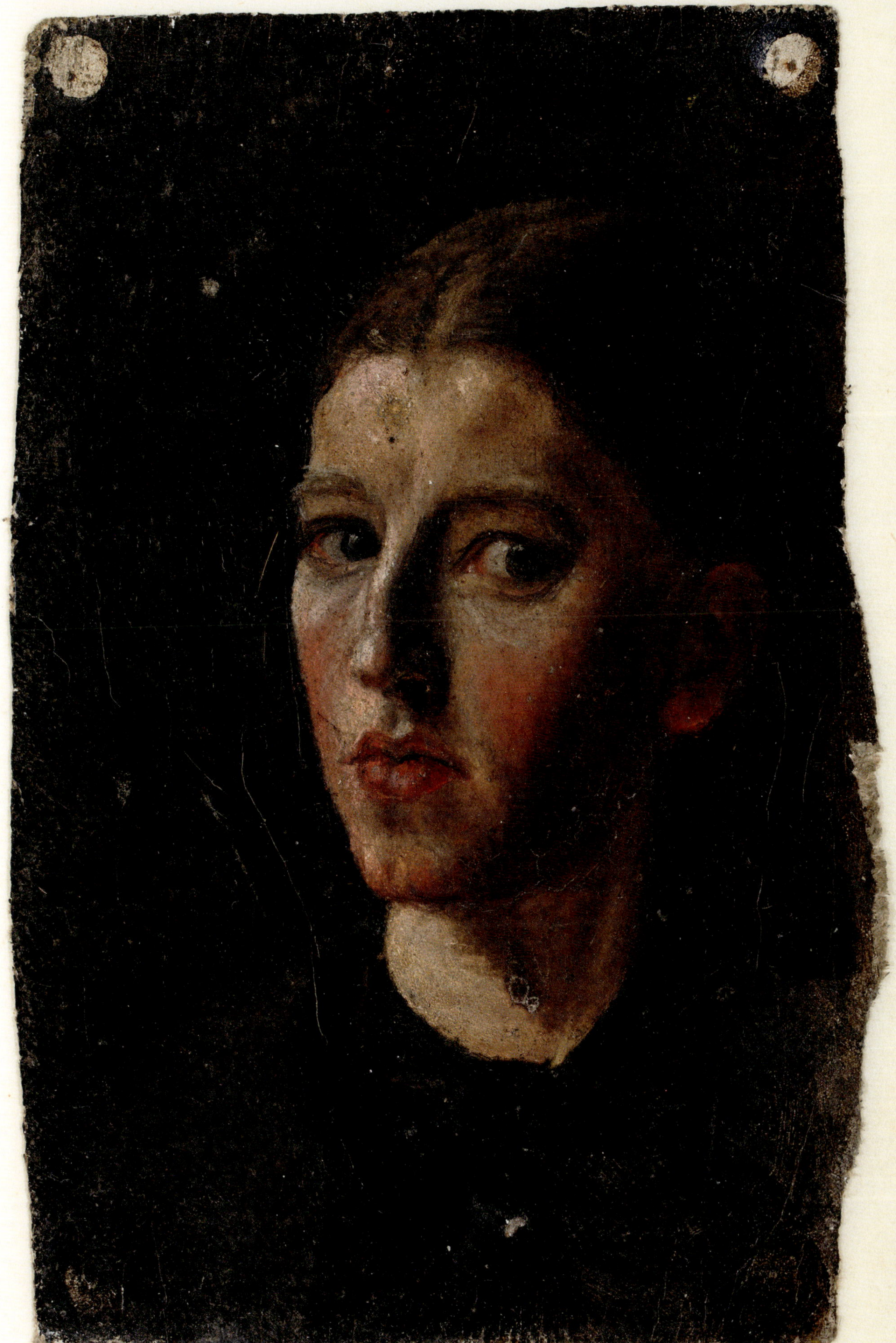

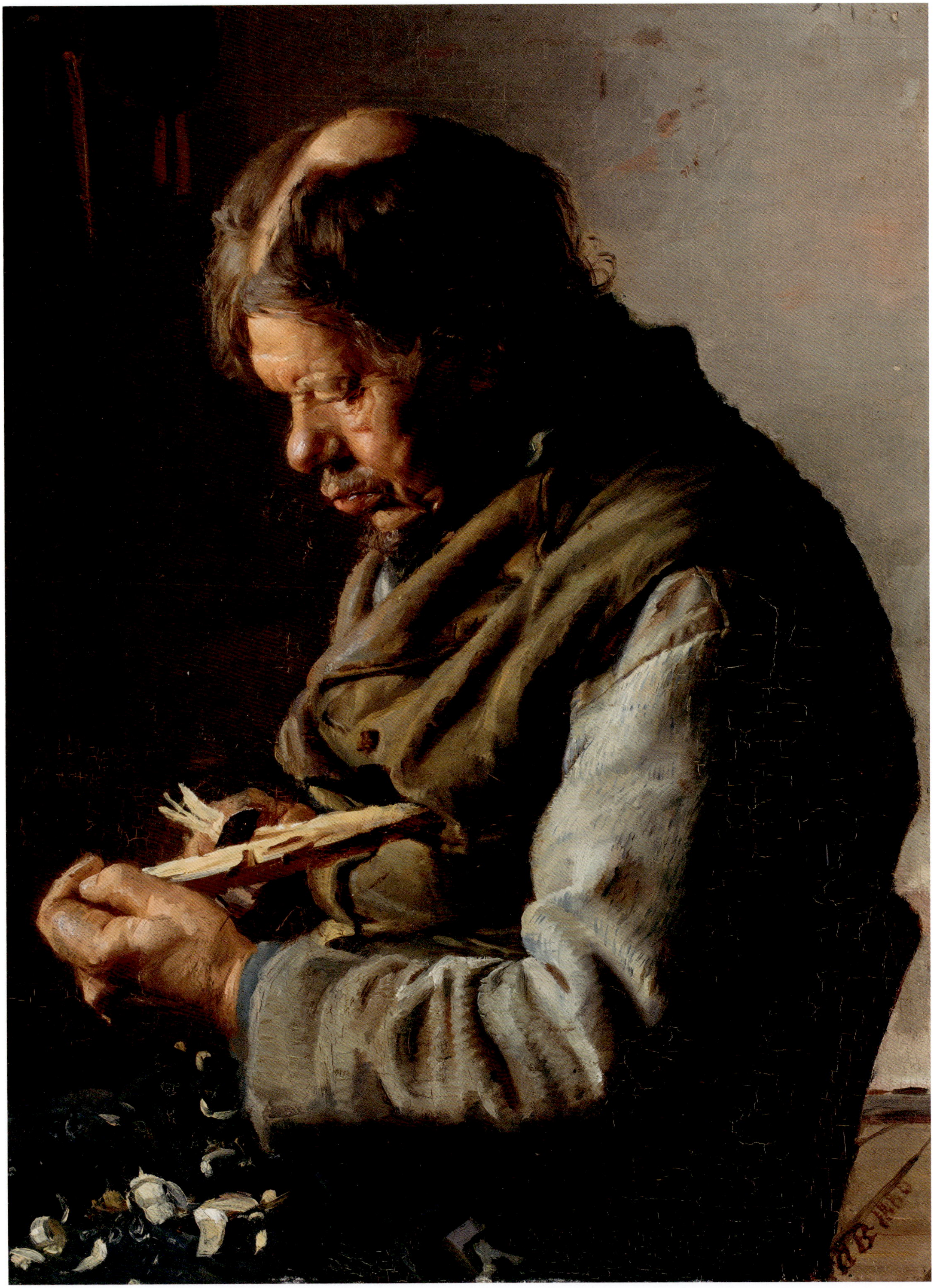

Anna Ancher and the Artist Colony

Anna Ancher (née Brøndum, 1859–1935) was, without comparison, the greatest female artist in Denmark at the end of the nineteenth century. This was despite the odds being against her from the start. She was born in a remote province and, of course, was a woman. She was born into a traditional family where it was common for men to take care of work while women managed the house and children. As such, she would have been expected to marry and live as her husband's wife. However, one might question how traditional her family truly was, especially given her mother's support of her career.

Anna Brøndum was the fifth of six siblings, and her parents owned the only hotel, Brøndum's, in the fishing village of Skagen at the remote northernmost point of Denmark. It was a middle-class home and her mother, Ane Brøndum (1826–1916), was deeply committed to the 'Home Mission', a Christian movement that had recently swept across the country. Her father, on the other hand, left little trace in history, though he lived until she was an adult.

Anna Brøndum was still a child, aged 12, when the first painters of what would become the Skagen artist colony arrived in 1872. These were the Norwegian painter Frits Thaulow (1847–1906) and the Danish painter, and later renowned poet, Holger Drachmann (1846–1908). Other artists soon followed in their footsteps. They stayed at Brøndum's Hotel, and even this first year, Anna Brøndum took interest in the studies the two artists hung on the walls of the hotel.[1] Later, she recalled in an interview that it was the arrival of Danish artist Karl Madsen (1855–1938), who became a lifelong friend, and the Norwegian artist Christian Skredsvig (1854–1924) in Skagen in 1873, that sparked her own interest in painting.[2]

In 1874, the young Danish painter Michael Ancher (1849–1927) travelled from Copenhagen to Skagen to find inspiration and new subjects for his art. He became friends with the young girl that turned 15 that August. He and his artist friends, among them Madsen, had been instructing her and her two cousins in drawing.[3] When he returned the year after, they began courting. Michael Ancher stayed in Skagen until January 1875. Back in Copenhagen, he bought her a pochade box as he had promised her and wrote in a letter: 'Now be diligent about drawing and let it be your goal to become a painter, and everything will most likely go well.'[4] Already at this point, it seems that the young Anna Brøndum had the support of her future husband and the encouragement of the artists who came to Skagen. Michael Ancher's support did not appear to be motivated by superficial charm or hopes of a summer fling but seemed more fundamental. She was also supported by her mother, who had never wished for her children to marry.[5] Having been unhappy in her own marriage, her mother did not encourage her children to follow her path. This fact was likely more important for Anna Brøndum's profession than often assumed, as forging an artistic career in a patriarchal society without being married would have posed significant challenges. Perhaps by focusing on a career, and with the family supporting each other, it became possible to navigate the constraints of society and create opportunities that might otherwise have been out of reach. None of her siblings ever started their own families; as three of them, like their mother, worked at the hotel, Anna Ancher could always turn to them for help.

After her Confirmation in the autumn of 1875, Anna Brøndum went to Copenhagen to study at the painter Vilhelm Kyhn's (1819–1903) private school of drawing

Cat. 2
Old Man Whittling Sticks, 1880
Oil on panel
39 × 29.2 cm
Skagens Museum

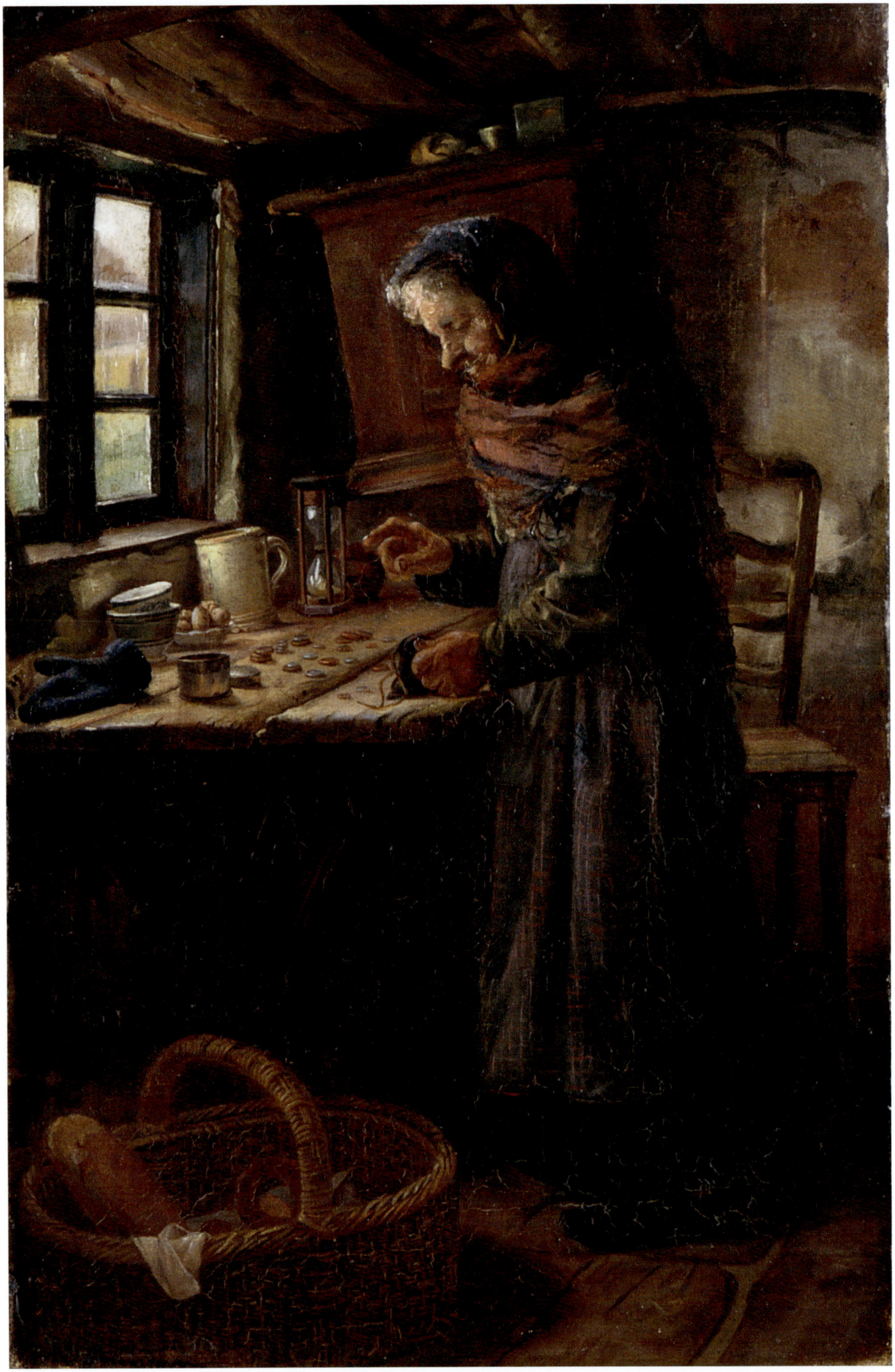

and painting for women. The Royal Danish Art Academy in Copenhagen did not accept female students, so attending the private studios of renowned painters was the best artistic education women could receive. Soon after Anna's arrival in Copenhagen, her mother wrote: 'for future, you must write and say what you need. Nothing is dearer to me than to pay for your learning; you know that'.[6] Anna Brøndum attended the school for three winter seasons. In the summers, she returned home to Skagen, where she had conversations with the travelling painters and received unofficial drawing lessons from some of them.

In the autumn of 1877, Anna Brøndum and Michael Ancher were engaged. In December 1878, she exhibited for the first time in a sales exhibition in Copenhagen, and again the following year. However, her formal debut as an artist was at the spring exhibition at Charlottenborg, Copenhagen, in 1880, where she presented *Old Man Whittling Sticks*, signing her paintings 'A.B.' [cat. 2].[7] Her first reviews were positive, praising her painting for its strong realist qualities, an air of truth and calm, and her high skill, describing her as a promising young artist.[8] Her only known self-portrait is from these years, and although it is small in size, it also shows a self-confident young artist [cat. 1].

The artist colony in Skagen developed significantly in those years, and in 1879 several painters arrived with fresh inspiration from France. Among the lively company were Thaulow, Madsen, Drachmann, the Norwegian artist Christian Krohg (1852–1925), the Swedish artist Wilhelm von Gegerfelt (1844–1920), and the French artist Émile Barau (1851–1930), who came with Gegerfelt.[9] As Michael Ancher was delayed and only arrived in Skagen in October, letters from Anna Brøndum to him reveal that she was being influenced by the other artists and their enthusiasm for the exciting new direction in art. She tried to encourage him to adopt this new perspective.[10] In a small painting from that year, one can see one of the poor members of the local community, Stine Bollerhus, counting the small coins she had earned from selling the baker's bread around town [cat. 3]. The new direction in Danish art was naturalism. The artists sought to portray nature and people with greater truthfulness and honesty in their paintings. This development was also inspired by the Danish author and critic Georg Brandes (1842–1927) who, like the Danish artist Peder Severin Krøyer (1851–1909), became associated with the Skagen painters. In this way, the artist colony in Skagen played a significant role in Denmark's 'Modern Breakthrough' from the beginning of the 1880s.

Challenging Expectations: Navigating Success in a Male-Dominated World

After their wedding in Skagen on 18 August 1880 – coinciding with Anna's twenty-first birthday – Anna and Michael Ancher began their life together in Skagen. For a female artist in Denmark during this period, marriage often meant giving up her career to devote herself to managing the household and raising a family.[11] However, Anna Ancher defied these expectations. Without rebellion or confrontation, she continued painting and exhibiting. How was this possible? What made the Anchers' relationship different? There are visible indications of the dynamic in their marriage and the kind of home they created. The painting *Judgement of a Day's Work* depicts the young artist couple in their living room, assessing the day's work together [fig. 1]. They are portrayed as equals, engaged in conversation with equally important voices. Anna Ancher, relaxed and leaning

Cat. 3
Stine Bollerhus Counts the Money Earned Selling Bread, 1879
Oil on canvas
52.7 × 35.5 cm
Skagens Museum

back in the armchair, exudes authority. In this way, the painting appears to be a subtle statement recognising her as an artist. To underline this point, the work was created collaboratively and signed by both of them.

As a newlywed, motherhood loomed as a potential obstacle for Ancher's career. For a talented artist of her time, who happened to be a woman, it was often assumed that motherhood would overshadow artistic ambitions. What Ancher herself thought about this is lost to us today, but there is no reason to believe she did not look forward to becoming a mother. During her pregnancy, Anna and Michael Ancher seized the opportunity to create a provocative statement through art. Michael Ancher painted the pregnant Ancher in the doorway, a bold and controversial work for its time [fig. 2]. The large painting depicted Ancher as obviously pregnant – a contemporary and unapologetic representation of the pregnant body, which at the time was an all-too-clear reference to the sexual act that had preceded it. Therefore, it was an unusual motif to display at the Copenhagen salon, sparking debate as the couple likely anticipated. The Danish writer Henrik Pontoppidan (1857–1943), who later won the Nobel Prize in Literature, wrote to Michael Ancher before the painting was exhibited:

> I am now looking forwards to the spring exhibition. I hope a lot of good things will appear there. At least I know that from your hand something valuable will come; because you still intend to send your wife's portrait, don't you? For God's sake, don't let yourself be deterred from it by pedants who may have had audience with you.[12]

This shows that Ancher let herself become visible in the ongoing debates of her time, albeit in her own quiet way. However, the couple received support from their artist friends, as evidenced by a letter from Peder Severin Krøyer to Michael Ancher after the exhibition opened. In the letter, Krøyer praised the painting and wrote: 'It's comical that it offends the audience, especially the female audience, it offends their "feelings of decency", isn't it lovely?'[13] At the birth of Ancher's first and only child, Helga Ancher (1883–1964), who became a painter like her parents, her former teacher Kyhn sent her a present accompanied by a letter. In it, he suggested she should now launch her pochade box into the sea, implying she should give up all artistic ambitions and dedicate herself entirely to motherhood. The letter itself is lost, which is perhaps not surprising, but it is known from a lengthy quotation included in an indignant letter from Michael Ancher to the free-spirited Georg Brandes.[14] Michael Ancher was furious, expressing his outrage at length. Fortunately, Ancher simply continued painting while ensuring that their daughter was well cared for – by herself, by Michael Ancher, and by her mother and sisters.

In 1885, Anna and Michael Ancher embarked on their first trip to Paris to experience the huge Salon of contemporary art and the smaller international exhibition at Galerie Georges Petit. They had previously visited Vienna in 1882, where Ancher had immersed herself in Dutch seventeenth-century art, which had already begun to influence her paintings alongside inspiration from France. During these travels, she connected with other painters. In Vienna, the couple met Krøyer for the first time. He would go on to become a close friend, a frequent guest in Skagen, and a part of the artist colony later the same year. In Paris, the Anchers became familiar with French art and

Fig. 1
Anna and Michael Ancher,
Judgement of a Day's Work, 1883
Oil on canvas
85.5 × 103 cm
Depositum at Skagens Museum from the National Gallery of Denmark

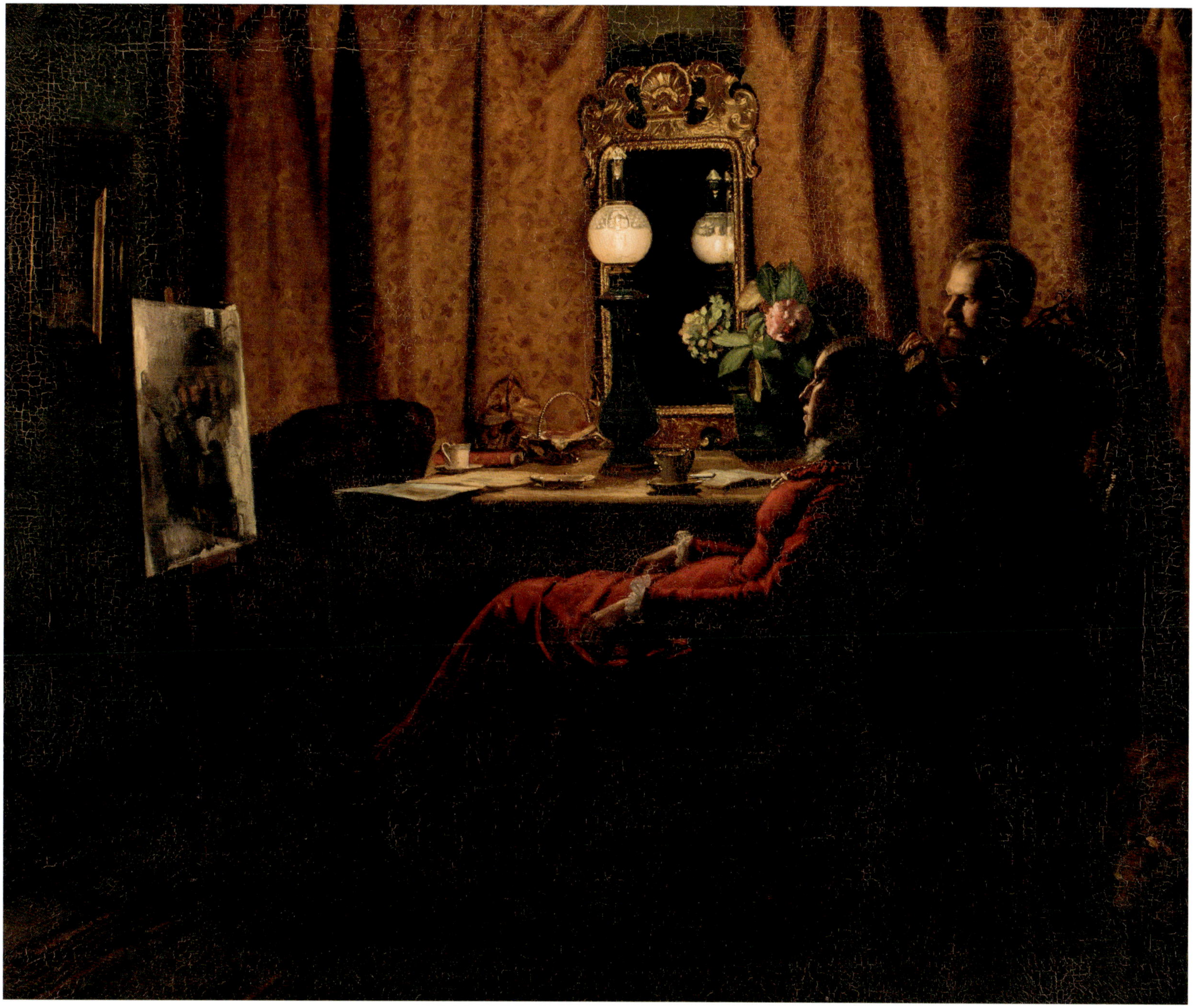

During her pregnancy, Anna and Michael Ancher seized the opportunity to create a provocative statement through art.

Fig. 2
Michael Ancher,
Anna Ancher Standing in the Doorway. Study for 'Portrait of My Wife', 1883
Oil on canvas
103.2 × 91.1 cm
Skagens Museum

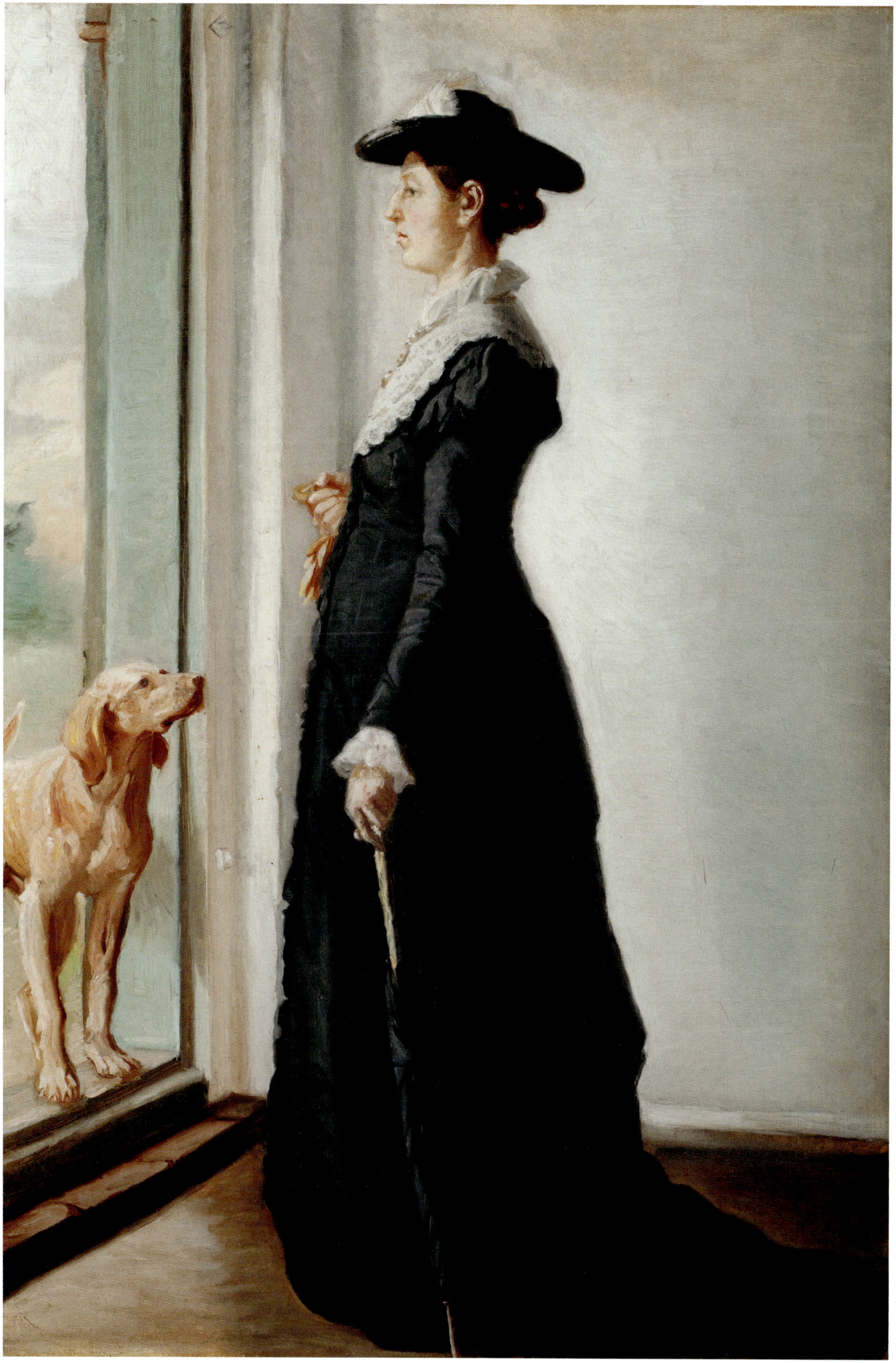

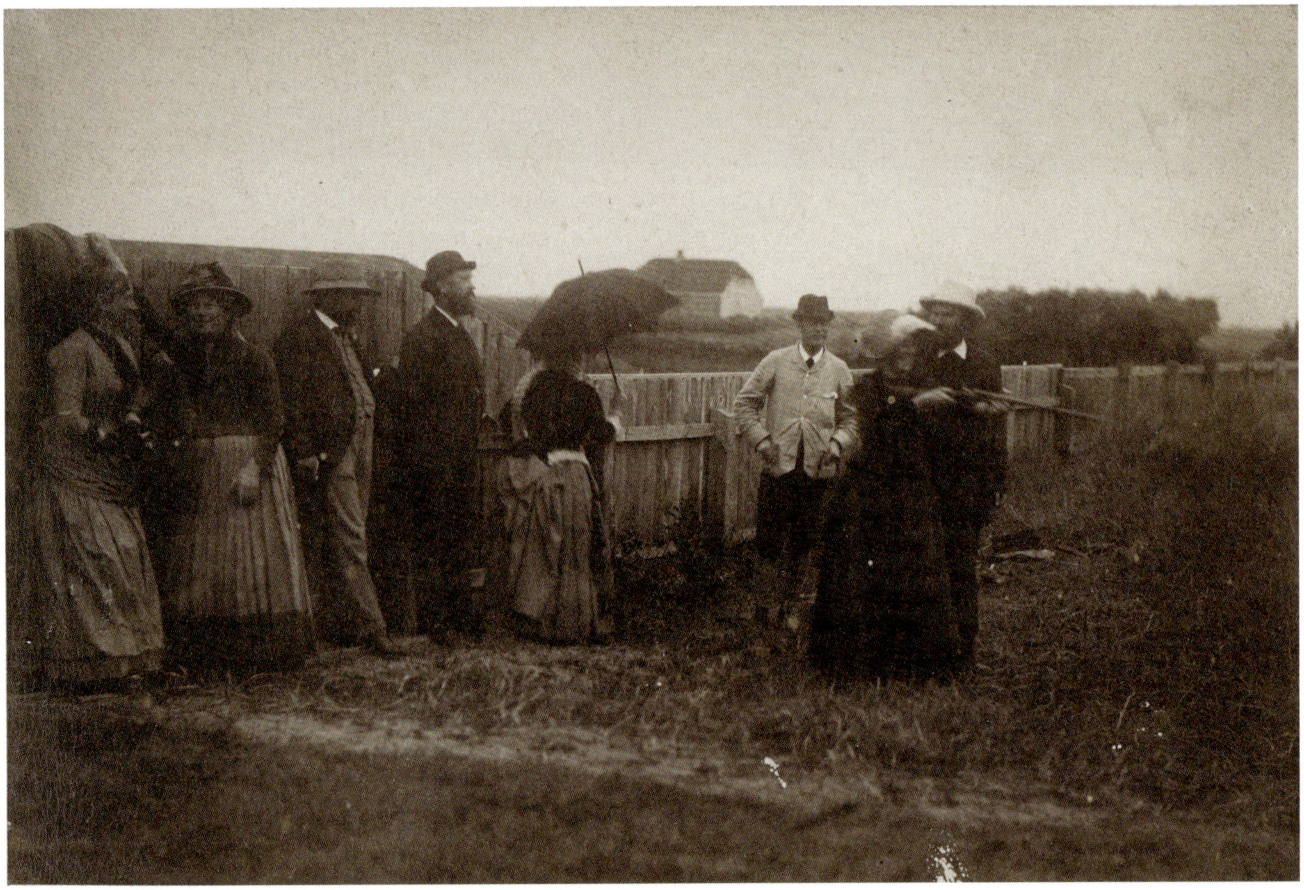

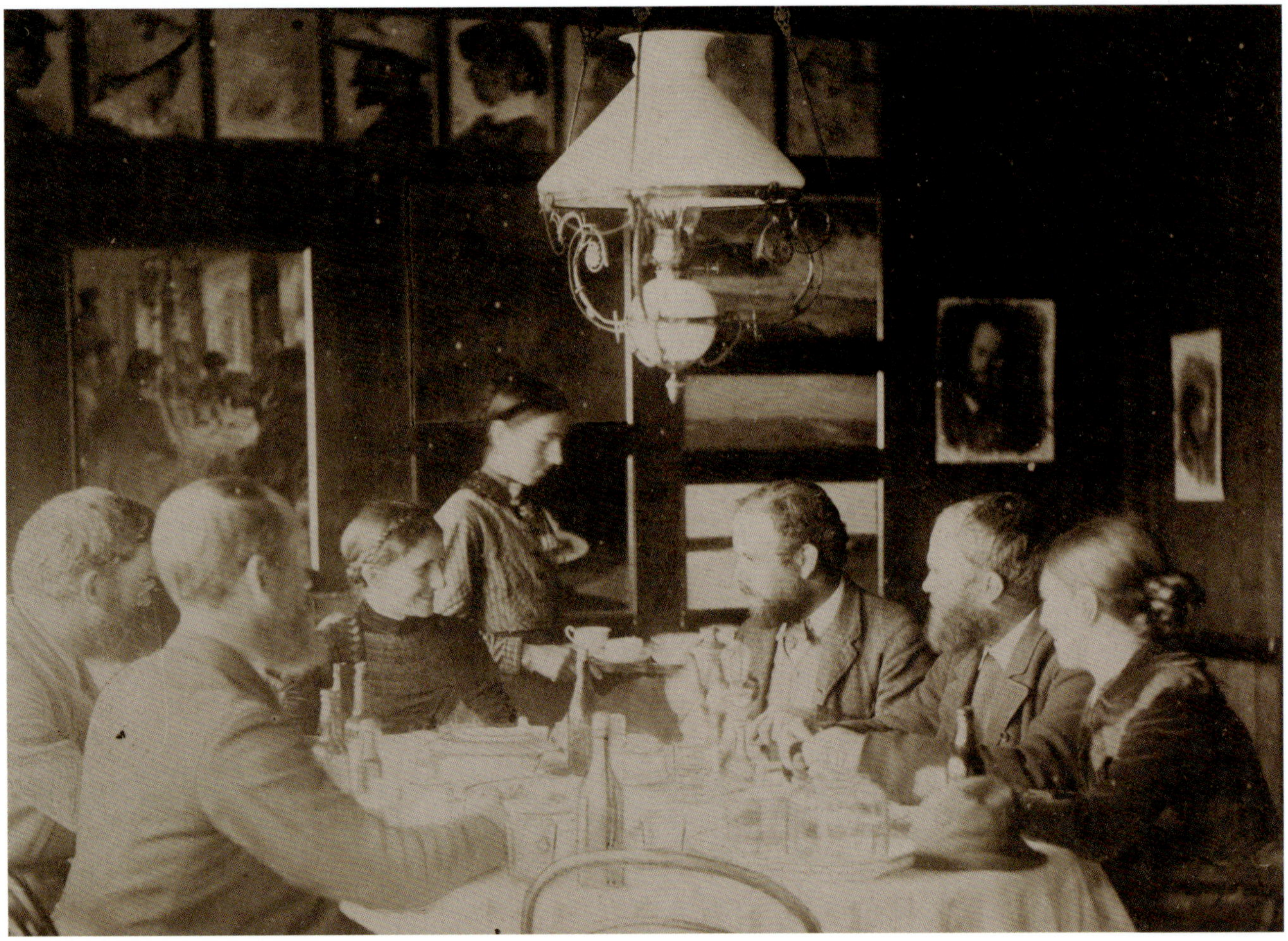

artists. Their connections led to the 1886 visit to Skagen by the Austrian-British artist couple Marianne Stokes (née Preindlsberger, 1855–1927) and Adrian Stokes (1854–1935), who had arrived from Brittany. The couple quickly became part of the artists' festivities in Skagen and left their mark by appearing as models in paintings and drawings by their new friends [figs. 3 and 4]. They also left behind their own works.

The allure of Paris, the city of artists, drew the couple back in 1889 [fig. 5]. This time, they stayed from the beginning of January and until June, during which time Ancher attended the school of Alfred Philippe Roll (1846–1919) and received corrections by Pierre Puvis de Chavannes (1824–1898). Krøyer, who was already working in Paris that winter and had a close relationship with Roll, likely facilitated her introduction to the studio.[15] Unfortunately, Ancher's letters from Paris appear to have been lost, leaving little information about her further education there. However, upon her return to Skagen, her colours seem to have become lighter and brighter, and her compositions grew larger and more complex, as seen in the painting *A Funeral* finished in 1891 (National Gallery of Denmark, Copenhagen).

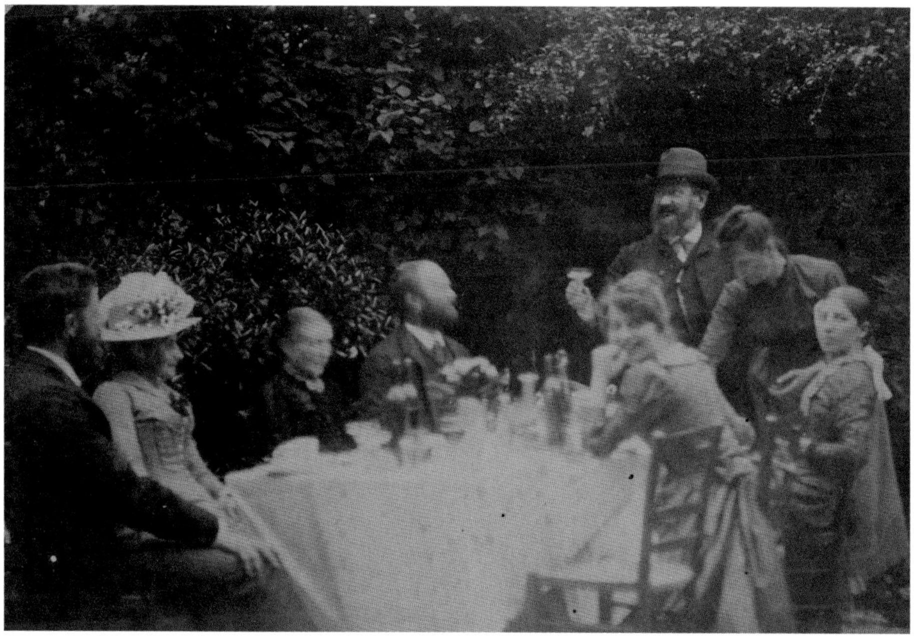

This stay in Paris was her longest stay abroad. Later, she travelled for shorter periods to Germany and the Netherlands in 1891, Italy in 1897, Germany again in 1900, Britain in 1907, and Italy again in 1924. The trip to London in 1907 is an interesting story in terms of her supporting network and her humorous and spontaneous personality. In a later interview, she laughed while recalling that she was at the train station in Copenhagen, saying farewell to the Danish painter Laurits Tuxen and his wife, who were travelling to London for the opening of the *Exhibition of Works by Danish Painters* at the Guildhall Art Gallery, where

Fig. 3
Peder Severin Krøyer (photographer)
Anna Ancher Takes Aim with the Shotgun (Vilhelmine Bramsen, Helene Christensen (behind her Marianne Stokes), Adrian Stokes, Degn Brøndum, Beatrice Diderichsen, Alfred Bramsen, Anna and Michael Ancher)
1886
Albumen print
114 × 173 mm
Skagens Museum

Fig. 4
Peder Severin Krøyer (photographer)
Lunch at Brøndum's Hotel (P.S. Krøyer, Degn Brøndum, Marianne and Adrian Stokes, Michael and Anna Ancher. Hulda Brøndum is Serving.)
Albumen print
121 × 177 mm
Skagens Museum

Fig. 5
Peder Severin Krøyer (photographer)
Lunch, Presumably in Asniéres, Paris (Laurits and Ursule Tuxen, Ida Schandorph, Michael Ancher, Marie Krøyer and Anna Ancher. Standing: Sophus Schandorph and an Unknown Woman), 1889
Albumen print
115 × 172 mm
Skagens Museum

Ancher was also represented. Right then and there, she decided to go with the Tuxens to London with no extra clothes and no money. The party at the station encouraged her, and a message was sent to her family about her departure. They sent her clothes, and money was borrowed from the Tuxens.[16]

In London, she most likely attended a dinner after the opening of the exhibition hosted by the Danish consul general, to which she and her husband were invited.[17] Laurits Tuxen had teased her that she would be sent back on arrival in London, but from a letter from Ancher's mother to Michael Ancher, we can understand that this trip was immediately accepted, and help was sent.[18]

One of the paintings Ancher exhibited at the Guildhall was *The Maid in the Kitchen* from 1883/86 [cat. 4]. It was one of her most important works, as it had been displayed in several exhibitions around Europe and was purchased by the Danish collector Heinrich Hirschsprung (1836–1908), the founder of The Hirschsprung Collection where it is housed today. The motif is from her home in Skagen, and the colours and light play a major role, typical for Ancher's works. The painting features the maid's bright red skirt, the sunlight filtering through the yellow curtain and the green cabbage and orange carrots in the foreground. The woman is depicted backlit against the window, enhancing the contrasts between light and shadow. Because the maid looks away from the viewer towards the window and her work, it amplifies the overall sense of her being embraced by the light, the colours and the warm atmosphere.

Cat. 4
The Maid in the Kitchen, 1883/1886
Oil on canvas
87.7 × 68.5 cm
The Hirschsprung Collection

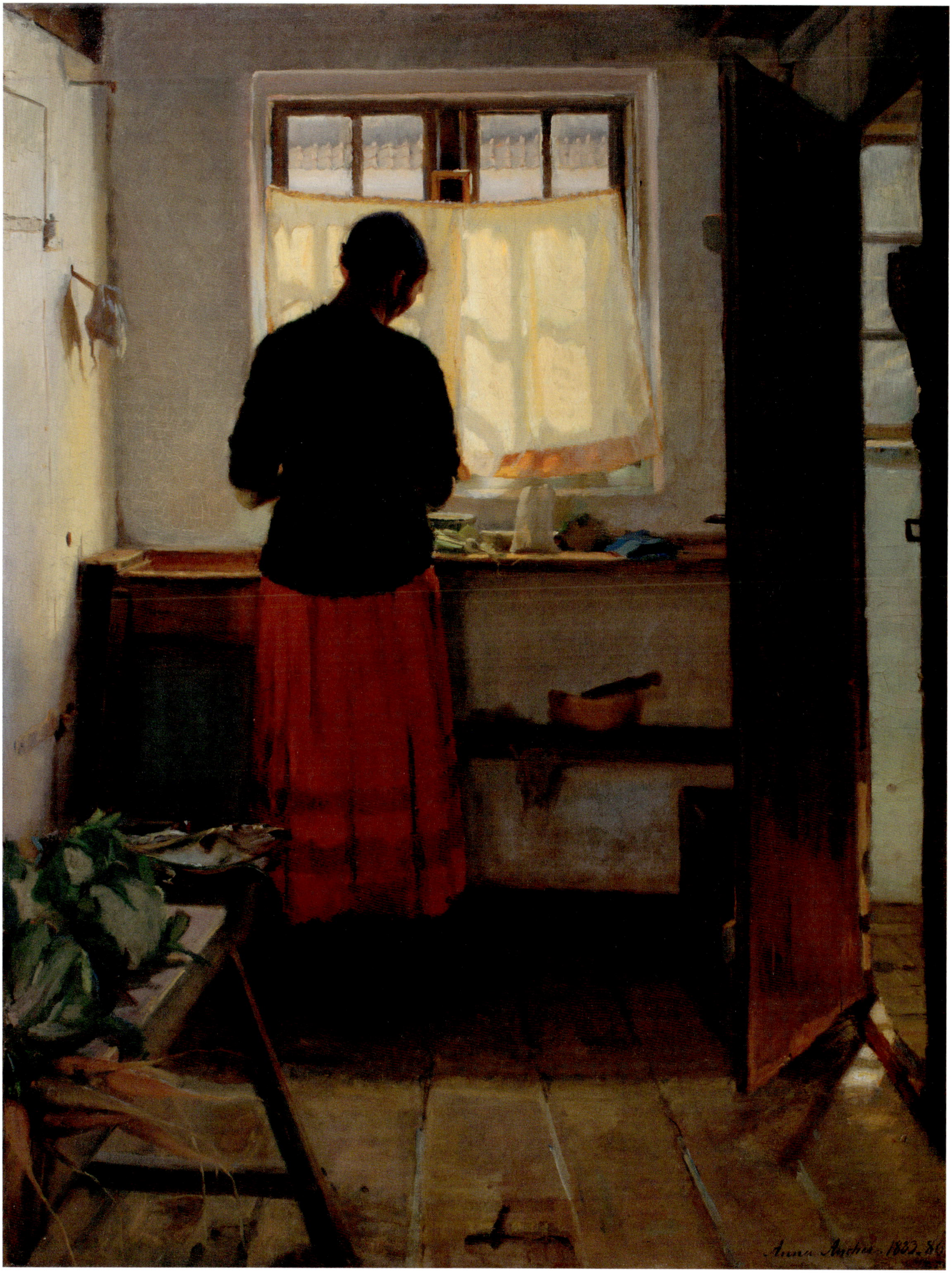
Anna Ancher. 1883-86

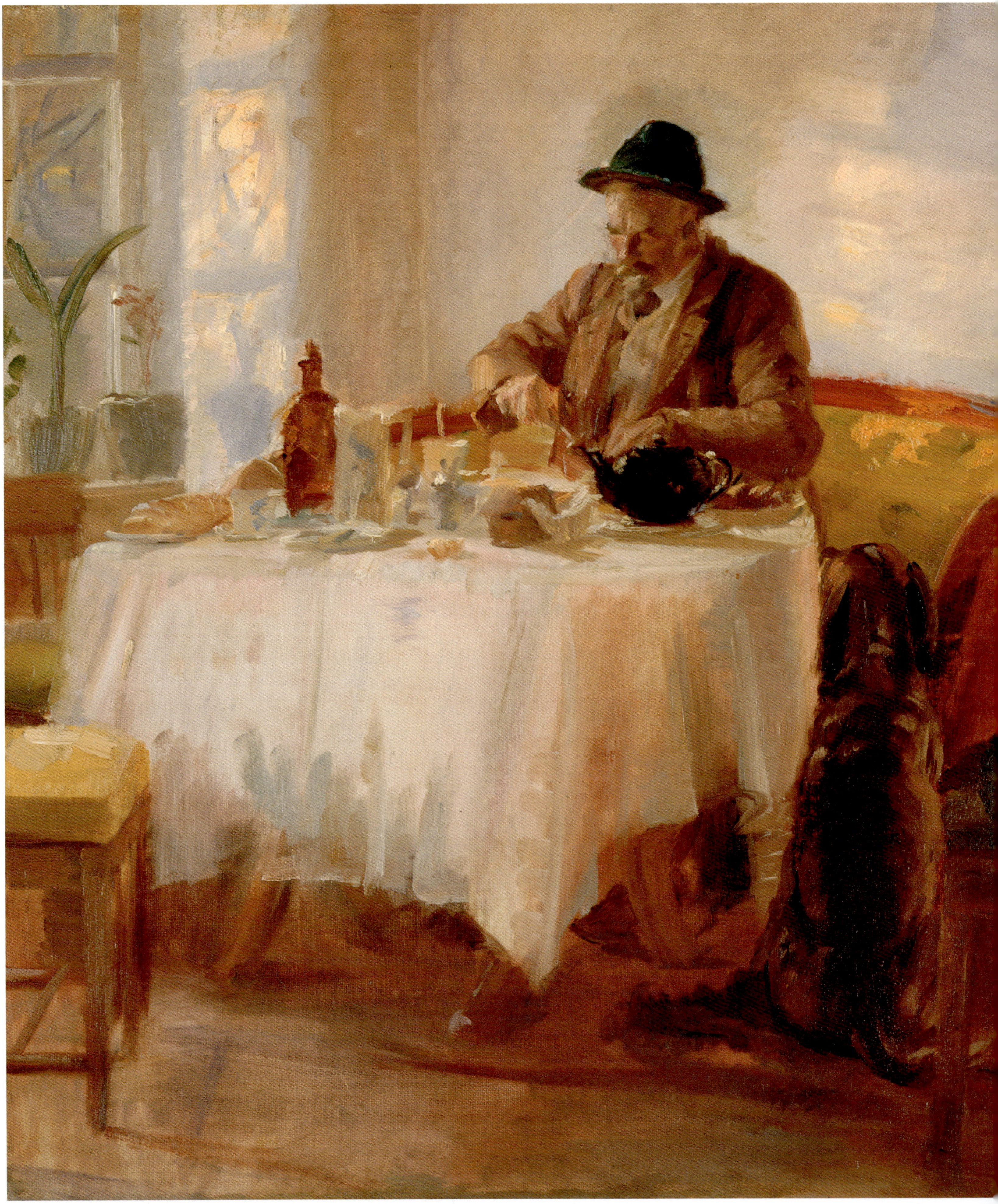

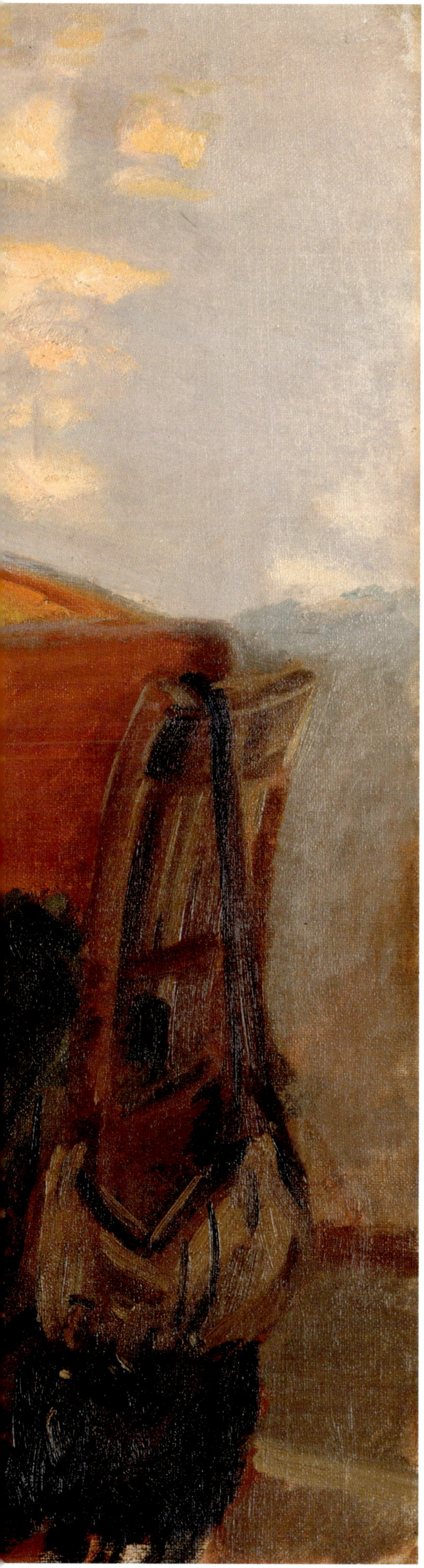

Talent for the Future
Though Ancher travelled throughout her career, and during a period from 1898 to 1913 the couple owned a villa in Copenhagen, her motifs were always from Skagen: her home, the homes of the locals, the city, or the area surrounding the fishing village.

Her home, and the home of her husband and daughter in Skagen, is a museum today and open to the public. Walking through the house, you can see that, though Ancher was born and raised in Skagen, she had a broad perspective on the world. The house is filled with their paintings as well as works by friends and colleagues from near and far. Numerous Japanese objects are seen around the living rooms, including a large paper lamp, samurai swords and lacquered boxes. In Ancher's studio, you can see the Hokusai manga book collection, containing thousands of sketches of various subjects by the Japanese artist Katsushika Hokusai (1760–1849). Piles of the British magazine *The Studio* are also found on the shelves in the Anchers' house and served as inspiration for interior design. In this way, Ancher balanced tradition and modernity. She depicted the local environment with its landscapes, people, religion and workspaces while simultaneously engaging with new trends and international impulses, which she processed in groundbreaking ways, especially in terms of light and colour [cat. 5]. She appears to have remained unaffected by others – not her husband or her teachers, Kyhn and later Puvis de Chavannes – but stayed true to her own path. This may have been easier for her than for her male colleagues, as she had not undergone the formative training provided by the art academy. She continued to work with the elements she found interesting in terms of inspiration from old masters, contemporary techniques and new 'isms', while adding her own personality, warmth and humour.

Cat. 5
Lunch Before the Hunt, 1903
Oil on canvas
48.2 × 56.8 cm
Skagens Museum

A Modern Woman
Ancher was, in many ways, a modern woman in the sense that she painted works that pointed forwards in time to a much greater degree than most painters associated with the artist colony in Skagen. Her paintings remain widely popular today and are still relevant for contemporary audiences. She also lived a more modern life than some of her female colleagues, continuing her career after marrying and becoming a mother. Supported by her family and a network of prominent friends, colleagues and patrons, she demonstrated a strong drive, unwavering self-confidence and a clear sense of purpose [fig. 6]. Evidence of her success includes consistently passing the censorship for the spring exhibition in Copenhagen, and exhibiting there almost every year from debut to death, and the sales of works to the National Gallery of Denmark and The Hirschsprung Collection.[19] She was represented at several World's Fairs, where she also took home medals. In 1921, she was named an honorary member of Kvindelige Kunstneres Samfund (The Danish Women's Artist Association) and later held a board position at Skagens Museum from 1928. Shortly before her death, she successfully placed her old friend and colleague, Madsen, to be appointed as the first director of Skagens Museum. Today, her estate and large collection of paintings form a significant part of the Skagens Museum's collection and Denmark's art historical heritage.

Fig. 6
Unknown Photographer
Anna and Michael Ancher in the Door to the Old Studio, 1890s
Collodion or gelatin silver print
154 × 112 mm
Skagens Museum

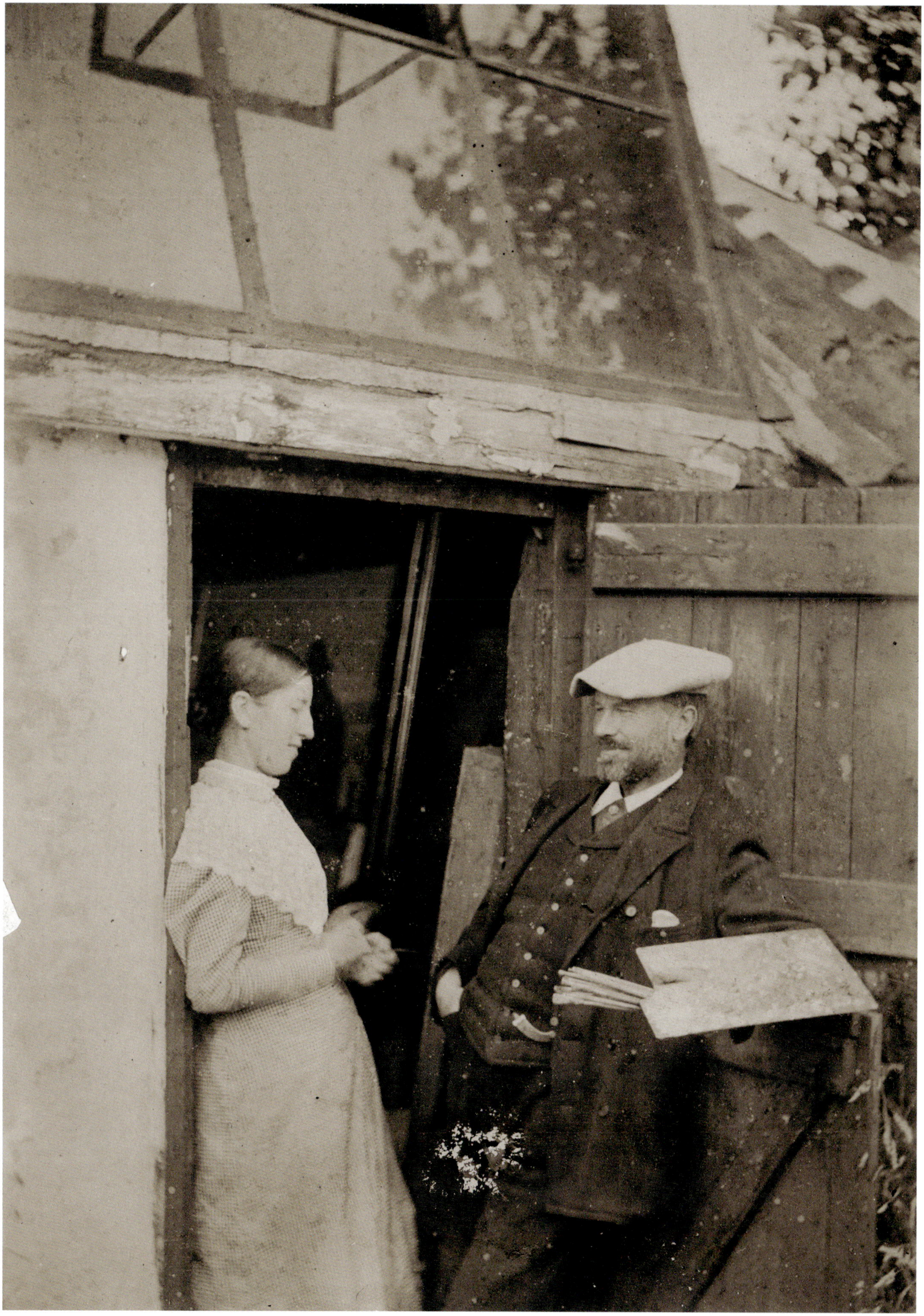

LIFE IN A SUNBEAM

Mette Harbo Lehmann

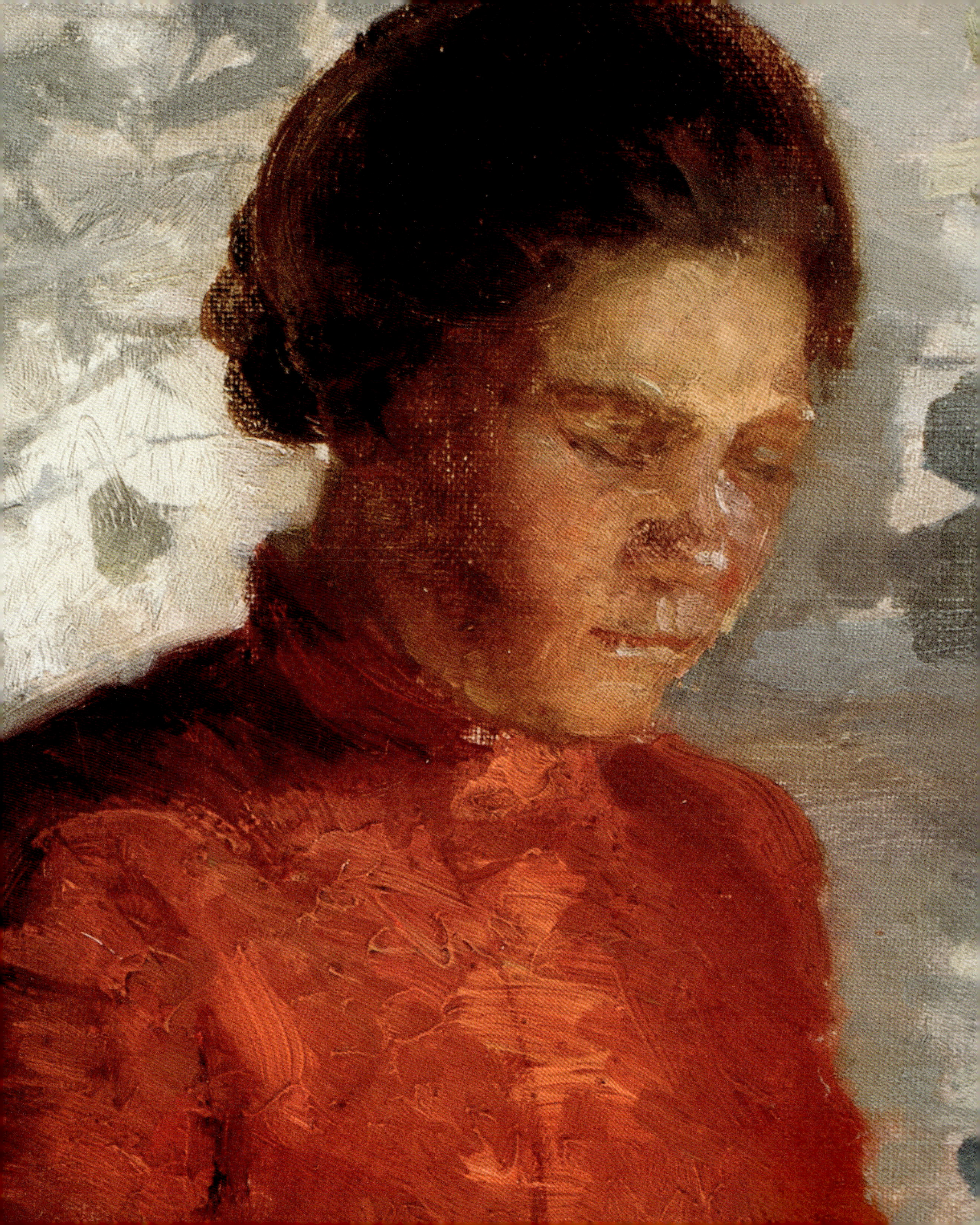

‘She was the first in Danish art to really understand how to capture a ray of sunlight.’ That is how Danish art historian Karl Madsen described Anna Ancher in 1929.[1] Her treatment of light, as it fell through the windows and drew patterns on the living room wall, was unique. Her use of bright colours was exceptional for a naturalist painter, whether it described the local interiors of Skagen, workers in the golden grain fields or the serene sunsets over the moor.

But what was Anna Ancher's focus? What did she have her eyes and mind fixed on? Was it the farmers, the piety of the churchgoers, her daughter – or were these motifs merely an excuse for catching sun rays and experimenting with colour? Ancher was a product of her upbringing in Skagen; she saw and knew the local farmers, fishermen and women, and she adored her daughter. Yet, she was also an artist with a capital 'A', possessing the courage to stand out.

The Sketch as Artwork

What can an art museum permit itself to display when managing an artist's legacy? In the house that Anna and Michael Ancher left behind, thousands of sketches were discovered. Anna, in particular, had hidden her oil studies away in drawers, cupboards and closets. Can we simply take these works out and put them on display today when the artist herself was so meticulous in hiding them? This is a question the museum organisation must continuously ask itself while managing this vital piece of cultural heritage in Skagen. Each and every sketch chosen for exhibition influences the public perception of Ancher as an artist. The dilemma lies in the fact that many of the hidden sketches are exceptional and deserve to be seen. Yet, like any artist, she occasionally had bad days or experiments that did not succeed. Deciding whether a sketch belongs to one category or the other often depends, to some degree, on subjective taste. Another challenge is that Ancher frequently revisited themes, creating multiple variations of the same motif over several years, and it can be difficult to determine which piece represents the 'finished' work, if such a thing exists. Was it the one she painted last, first or somewhere along the way? In some cases, it may not be possible to decide. One example is the portraits of her mother in the blue room at Brøndum's Hotel [cat. 6]. These exist in several variations, viewed from different angles, cropped in various ways, and with a view to living rooms with other colours.

One must also consider that, throughout the nineteenth century, the status of the sketch evolved, gaining significance and value as an independent work of art. This shift had a knock-on effect on how Ancher's studies were perceived in her own time and continues to shape our view of her sketches today, especially

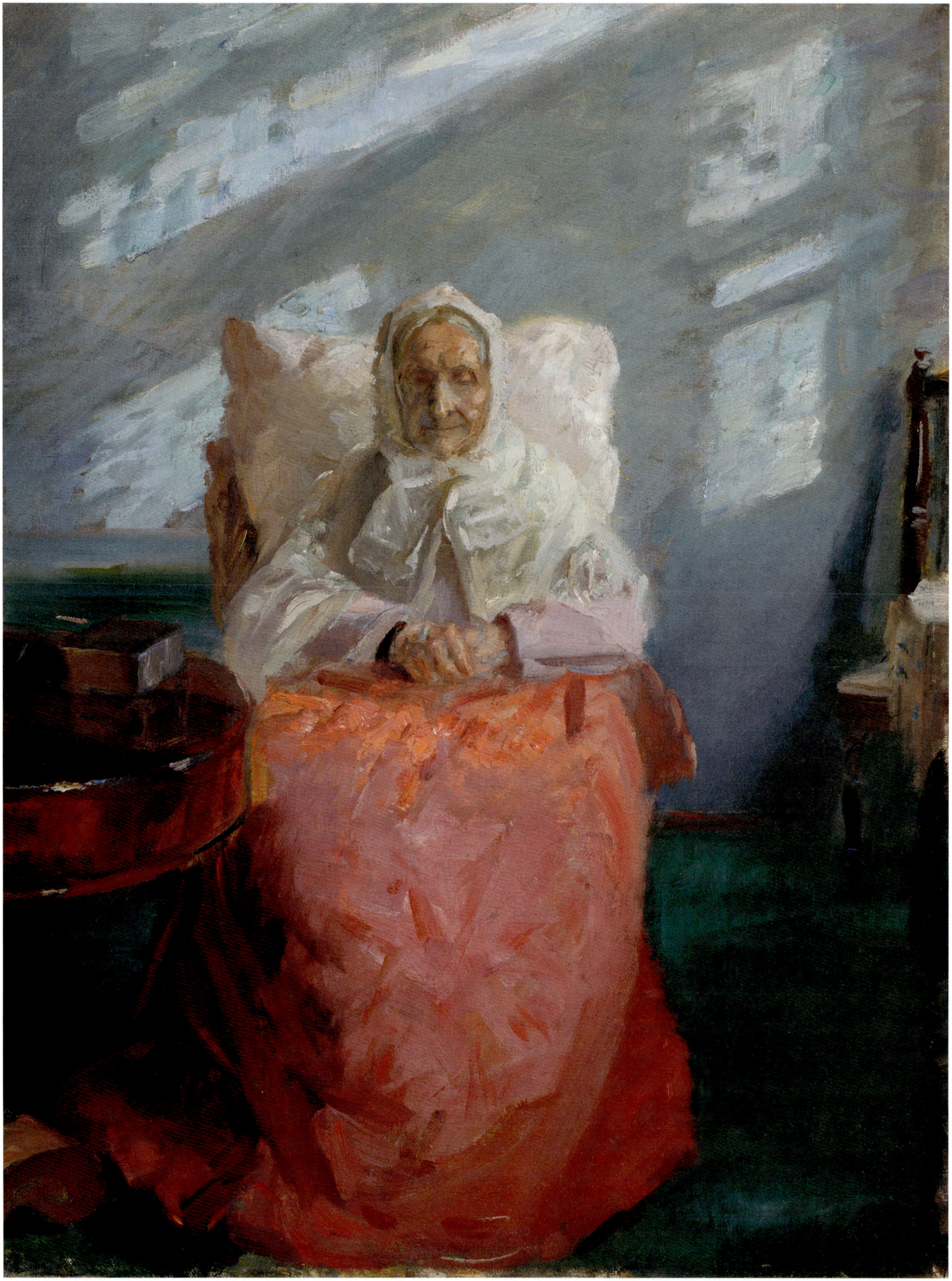

after the hidden treasures were uncovered in the 1970s when her home was opened as a museum. The American art historian Albert Boime (1933–2008) explains this development in the context of French Academy painting.[2] At the beginning of the century, the Academy style was predominant. In this tradition, the finished work was regarded as the only 'real' work, while the oil sketch served merely as a tool to achieve that goal. The sketch would always be private, and only the finished work was displayed. However, a discussion eventually arose about the characteristics of the sketch that fundamentally shifted the perception of its importance. It was argued that the oil sketch had advantages in terms of representing the idea and in possessing immediacy, freshness and originality, whereas the finished work represented the artist's craftsmanship in relation to execution. This debate slowly started a movement whereby the finished work sought to preserve the qualities of the sketch. By the end of the century, the status of the sketch was so established that it could be exhibited as a work of art in its own right. In this way, the boundaries between oil sketch and finished work were blurred.

Ancher found herself artistically in the middle of this development. Even among her close friends, she was infamous for hiding her studies and being immensely secretive about her process in the studio.[3] One of the hidden oil studies discovered in the artist couple's house after her death was *Evening Sun in the Artist's Studio at Markvej* [cat. 7]. Its qualities are so remarkable when viewed today that it is almost breathtaking to think it might never have been shown to the world. But known as it is today, it has become an integral part of the artist's story, which has consequently changed to a certain extent since the time when she herself controlled what left the studio. The painting is a study

Cat. 6
Mrs Ane Brøndum in the Blue Room, 1913
Oil on canvas
5.8 × 42.7 cm
Skagens Museum

of the light that falls into her studio, a space added to their old house as part of a larger extension completed in 1913. In this work, she explored how the rays of the low-lying sun, filtering through the window, affect the colours in the room. It is seen partly in the impasto highlights and partly in the muted shadows of the corners. The work is strikingly simple in composition and does not seem to possess any other narrative beyond the flicker of sunlight and play of colours.

What Ancher herself considered to be her primary works remains largely unknown, as she never wrote about her thoughts on the matter. However, in a letter from her husband to a journalist in 1906, he cites her as mentioning what she sees as her most important paintings – or more accurately, the paintings she believed had the greatest artistic value.

> As regards the question of which paintings we attribute the greatest artistic value to, the answer, as far as my wife is concerned, would be:
>
> *A Blind Woman in her Room. Evening Sun*, The Hirschsprung Collection. *The Girl in the Red Skirt*, The Hirschsprung Collection. *The Gull Pluckers*, The Hirschsprung Collection. *Portrait of an Old Woman*, Kunstforeningen. *A Funeral*, The Art Museum. *A Field Sermon*, The Art Museum. *Kyhn in his Studio*.[4]

Common to the seven works she mentions is that they had all been exhibited and subsequently sold to museums or otherwise gained visibility and publicity. This selection of works must be understood in the context of her time, which largely wanted finished exhibition pieces. Today, however, we can more easily appreciate both her elaborate exhibition works as

Cat. 7
Evening Sun in the Artist's Studio at Markvej, after 1913
Oil on canvas
52.6 × 39.2 cm
Skagens Museum

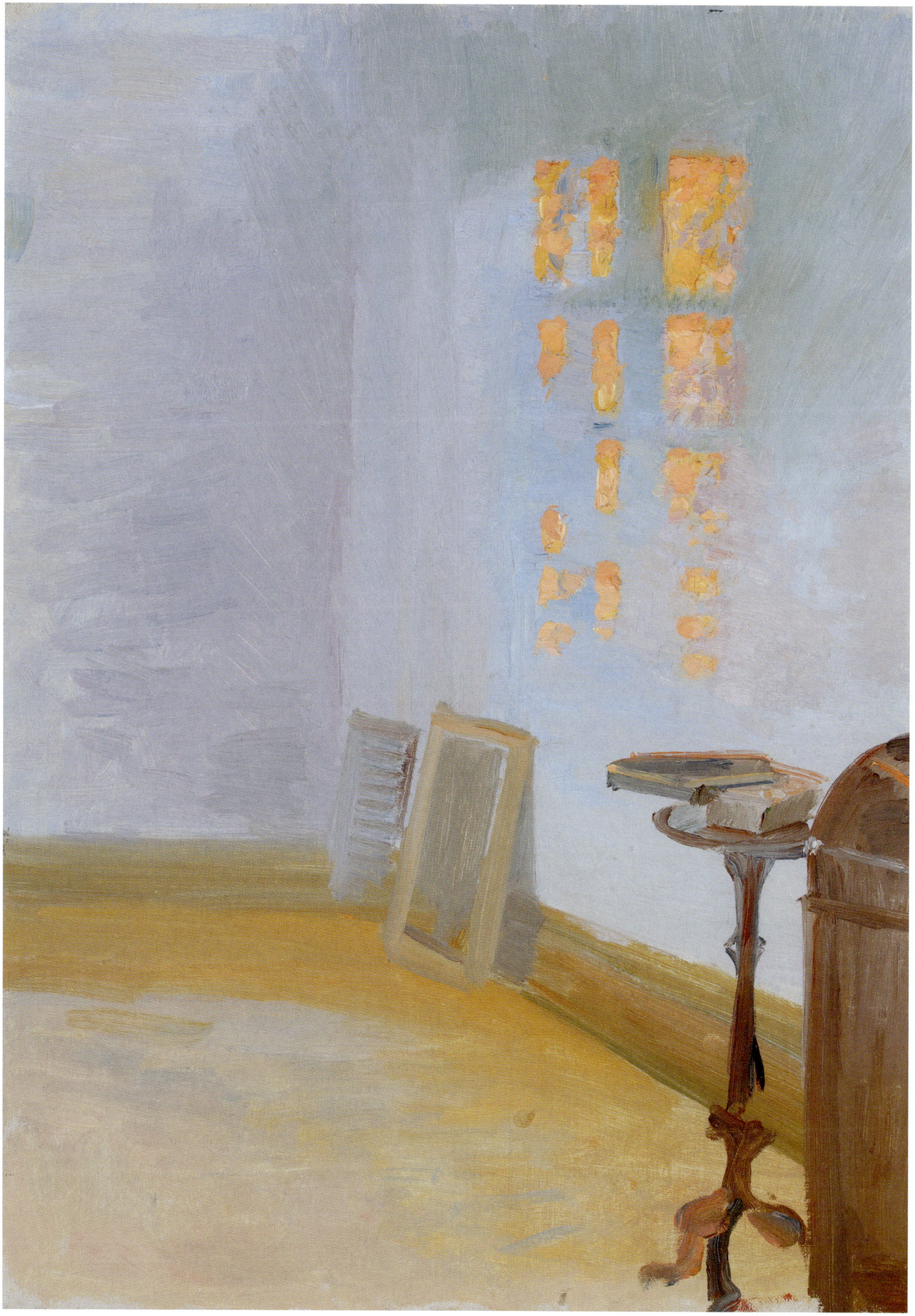

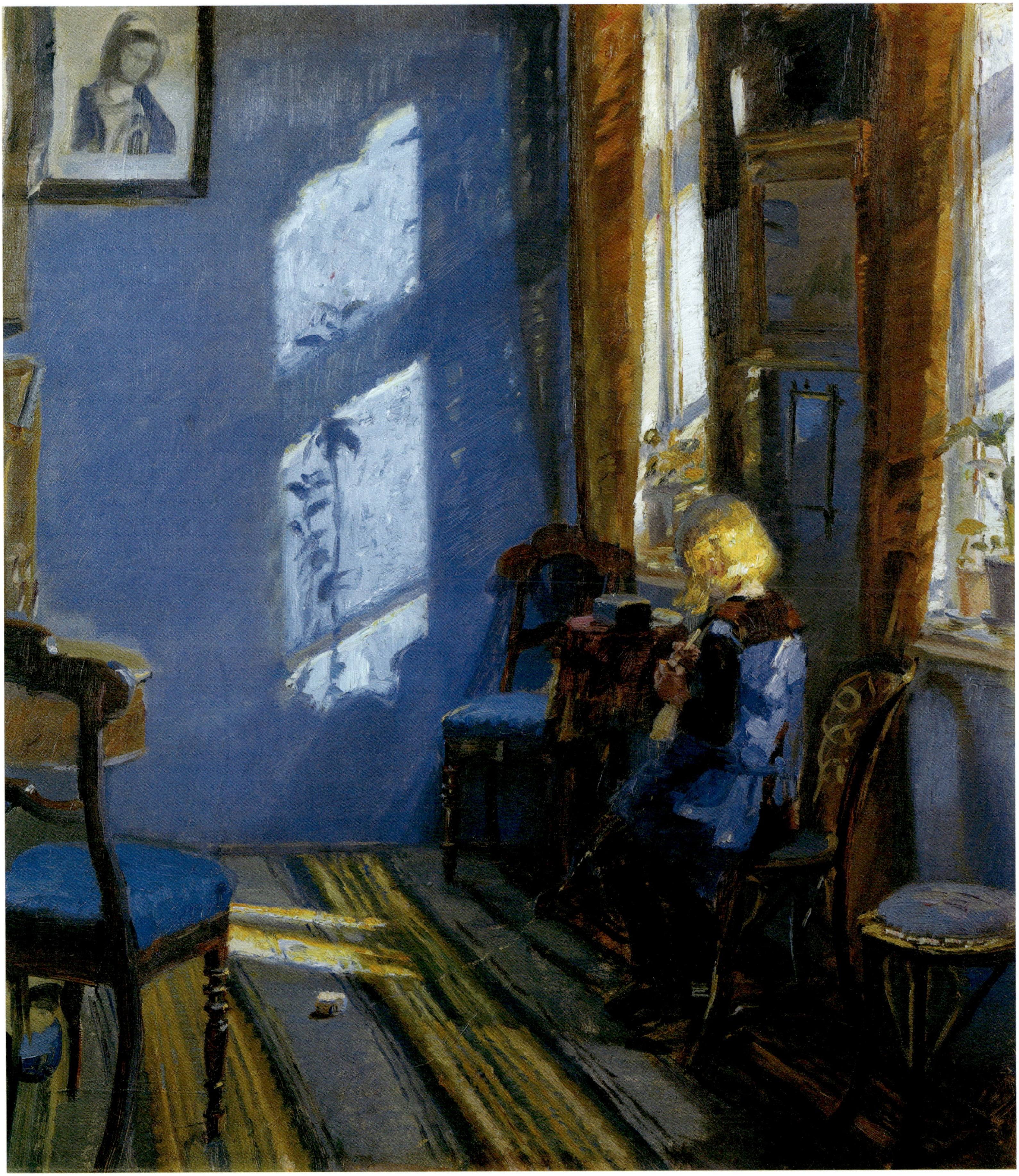

well as her hidden oil studies, which exude immediacy, personality and passion for colour. Does it matter whether a painting is an oil sketch or an 'exhibition piece', as long as it possesses its distinctive qualities?

The Light and the Critics

What did the contemporary critics say? Since the beginning of Ancher's career, critics noticed her. The first reviews and descriptions of her as a young and promising artist mention her talent, realism and use of light. They write that one should keep an eye on her in the future, because she might be able to make her mark with even better works.[5] One review from a national Danish newspaper in 1883 states that Ancher, 'in recent years has made a name for herself at our exhibitions':

> The 'Two old people plucking Seagulls'[6] are thus by no means beautiful specimens of the type that Mrs. Ancher has chosen to produce here, but there is nevertheless so much feeling, picturesque whole, and despite a perhaps somewhat weak treatment of form such a beautiful harmony in this picture, that one can only regard it with sympathy, and this is so much the more pleasing to admit, as these qualities belong to the most important of a work of art. How pleasantly the two poor old people sit there at their anything but pleasant work, how funny and jovial he laughs at the whole thing, and how calmly and seriously she sits with her long arms outstretched over the big dead birds, plucking the white down, that cover her hands and clothes. How clear and warm the daylight shines in through the blinds that cover the window, and what a friendly atmosphere of still life is spread over the whole.[7]

The critic sees that she operates within naturalism or realism as a genre; a genre that he personally, as a slightly conservative individual, does not appreciate, as it produces unpleasant or downright ugly things, which, in his view, are not suitable for fine art. However, he also sees a deviation from that, in the form or in the natural resemblance, which is counterbalanced by Ancher's other qualities in her way of painting. What appeals to him is her harmonious composition, which lends a sense of calmness to the image.

Nine years later, Ancher's painting had evolved. She had exhibited her works numerous times, engaged in many conversations with like-minded contemporary artists, travelled abroad, and in 1889 continued her education in Paris. Her paintings began to display more vibrant colours, greater courage to experiment and a stronger willingness to stand out. When she exhibited what we today regard as one of her most important paintings, *Sunlight in the Blue Room* from 1891 [cat. 8], at the Spring Exhibition in Copenhagen in 1892, she therefore also received mixed reactions. When we look at the painting today, we may perceive it as uncontroversial, unproblematic, beautiful and even idyllic, with its warmth of colour and pleasant sunbeams that fall across the tranquil room. However, this was not how everyone saw it at the time. In a review of the Spring Exhibition, an anonymous critic in a national newspaper complained that certain artists had become too modern and should leave their paintings at home in the private confines of their studio. He argued that they appeared as if they had the sole right to assess and understand the 'experimental art':

> Otherwise, the skilled and talented artist Anna Ancher for example did not meet with her 'Sunlight in the Blue Room', where the poor child's

Cat. 8
Sunlight in the Blue Room, 1891
Oil on canvas
65.2 × 58.8 cm
Skagens Museum

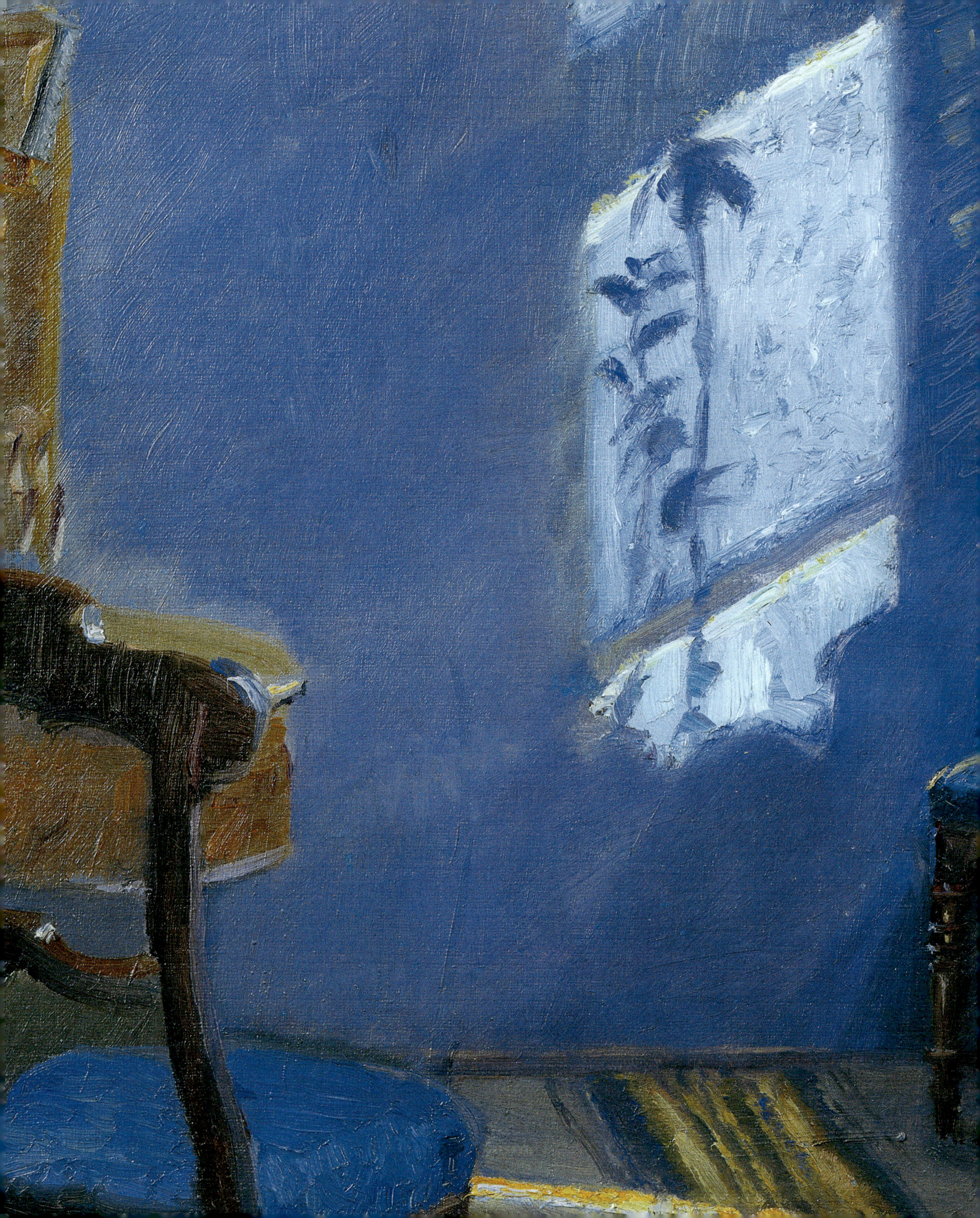

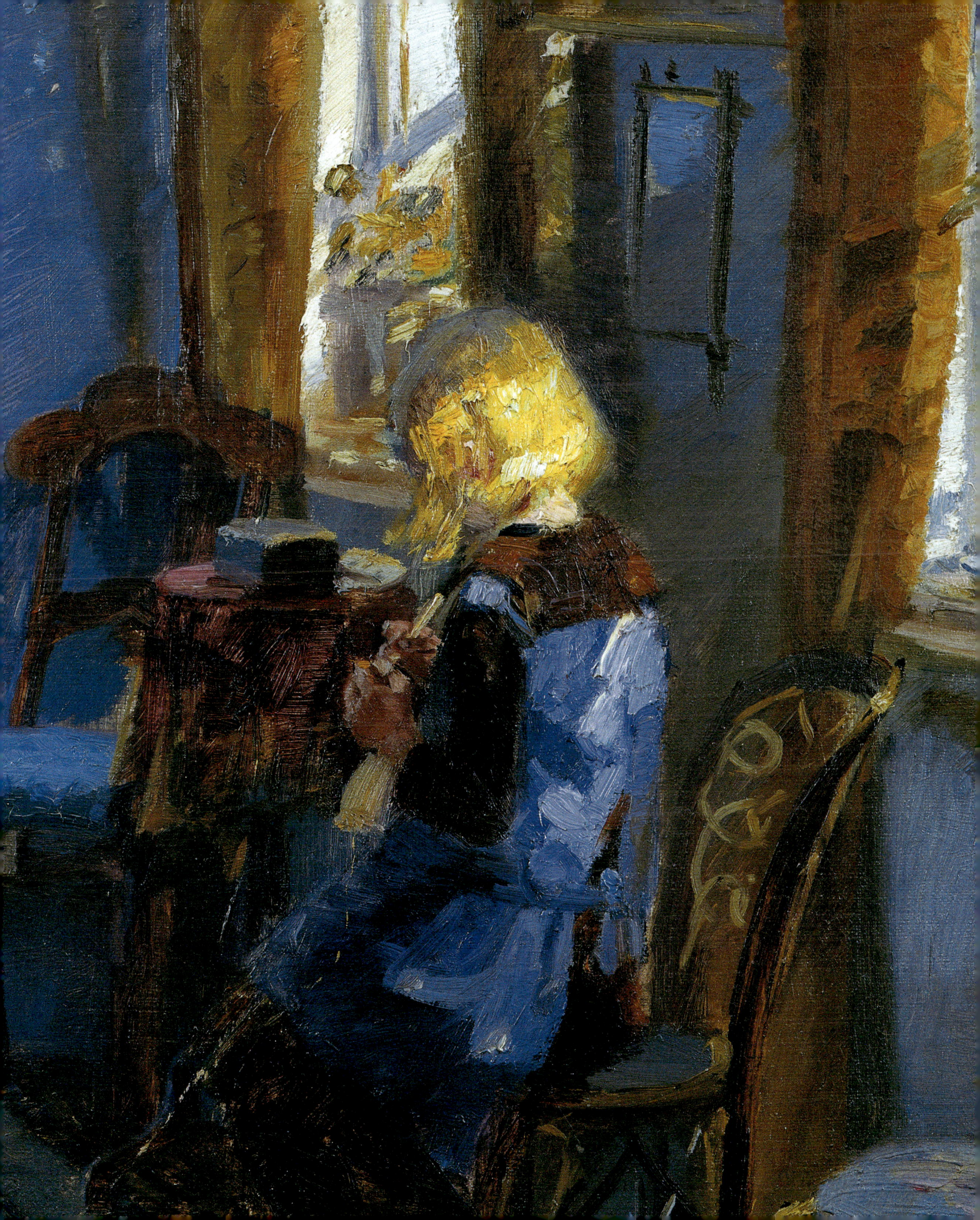

> yellow hair is eaten up by the sun to the scalp, or with her half-length portrait of 'A Young Girl Against a Sunlit Background' [unidentified]. These works are, after all, only respectable titanic attempts, imperfect tests that do not stand up to criticism, memories of half- and completely failed efforts, or reminiscences from the struggle in the private chamber, which do not concern the public. One can at most demand private sympathy for and understanding of this flight of Icarus, but no more.[8]

The review is interesting because it offers insight into the contemporary perception of Ancher's painting. On the one hand, she is recognised as a skilled and talented artist worthy of filling newspaper columns. On the other hand, she has produced a work that is so innovative that the reviewer can hardly accept it. However, it is precisely in this borderland where great art fights its way to its place in the history of art as something that pushes the boundaries of what we accept as good art. The critical review, in this case, is far more interesting than the positive ones. The negative review shocks and amuses; this one is almost poetic with its reference to the Greek myth of Icarus, who flew too close to the sun with wings of feathers and wax. Nonetheless, there were more good reviews than bad ones. The journalist C.H. noticed some of the same things regarding form and treatment of light in Ancher's painting, but offered a more favourable opinion of it:

> Mrs. Anna Ancher, whose talent is also nearest for depicting the quiet, peaceful life indoors, has exhibited a couple of interiors, 'Sunlight in the Blue Room' and 'Kitchen Interior', both of which bear the unfinished character of the sketch, while on the other side also have the exuberant freshness of the sketch. Warm sunlight and picturesque content are there in the Picture of the Blue Room.[9]

Both critics acknowledged the sketch-like character of the work, but while the first saw it as a negative stylistic feature – an expression that the artist was unable or unwilling to finish it, which he found odd and uncharming – the second journalist saw it as positive feature and an opportunity to give the motif a more immediate expression. Other critics were more unambiguously pleased. An example read, 'By Mrs Anna Ancher, there is an absolutely lovely interior painting: "Sunlight in the Blue Room", in which the colour effect is extremely fine'.[10] In this sense, Ancher also had her defenders.

Ancher's Interiors

The interiors were an important group of motifs for Ancher. This type of subject matter allowed her to focus on the sunbeams as they fell through the windows into the living spaces – not only in her own home but also in the homes of people of Skagen. In this sense, she had the entire town, and the houses of the fishing village, as her studio. The blue room was a small semi-private dining room at Brøndum's Hotel. Brøndum's was Ancher's childhood home, and it was only a hundred metres from her own house in Skagen. Her mother and three of her siblings ran the hotel, so Ancher's daughter, Helga, is seen in a homely environment in the painting. The image of the Virgin Mary on the wall behind the girl reflects the piety of Ancher's mother and sisters. However, Ancher herself, along with her brothers, did not actively participate in religious life. In the painting, the Virgin Mary's downward view appears more like an artistic device, serving as an imaginary line in an X-shaped composition where two diagonal lines meet at the centre of the blue wall. The blue wall itself is a dominant feature of the painting, with the sunlight's outlines and the play of shadows on its surface taking centre stage. Interestingly, Ancher chose to exhibit this predominantly blue painting alongside a largely yellow motif. The exact yellow painting cannot be identified with certainty, but it was presumably a version of her seamstress motif, which she revisited over several years. The painting *Study of a Seamstress in Blue*, illustrated here, is a version from approximately ten years later [cat. 9]. The location of the yellow room remains unknown, but Ancher painted in various local settings, including private homes in Skagen, in the girls' sewing school, in the doctor's consultation rooms, as well as in the hotel and in her own home. This allowed her to adapt the dominant colour palette of an image depending on the setting in which she worked.[11]

Ancher worked with different motifs, which she repeated, varied and returned to over time. One recurring theme was the seamstress with the sunlit background, sometimes with a potted plant in the background. Similarly, she explored and repeated the motifs of her mother in the blue room [cat. 6]. Another cluster of motifs was the girls' sewing school, which exists in many variations, canvas sizes and with a number of models [cat. 10]. Other recurring themes included the vaccination theme [cat. 11], the breastfeeding mother and various types of locals engaged in knitting, reading, eating or plucking birds. She also created works centred on her own family or on the religious life of the village, as it unfolded in the church, in the dunes or in the cemetery. What many of these interior motifs have in common is the essential role of sunlight. One does not necessarily see the window itself, but rather the sunspot on the wall, which takes up a lot of space in the painting. The sunlit space often takes the shape of the window which itself is not seen and the shadow patterns hinting at flowers imagined to be on the windowsill. It is rare for the sunspot to become the sole focus of a painting, but *Interior. Brøndum's Annex* is an exception [cat. 12]. Here, the view outside the window is completely cropped out by the edges of the painting and the world beyond is only indicated through the sunspots on the interior walls. The work is predominantly rendered in shades of orange, but a green curtain has been added to the window in the background to provide contrast. Ancher experimented with varying brushstrokes, applying particularly thick layers of paint to the sunlit areas. The room appears completely empty. There is no furniture and no carpets to be seen. In this way, the emptiness and the suggestiveness in it is emphasised, while simultaneously the intensity of the colour overwhelms and captivates the viewer.

What was most important to Ancher in relation to her interior motifs? What was she truly seeking? Was it the depiction of real-life people and their activities, the essence of the living spaces themselves, or was it ultimately her studies of light and colour that most captivated her?

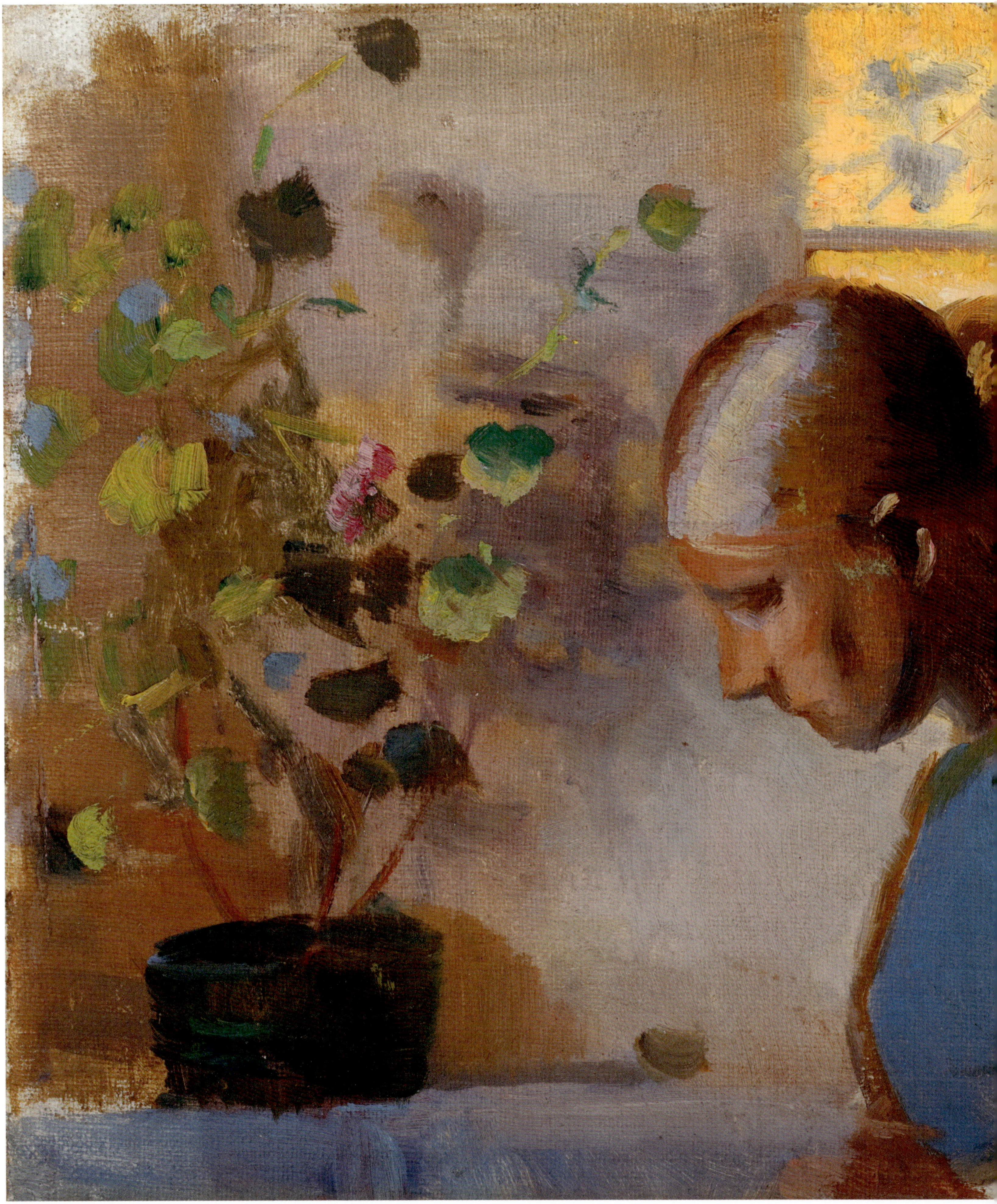

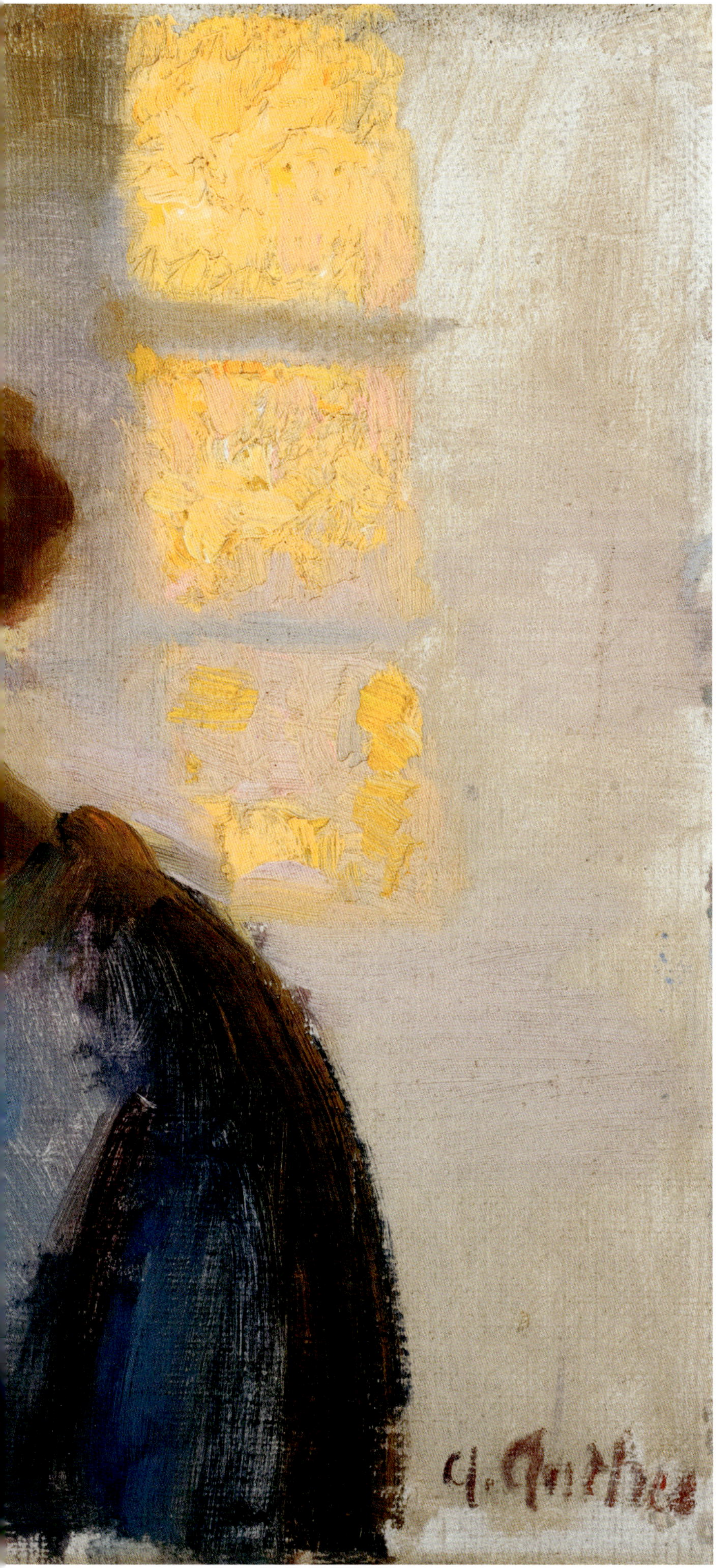

Cat. 9
Study of a Seamstress in Blue, c. 1899
Oil on canvas, glued on card
21 × 29 cm
Skagens Museum

Cat. 10
Two Little Girls Being Taught How to Sew, c. 1907
Oil on canvas
64 × 54.4 cm
Skagens Museum

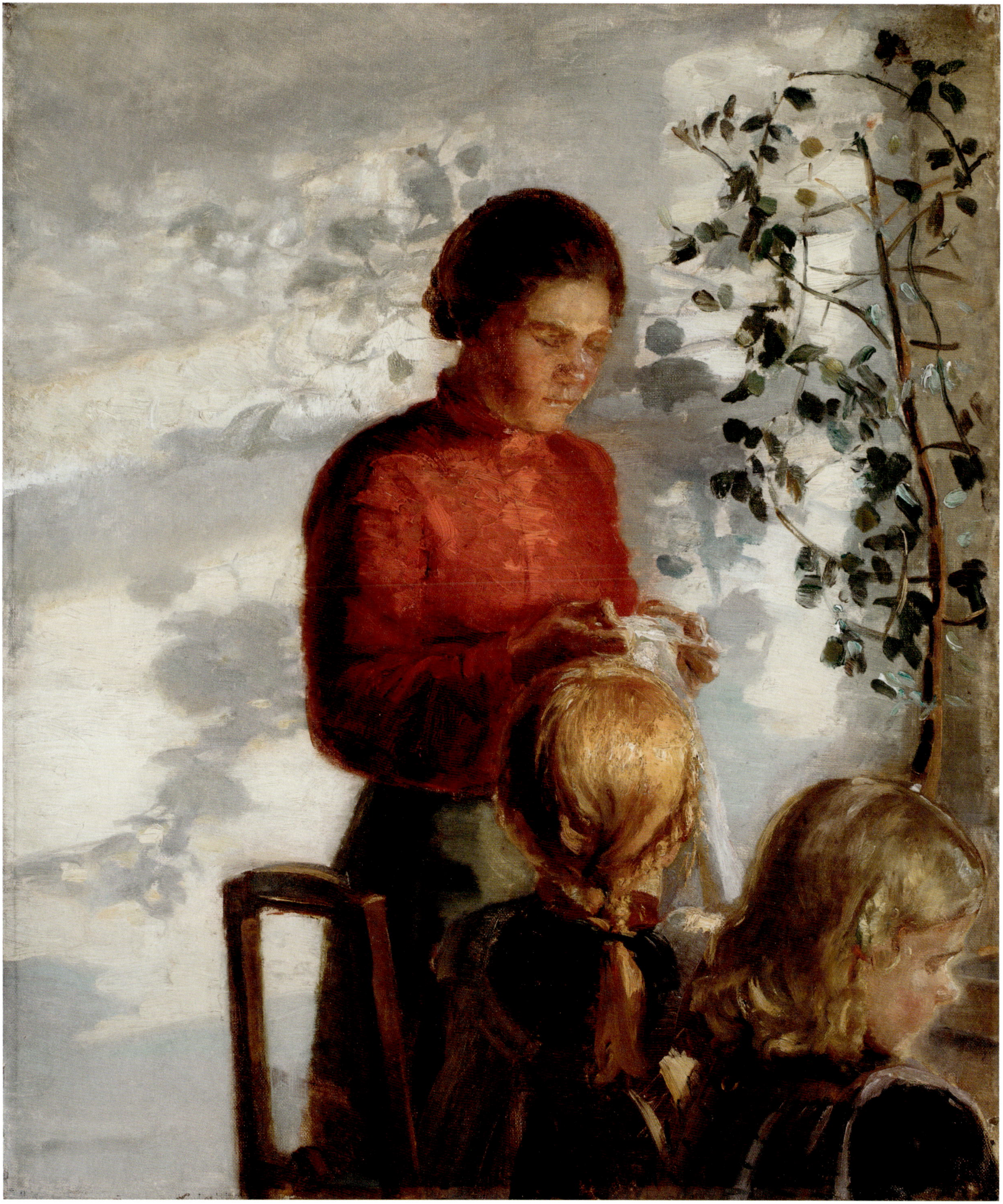

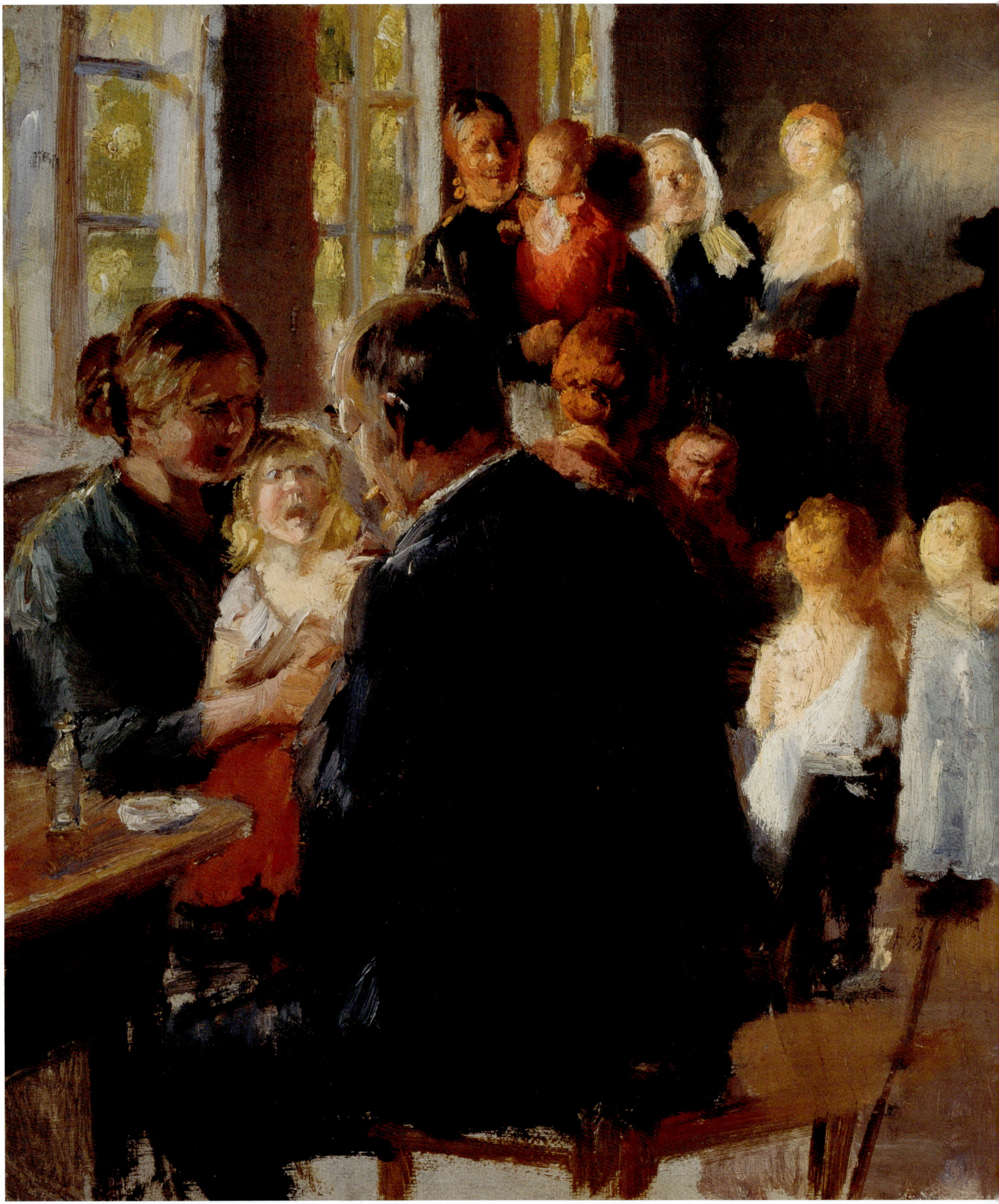

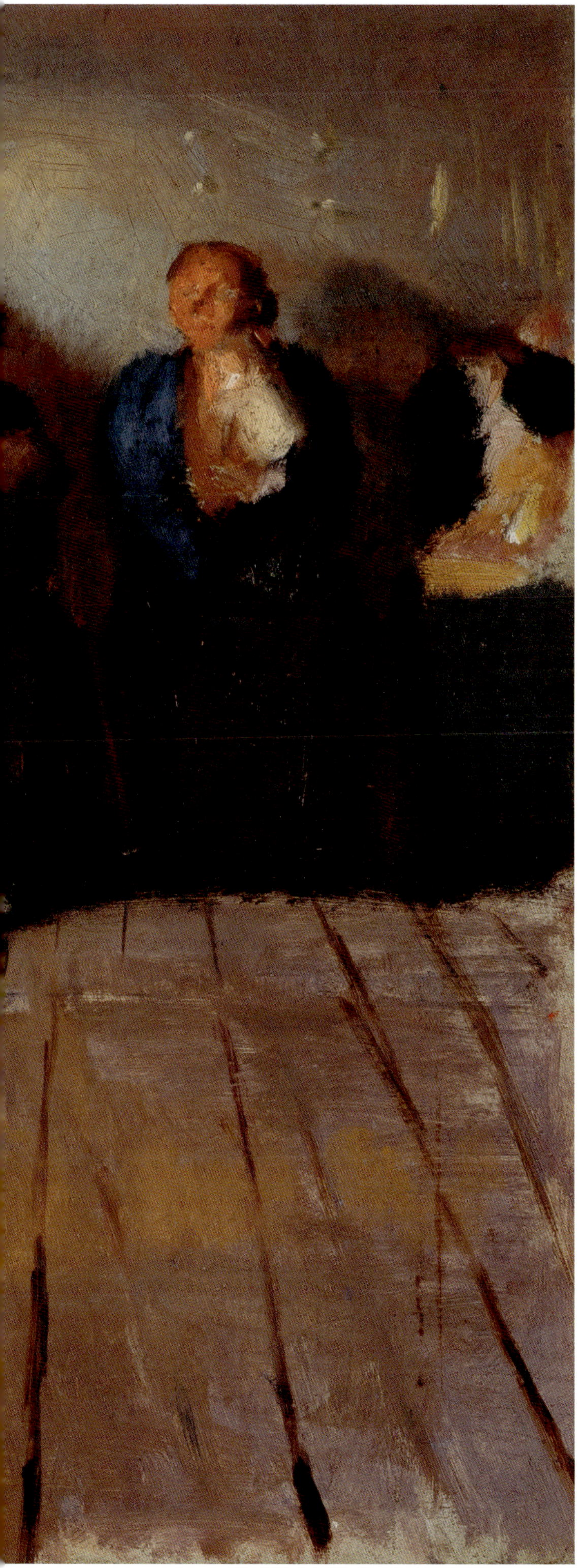

Cat. 11
A Vaccination. Study, 1898/1899
Oil on card
26.9 × 34.9 cm
Skagens Museum

Cat. 12
Interior. Brøndum's Annex, c. 1916
Oil on panel
44.4 × 37.9 cm
Skagens Museum

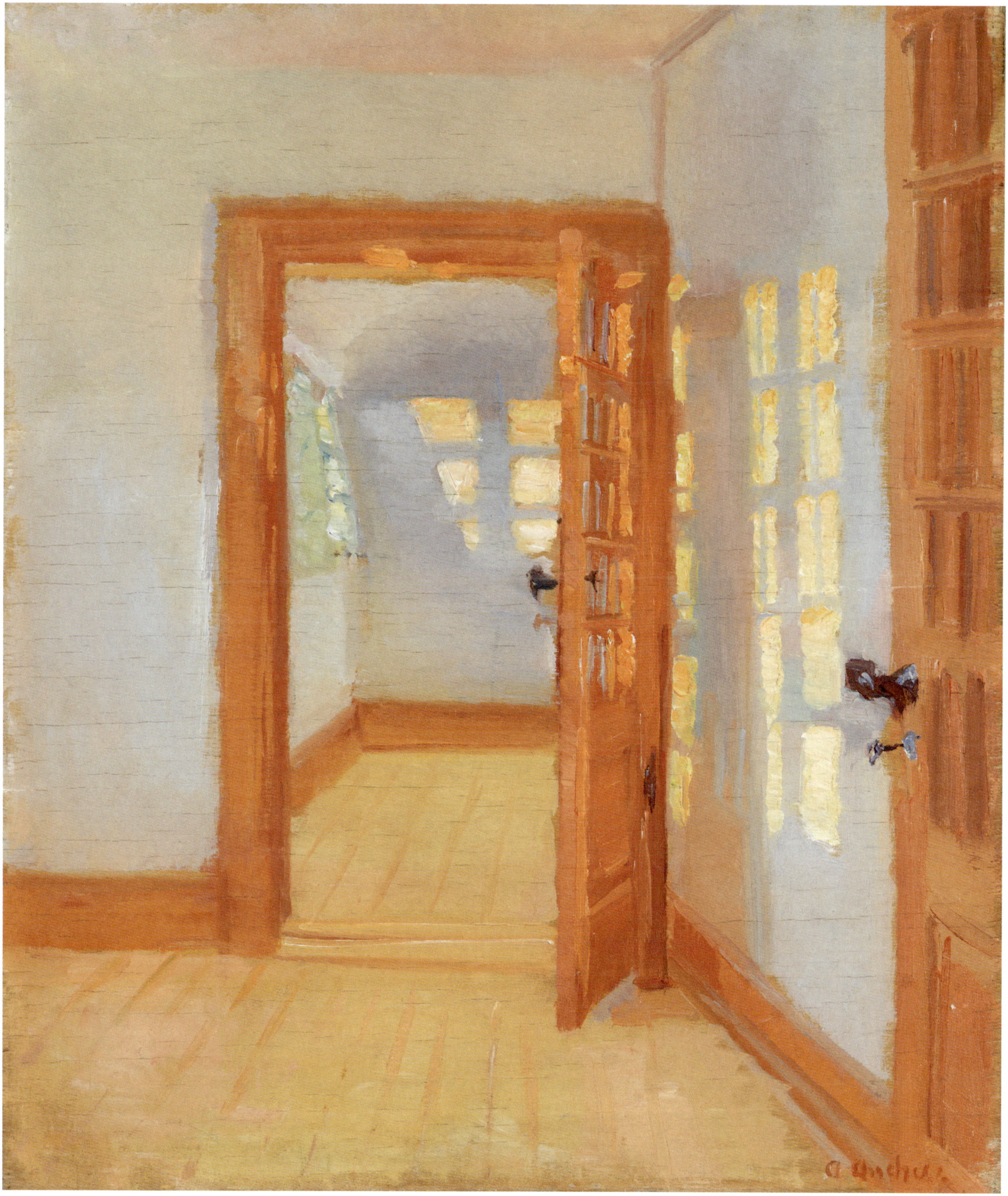

Numerous Exteriors

In Ancher's landscapes, her work with light and colour is also evident, though light as a central theme is less explicit than in her interior paintings. For many years, critics and art historians have uncritically reproduced the narrative that female artists of this period primarily worked with interior scenes, aligning with the gendered expectations of the time. It was assumed that women would not move too far away from home, and preferably not take on overly masculine motifs, such as complex figure paintings or landscapes. However, in recent times, there has been more focus on the fact that Ancher also painted quite a few outdoor works. While some of these have long been known, the fact that her exteriors were so numerous has not attracted much interest. But what did she see outside if light was not a pronounced theme? We find landscapes, cityscapes, gardens, the cemetery, the moor, beaches and the sea. The motifs vary as much as Skagen's surroundings allow. Small studies like *Moorland* (not dated), found in her studio, are abundant [cat. 13]. We also see larger works like *At the Grave* from 1913 [cat. 14]. The light is, of course, present in the exteriors but serves as an illustration of different hours of the day, such as sunshine, sunsets, dusk or moonlight, enhancing the atmosphere in the motif and highlighting different shades of colours.

One of Ancher's well-known motifs is the harvest workers moving through the field, as illustrated with the version of *Harvesters* from 1905 [cat. 15]. It is one of the motif groups she returned to several times and developed from 1900 to 1905. The painting is very simple in its composition. It is divided into two halves by the yellow, sun-ripened grain below and the blue sky with drifting clouds above. Midway between heaven and earth, the three harvest workers move from right to left through the field. Everything happens on one plane. There is

Cat. 13
Moorland, undated
Oil on canvas
22.5 × 27.5 cm
Skagens Museum

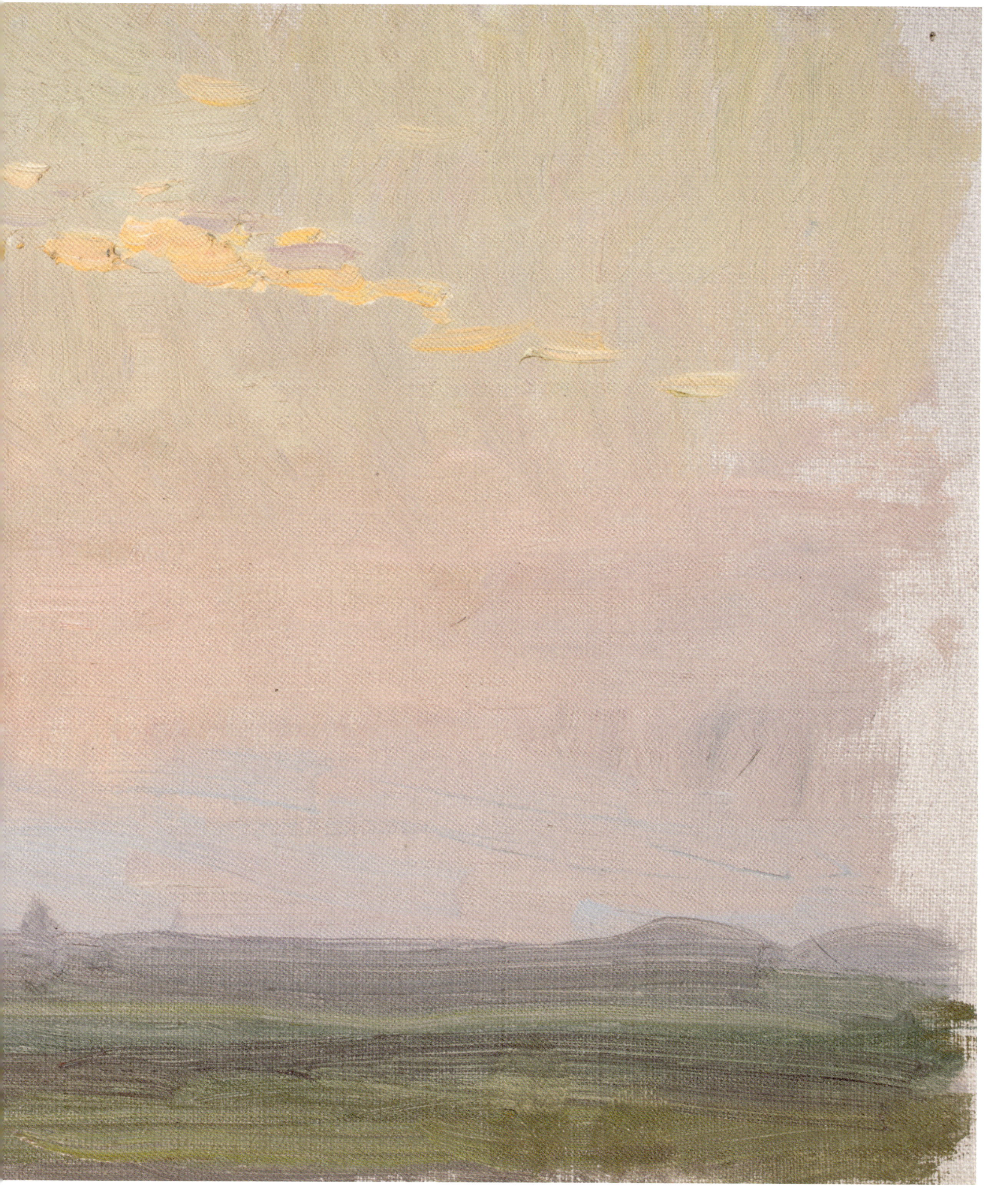

Cat. 14
At the Grave, 1913
Oil on canvas
79.5 × 61.4 cm
Skagens Museum

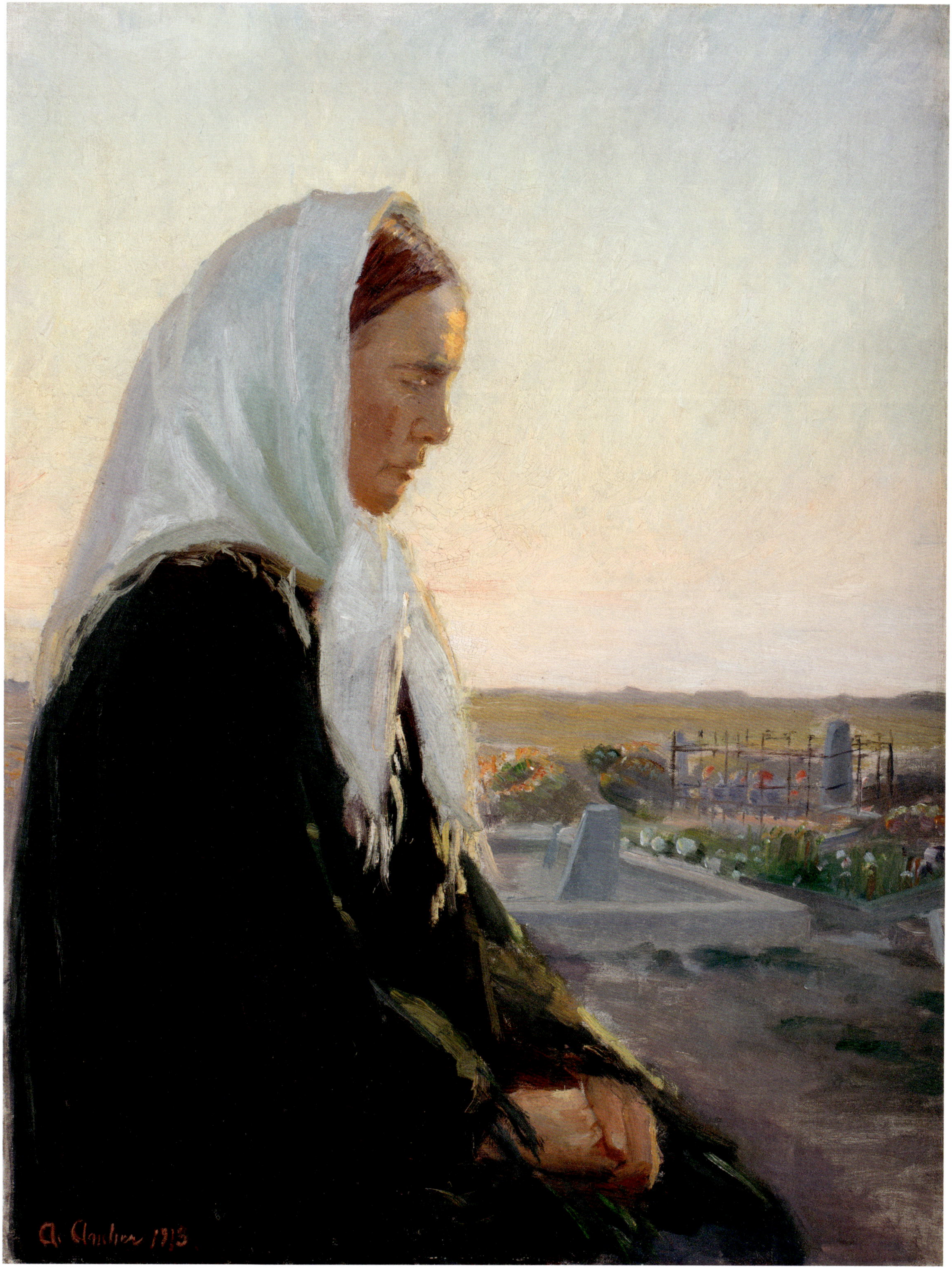

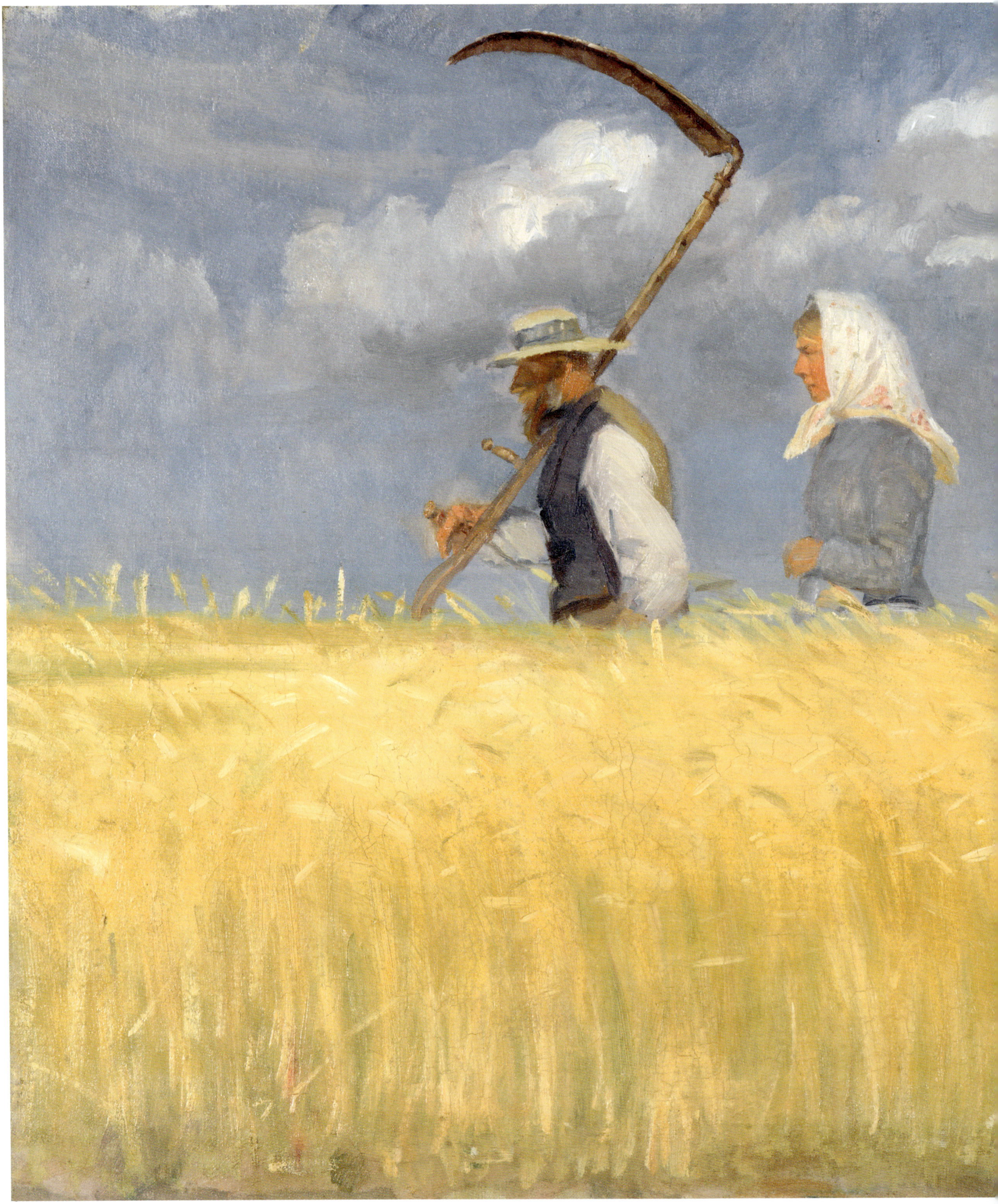

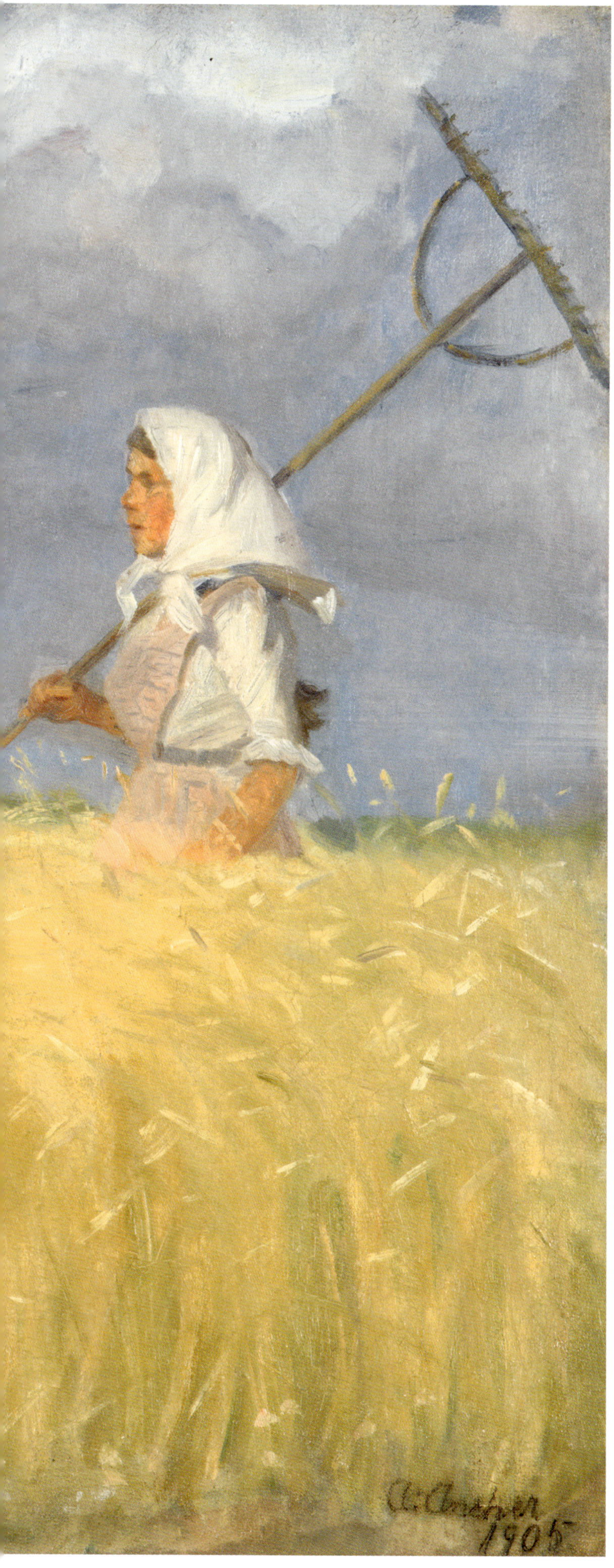

Cat. 15
Harvesters, 1905
Oil on canvas
43.4 × 56.2 cm
Skagens Museum

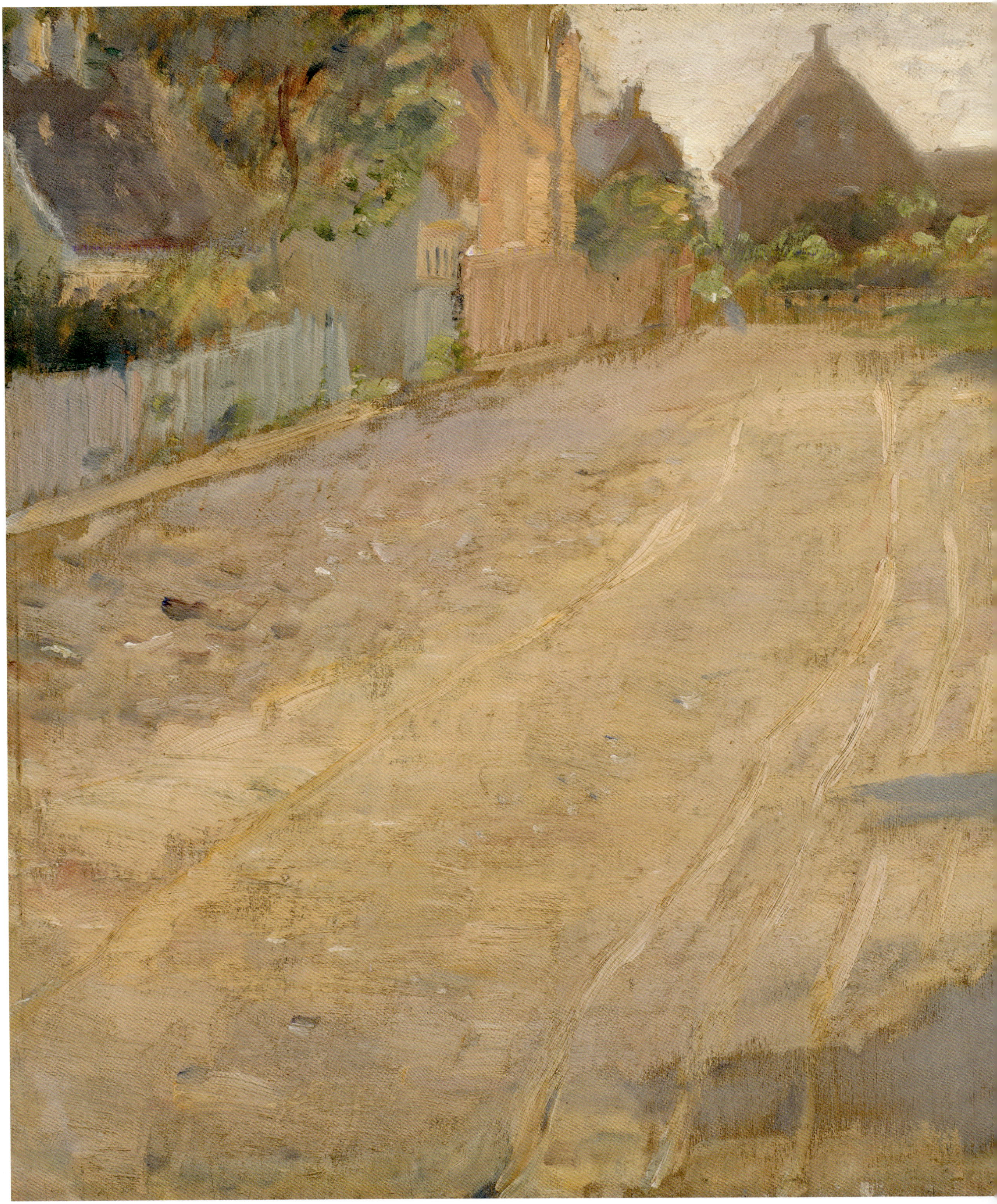

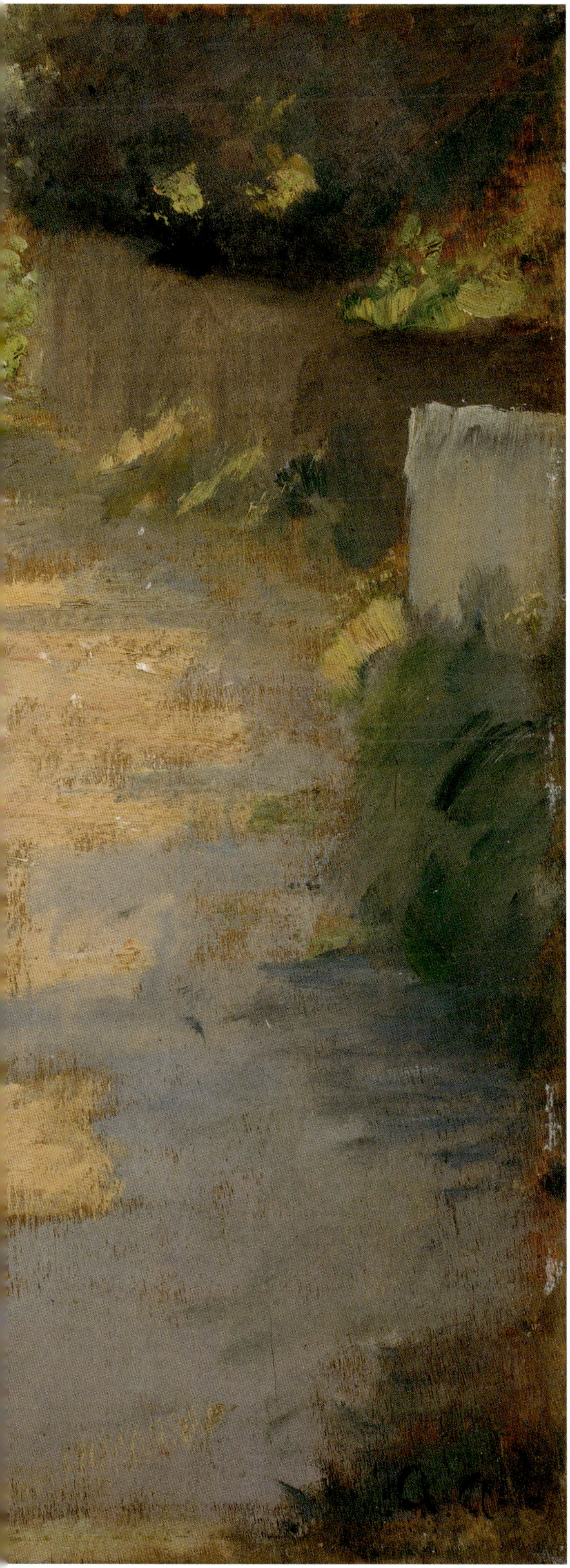

no depth or perspective leading into the image, lending it an almost symbolist character. Here, the identities of the figures are less important than what they represent: the motif evokes themes of nostalgia for traditional farming practices, fertility (symbolised by the ripe wheat) and death (represented by the scythe).

Another exterior, which is also, in its own way, a naturalistic representation of a location in Skagen, is *Daphnesvej* [cat. 16]. As in the harvest painting, the view is limited by the angle of view, so the focus becomes something other than the representation of nature. 'Daphnesvej' is the name of a street that runs between Ancher's house and Brøndum's Hotel in Skagen, named after a wrecked ship called *Daphne*. At the time, the roads in Skagen were unpaved and consisted of sand well into the 1920s. The houses were typically small, single-storey structures, characterised by a lack of good building materials. Here, Ancher has captured the atmosphere of the city on a hot summer's day, where traces of human activity are visible only as wheel tracks on the sandy road. Ancher revisited the motif in the painting *Østerbyvej* from the same year [cat. 17]. This street, named in the painting's title, runs from Brøndum's Hotel to the outskirts of the town, which is seen as a green hill at the end of the road.

In a small study from her own garden, *Helga Ancher and Ane Torup on the Garden Bench* from approximately 1890, we see a lush and green enclosed space [cat. 18]. Her daughter is engrossed in a conversation with her aunt, and only a glimpse of the open landscape appears in the background beyond the garden fence. In a later painting featuring the same garden bench, *A Girl in the Garden in Summertime. Skagen* a young woman is shown absorbed in a book, surrounded by colourful flowers [cat. 19].

Cat. 16
Daphnesvej, c. 1915
Oil on plywood
36.5 × 47 cm
Skagens Museum

Cat. 17
Østerbyvej, c. 1915
Oil on canvas, glued on card
34 × 41.5 cm
Skagens Museum

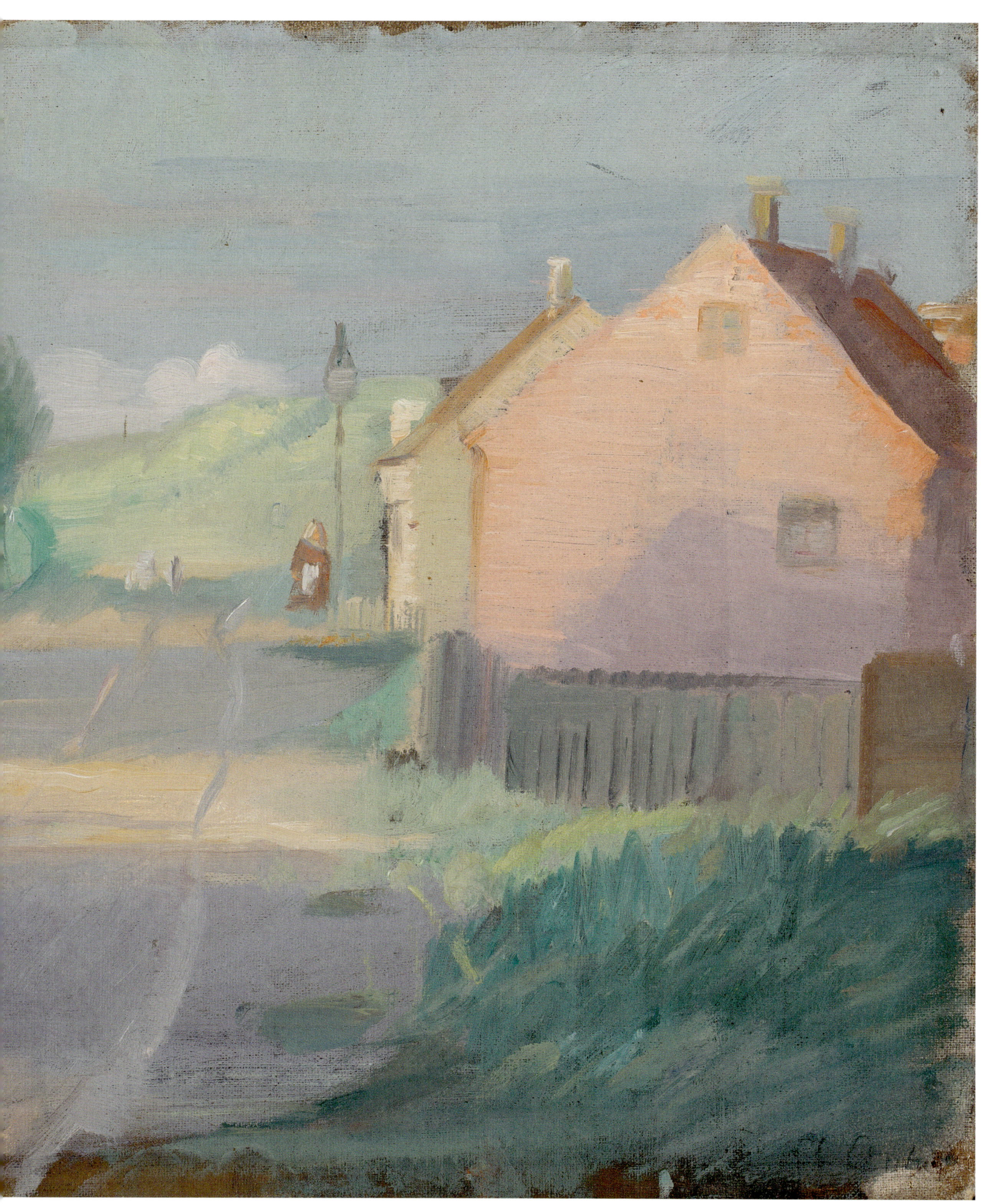

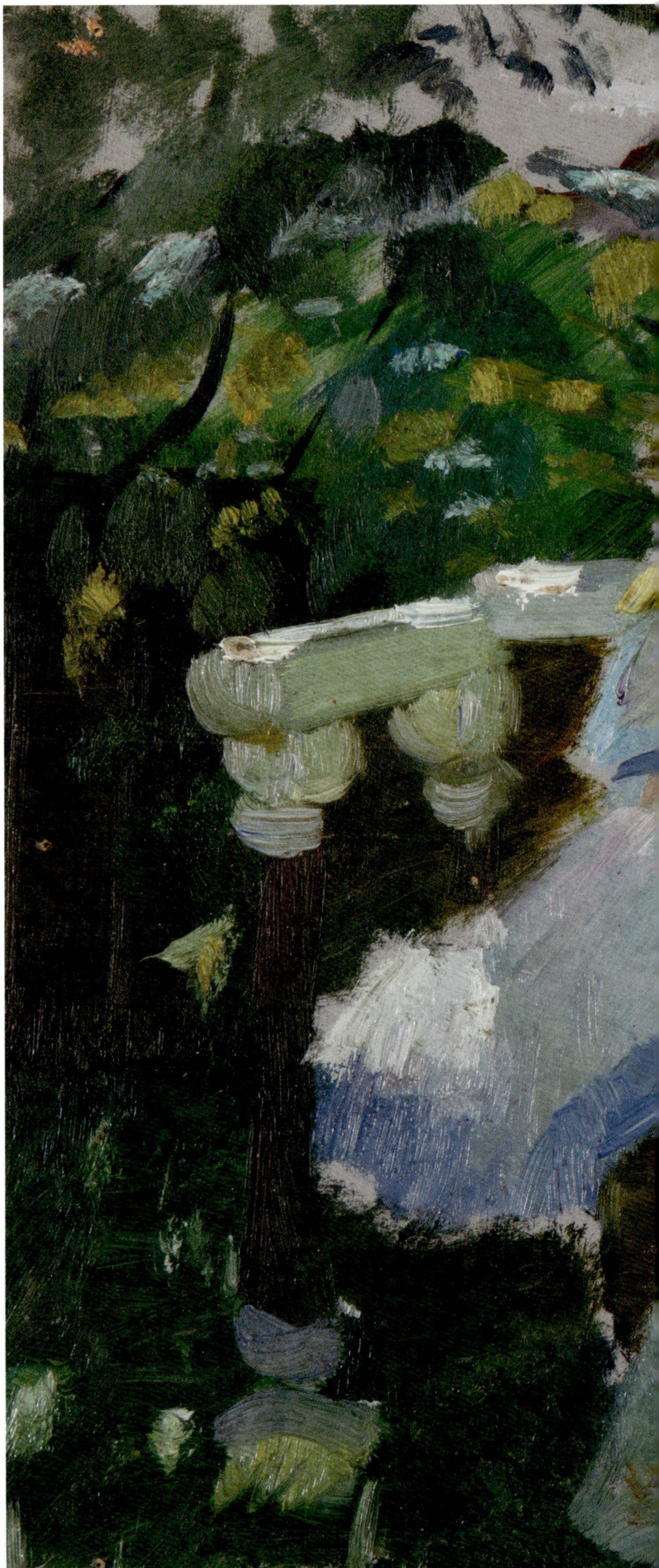

Cat. 18
Helga Ancher and Ane Torup on the Garden Bench, before 1892
Oil on card
23.8 × 32.8 cm
Skagens Museum

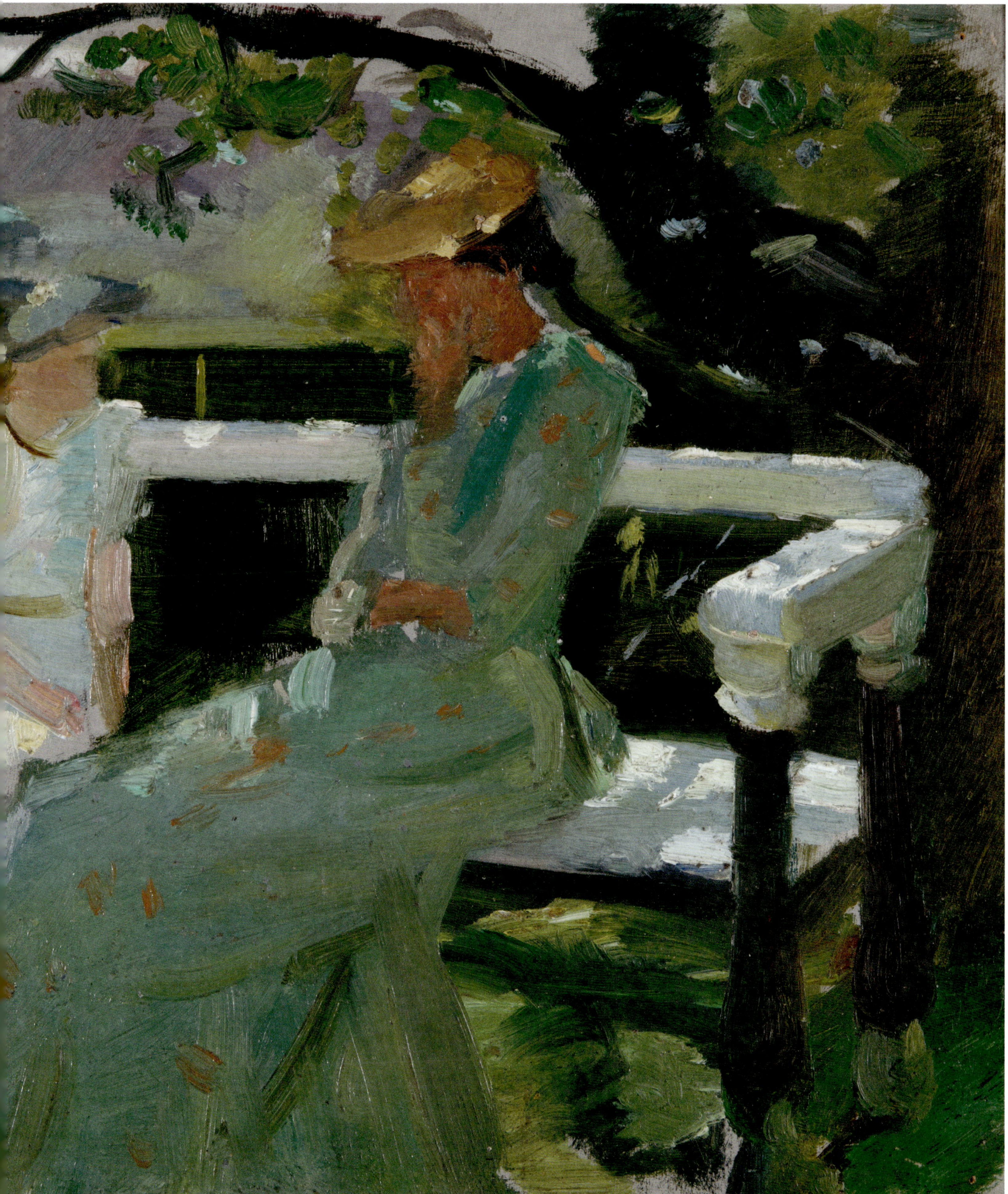

Cat. 19
A Girl in the Garden in Summertime. Skagen, 1914
Oil on card
35 × 28 cm
Skagens Museum

Overleaf:
Cat. 20
Blue Sunset, undated
Oil on canvas
43.3 × 68.5 cm
Skagens Museum

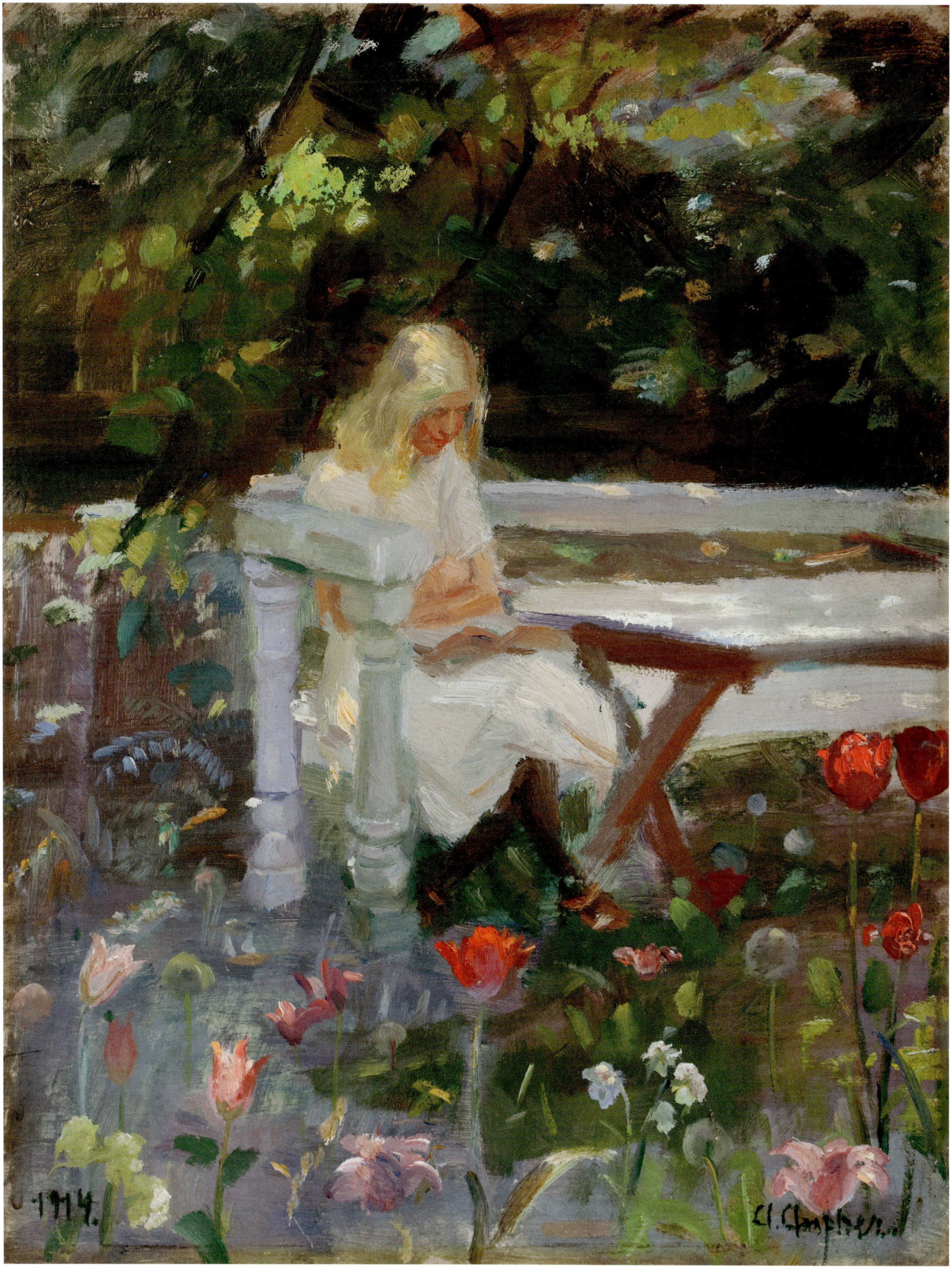

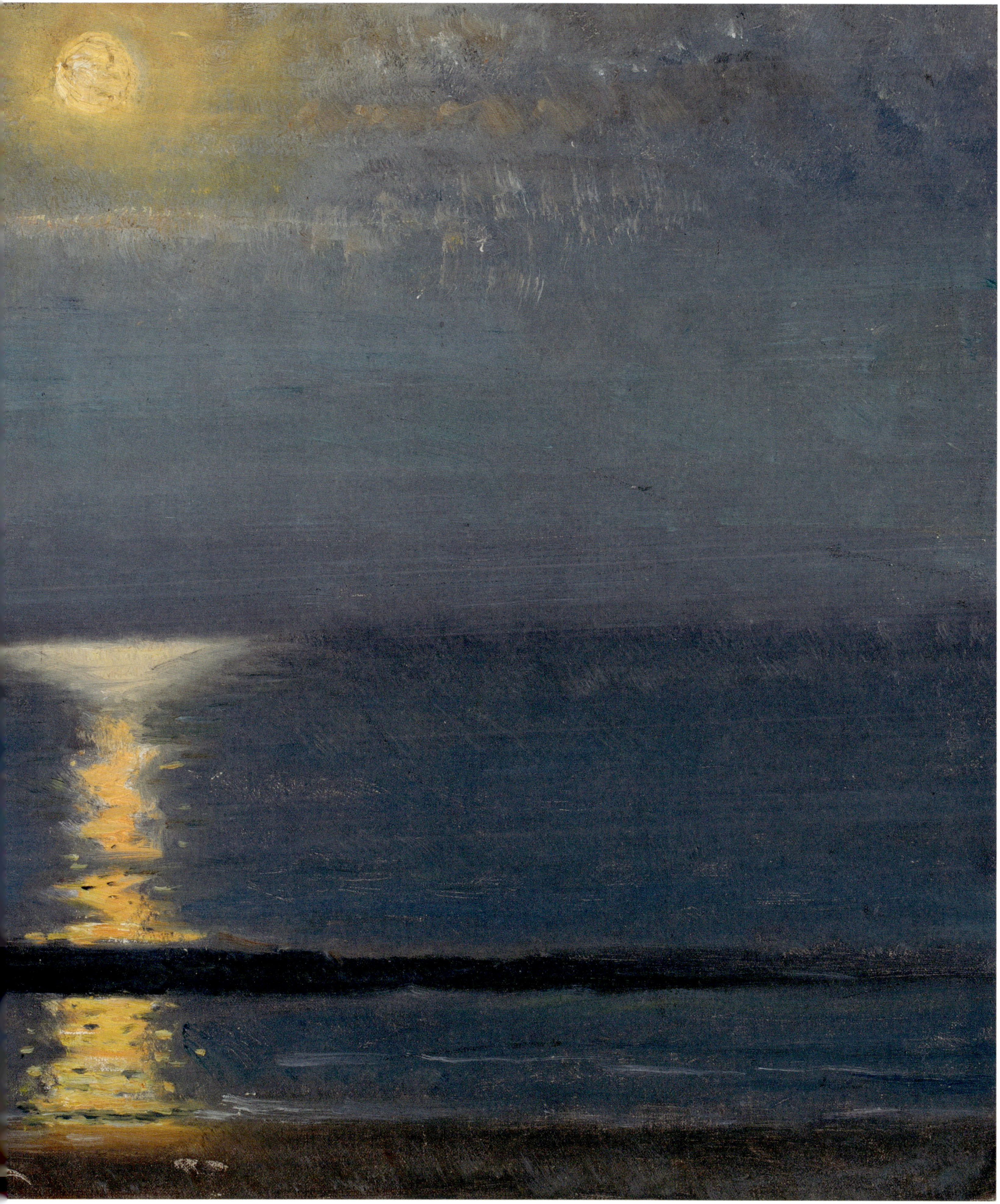

Anna Ancher had the courage to stand out. She did so every day her whole life. Her many repetitions of similar motifs and her many sketches reveal her persistence and dedication.

Cat. 21
Boats at Sønderstrand, Moonlight, c. 1883
Oil on canvas
25.2 × 19.5 cm
Skagens Museum

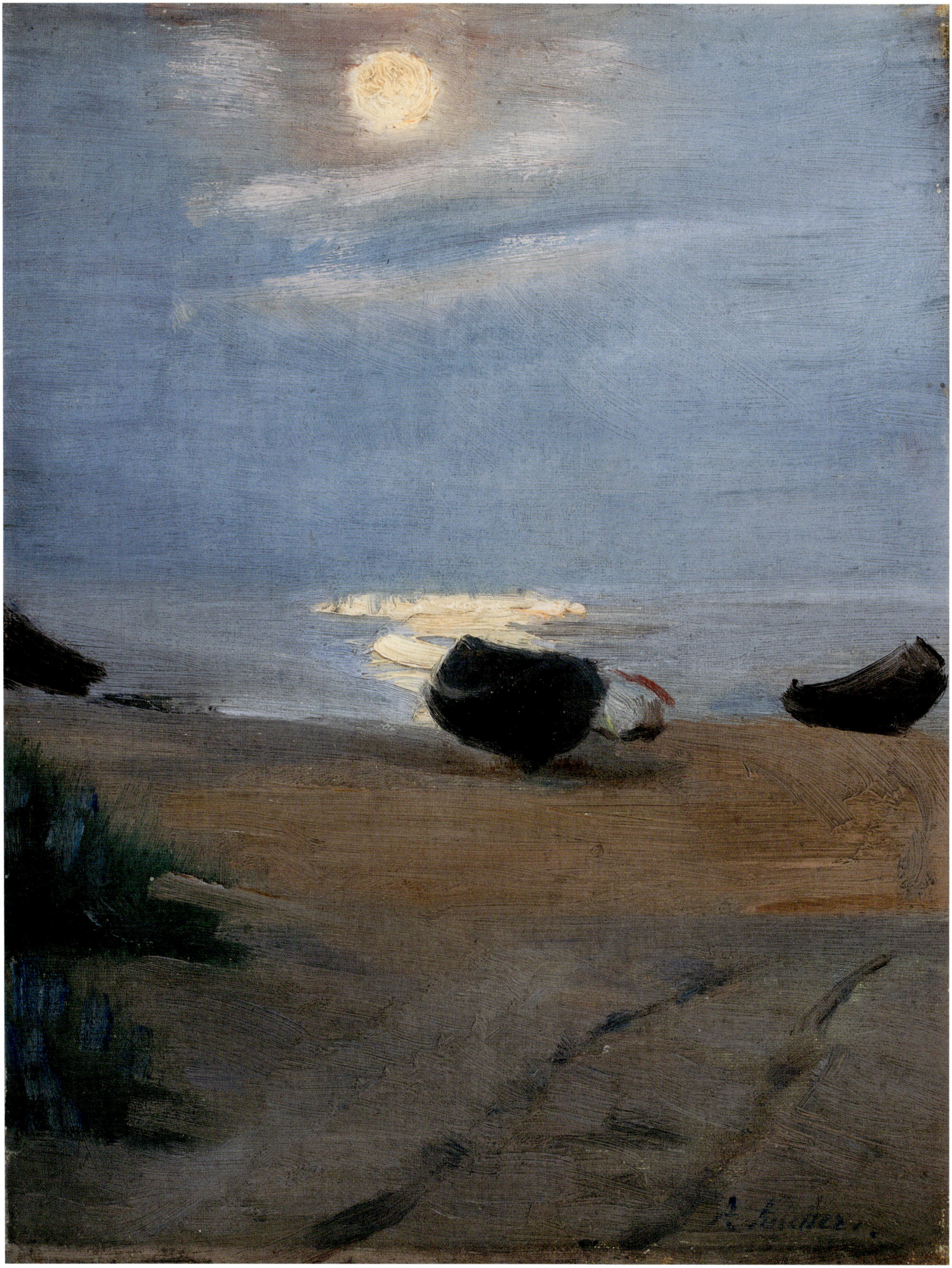

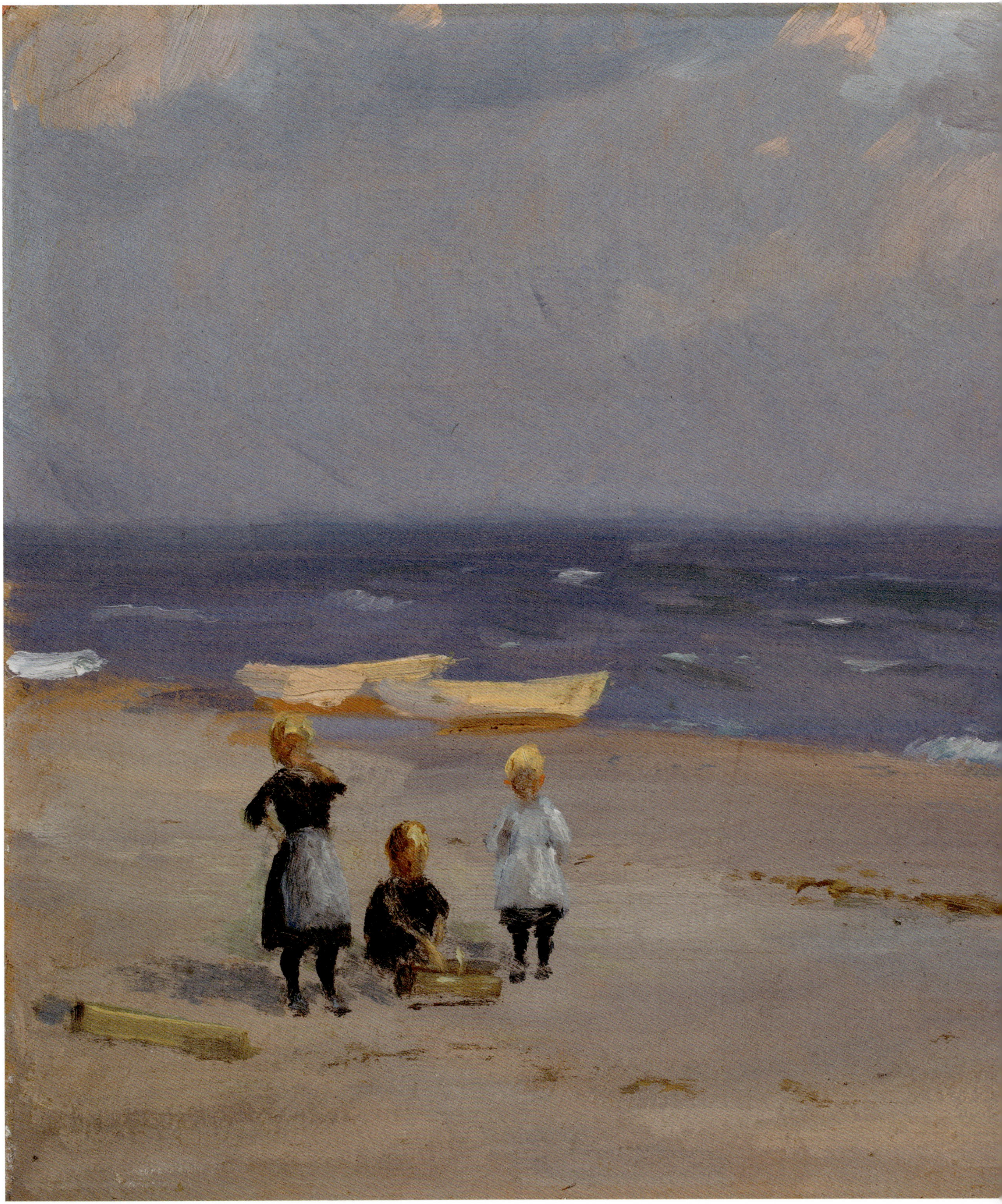

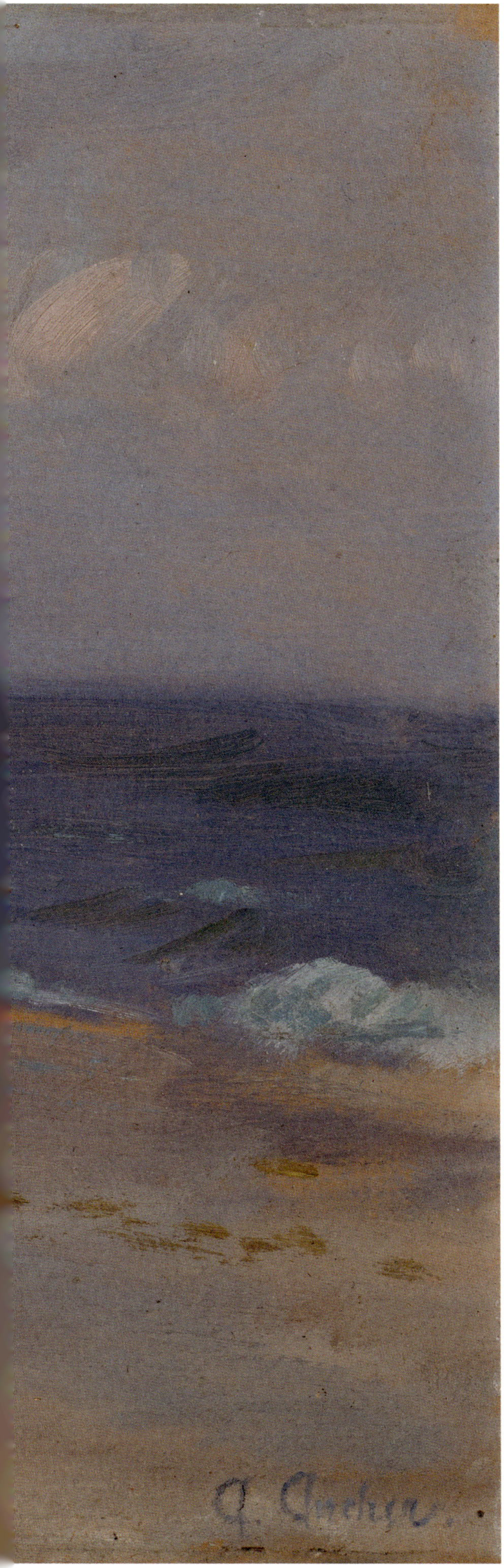

In predominantly blue shades we find the calm atmosphere of the Nordic summer evening in her painting *Blue Sunset* [cat. 20], as well as in the painting *Boats at Sønderstrand, Moonlight* [cat. 21]. In 1915, Ancher painted *Children Playing on the Beach* in broad daylight [cat. 22]. To capture this scene, she must have positioned herself in the public space of the beach, fully visible with her easel and painting tools. This is particularly noteworthy as it occurred during a period when tourism had begun to flourish in Skagen.

As is evident from Ancher's exterior paintings, she explored many different outdoor locations in Skagen and at various times of the day. She may not have painted exclusively landscapes in the traditional sense, but nevertheless, they are exterior paintings. So why has she been considered primarily as an interior painter? Could it be that painting *en plein air* was considered unfeminine at the time and long after her death? Evidently, that perception existed during her era. However, it did not stop Ancher. Perhaps these works did not receive much publicity, but they insist on existing. Moreover, she approached her exterior paintings in a way that aligned with her artistic perspective and distinctive style.

Cat. 22
Children Playing on Skagen Beach, c. 1905
Oil on card, glued on wood
24.7 × 31 cm
Skagens Museum

People of Skagen: Ancher's Models

Ancher's models appear both in her interiors and exteriors and, like her other motifs, are predominantly drawn from Skagen. They include not only friends and family but also numerous locals. Some of these individuals are known by name, while others remain anonymous. Some appear repeatedly in her works, while others are fleeting acquaintances. The painters who travelled to Skagen often used the same people from the village as models. The 'proper' fishermen were popular, perhaps because they fit artists' and audiences' expectations of what a typical weather-beaten and hardworking fisherman looked like. Similarly, unique individuals – those who were very poor, visibly different or otherwise stood out – were also favoured as models. Elderly and wrinkled figures, as well as younger, attractive members of the fishing community, were frequent subjects. Ancher's choice of models naturally had certain similarities with the other Skagen painters', but many also stood out. They were chosen less on the basis of being a type and more on the basis of being 'ordinary' or common citizens in the town. Some of her most distinctive models were Stine and Per Bollerhus, who lived in a dilapidated old shack and earned their living by walking around town selling wheat bread for the baker [cat. 3].[12] Other notable figures include the blind woman and old Lene [cat. 23]. However, several of her other models remain unidentified. For instance, the elderly couple feeding their rabbits, depicted with humour, as they gaze with childlike joy at the adorable animals, which have been brought right into their kitchen [cat. 24]. Similarly, *Three Old Seamstresses* working on a blue dress for a costume ball in a bright yellow living room, captures a moment of shared activity [cat. 25].[13] In the latter painting, one senses that Ancher placed greater emphasis on balancing and harmonising the colours in the composition than on telling us about the women, who therefore are dressed in clothes that are subordinate to the yellow colour of the room and the blue colour of the fabric, while still contributing with a rhythm.

Another type of model rarely seen in Ancher's works is her artist friends and colleagues. When she travelled to Paris in 1889 to further her education under Puvis de Chavannes, she met the Norwegian artist Kitty Kielland (1843–1914), who must have made an impression on her. She painted a portrait of Kielland while they were both in Paris, which now hangs in the living room of Ancher's house.[14] Another rare artist portrait by her is one depicting the Danish painter Valdemar Schønheyder Møller (1864–1905), which can be seen in the portrait frieze in Brøndum's dining room.[15] The dining room was furnished by the artists themselves, and later preserved in its entirety and transferred to Skagens Museum in 1946, where it remains on permanent display. These two artists may offer insights into Ancher's artistic interests. Kielland, like Ancher, had fought to secure a strong position in the European art world despite barriers of gender. She was inspired by French *plein air* painting and created landscapes with short, textured strokes and bright colours. Schønheyder Møller was, on the other hand, strongly preoccupied by painting the sunlight to such an extent that he eventually went blind from staring directly at the sun. Despite this, he managed to paint striking landscapes bathed in sunlight, both in Skagen and France, which must have appealed to Ancher.

Cat. 23
Old Lene Plucking a Goose, 1885/1890
Oil on canvas
70.5 × 54 cm
Skagens Museum

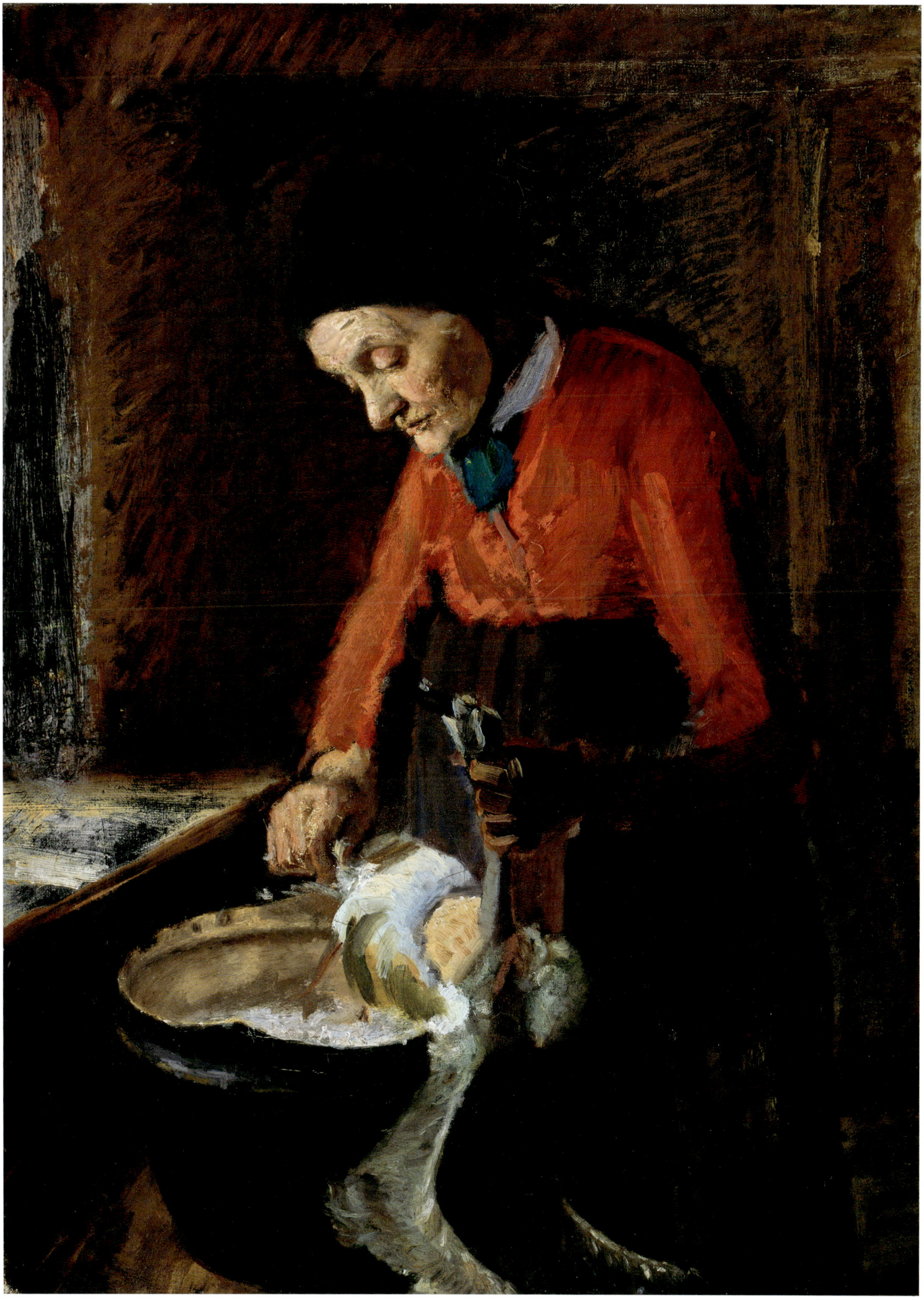

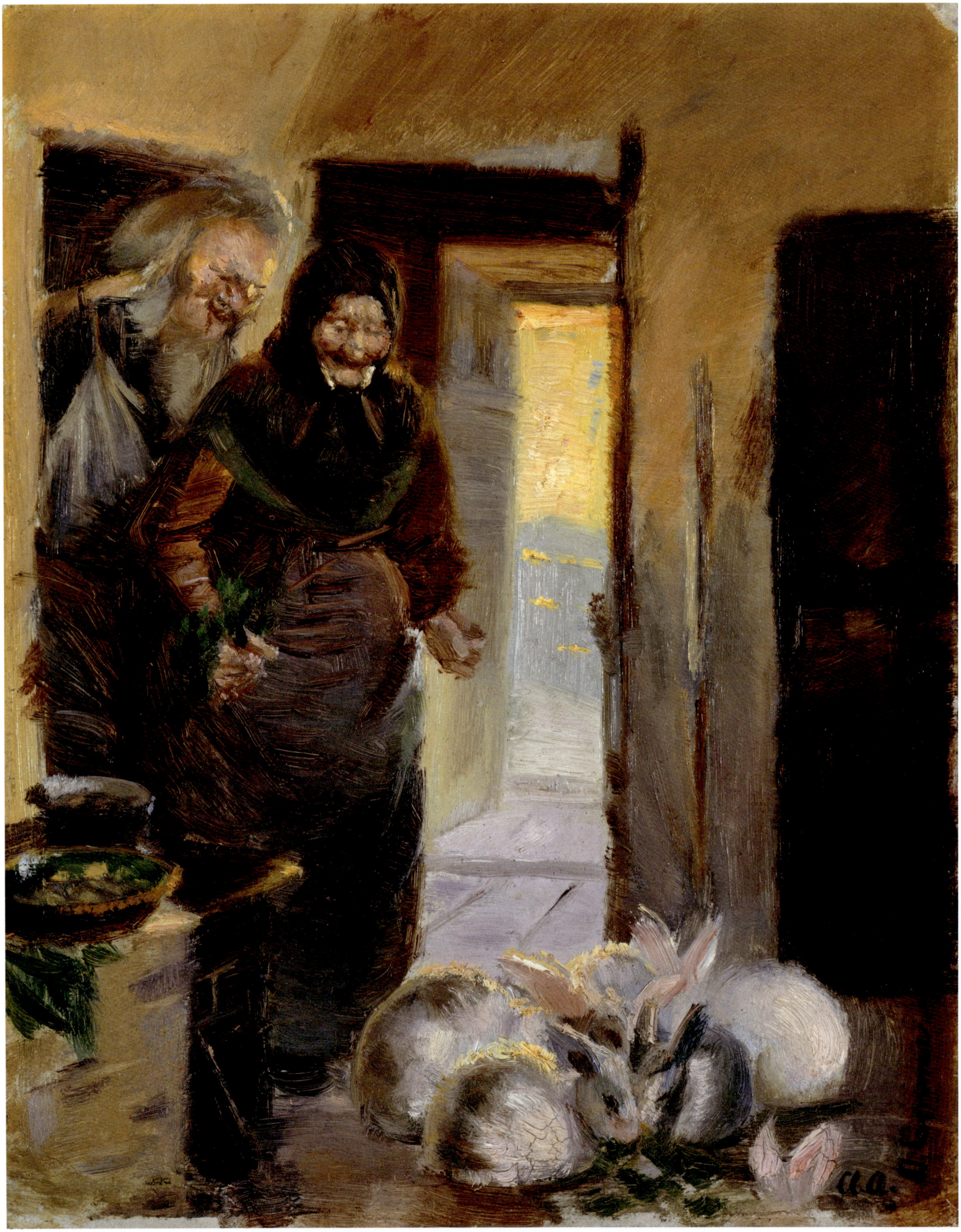

Life in a Sunbeam?

Anna Ancher had the courage to stand out. She did so every day of her life. Her many repetitions of similar motifs and her many sketches reveal her persistence and dedication. Today, many of these small studies can be admired as works of art in their own right. Her interiors and exteriors simultaneously show the naturalist's urge to document reality and the artist's technical experimentation with colour and light.

For Ancher, the entirety of Skagen was her studio, and its residents were her models. Her 'life in a sunbeam' extended beyond artistic choices and preferred motifs – it also reflected her privileged position in a broader sense. This privilege was not defined by monetary wealth but by being surrounded by a supportive network of family, friends and colleagues who provided her with the opportunity and framework to flourish as an artist. She received help and encouragement from many quarters because of her remarkable personality. She was talented, humorous and deeply passionate about the arts – a combination that inspired others to support her and contributed to her lasting legacy.

Cat. 24
An Old Couple with Their Rabbits, 1891/93
Oil on card
26.9 × 21.8 cm
Skagens Museum

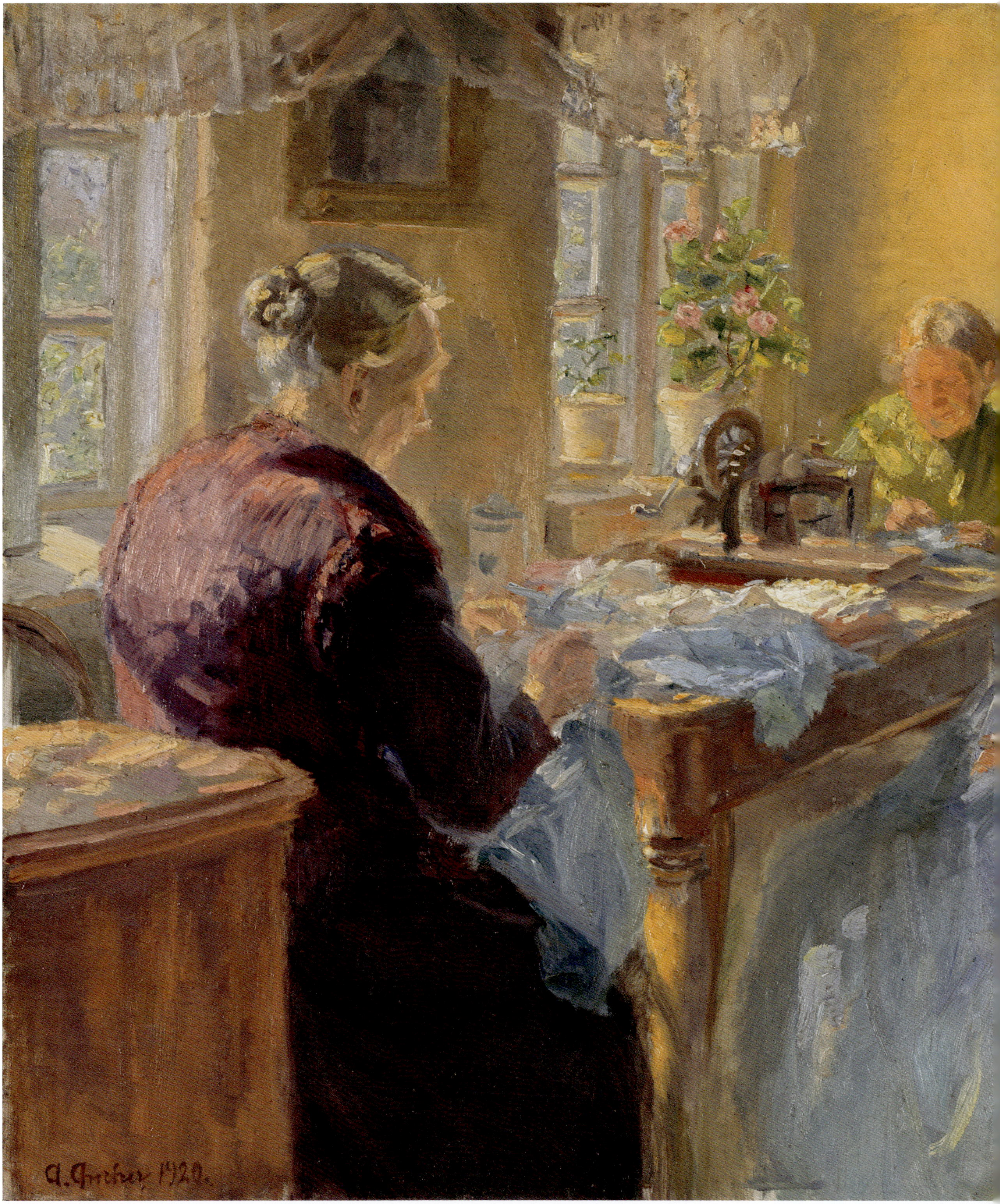
A. Ancher 1920.

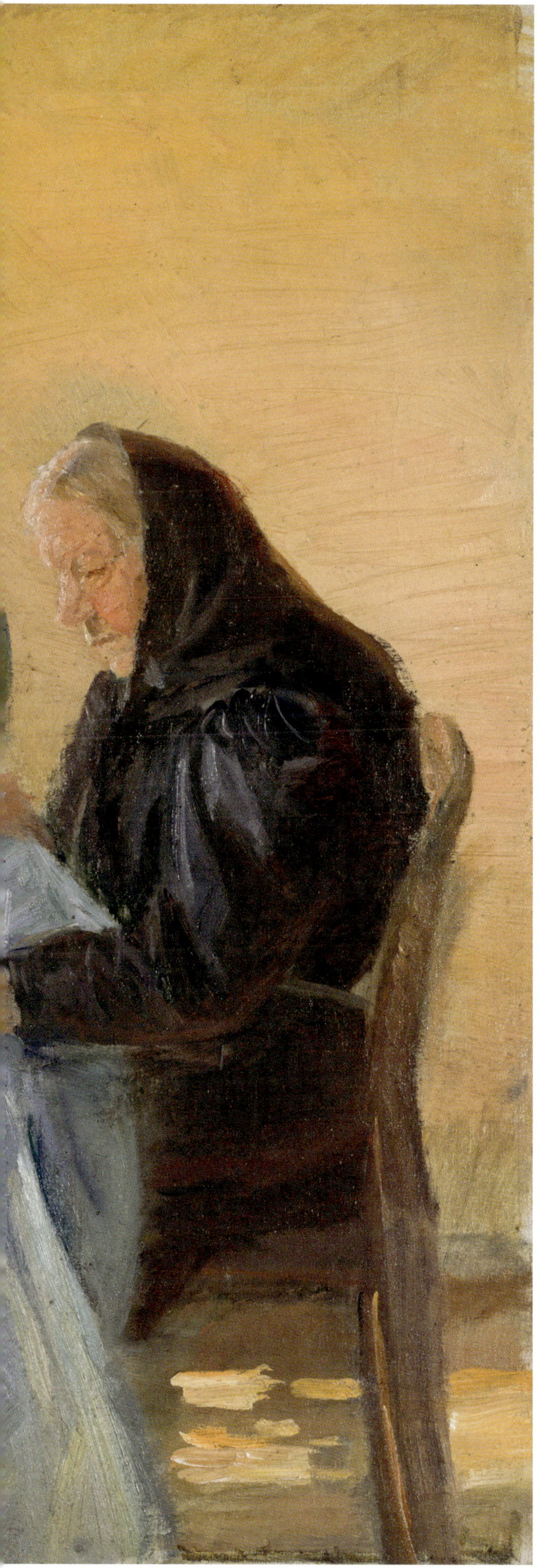

Cat. 25
Three Old Seamstresses, 1910
Oil on canvas
54.8 × 68.7 cm
Skagens Museum

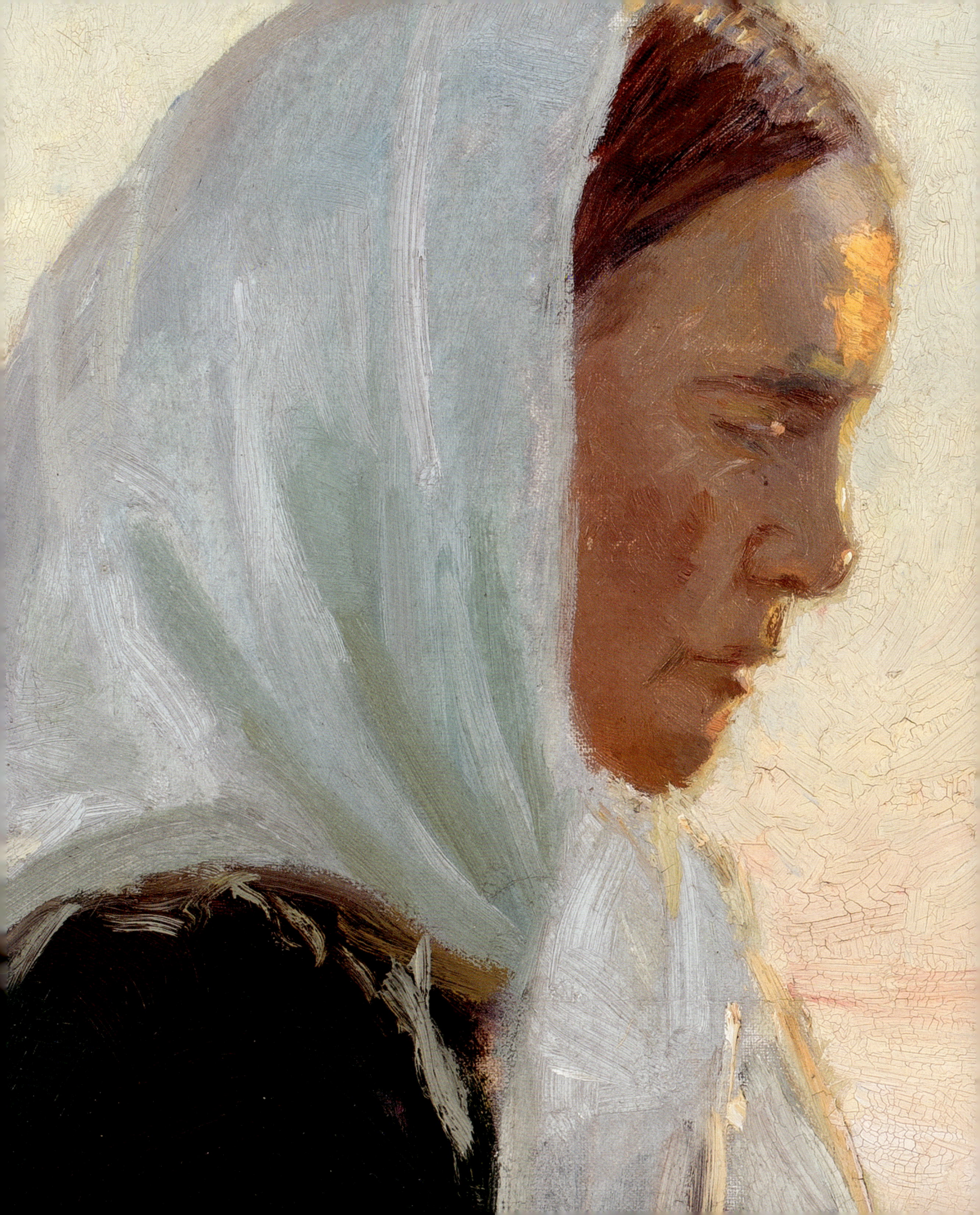

LOOKING BACK, LOOKING FORWARDS:

ANNA ANCHER'S ARTISTIC INFLUENCES

Helen Hillyard

‘Rembrandt goes so deep into the mysterious that he says things for which there are no words in any language. It is with justice that they call Rembrandt 'magician', that’s no easy occupation.’[1]

Vincent van Gogh on
Rembrandt’s *The Jewish Bride*, 1885

‘When we saw Rembrandt’s ‘Jewish Bride’ it was like having the nicest possible aquavit trickling through you... gloriously glorious’.[2]

Anna Ancher on
Rembrandt’s *The Jewish Bride*, 1891

In 1891, Ancher recounted in a letter to her cousin Martha the memory of seeing Rembrandt van Rijn's (1606–1669) masterpiece *The Jewish Bride* six years previously in Amsterdam [fig. 7]. Her description echoes that of her contemporary Vincent van Gogh (1853–1890), who rhapsodised about his own visit – in the same year as Ancher, 1885 – in a letter to his brother Theo. *The Jewish Bride* is among Rembrandt's most sumptuous works. Painted at the very end of the artist's life, Rembrandt employed the rich reddish-gold palette that characterised the work of his later years. *The Jewish Bride* is remarkable for its striking use of impasto, thick-raised paint that recreates the tactile quality of the fabric depicted. For both Ancher and Van Gogh, the experience of viewing *The Jewish Bride* elicited an intense physical reaction. They recognised in this Old Master – whose painting had been created over 200 years previously – an unknowable quality, which although both found difficult to put into words, was in equal parts emotive and visceral.

Ancher is often viewed as being one of the key figures to channel facets of impressionism and post-impressionism into a Nordic context.[3] In her bold use of colour and painterly interpretation of light effects, this visual connection is immediately recognisable when looking at the artist's work and is apparent to a greater degree than in the work of any other Skagen painter. And yet, what is equally radical about her art is the way she proactively selects and adapts historical motifs. We see Ancher looking back in order to move forwards, using lessons from the past to push new boundaries, while simultaneously incorporating developments at the cutting-edge of artistic practice.

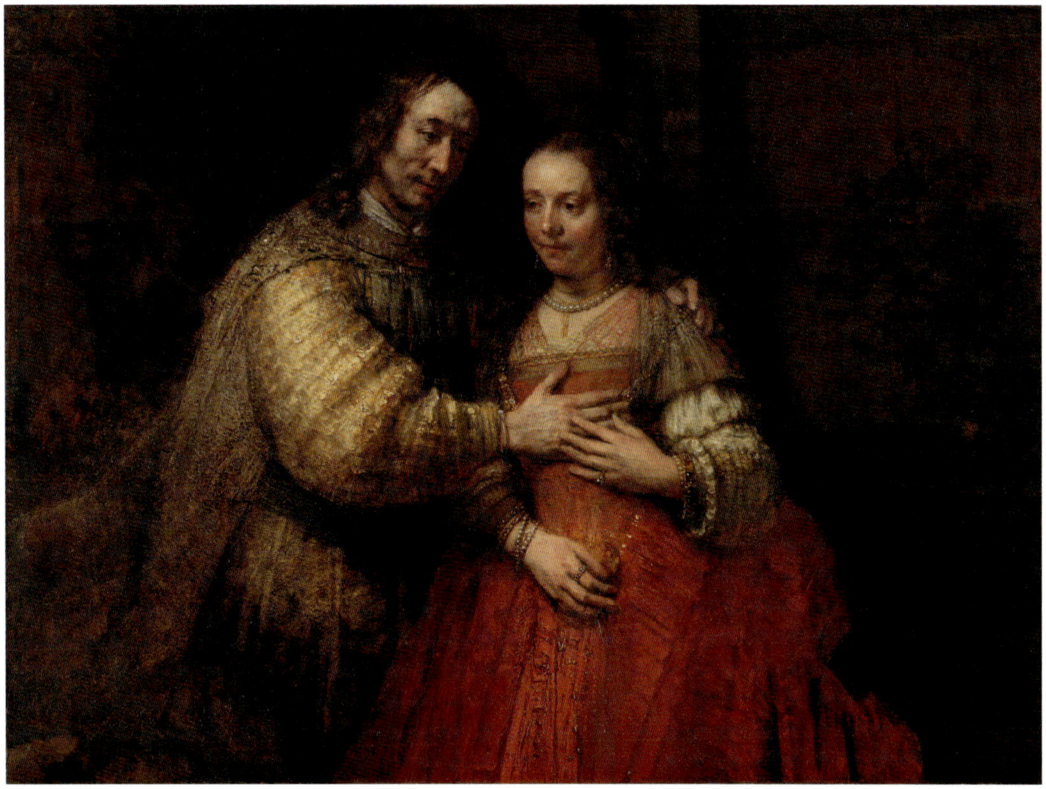

Fig. 7
Rembrandt van Rijn
Isaac and Rebecca, Known as 'The Jewish Bride', c. 1665–1669
Oil on canvas
121.5 × 166.5 cm
Rijksmuseum, Amsterdam

Facing the Past

Ancher's early artistic training would have been grounded in the Old Masters. Between 1875 and 1878, the young Ancher travelled to Copenhagen every winter in order to take classes at Vilhelm Kyhn's (1819–1903) school of drawing and painting for women. It was presumably during these classes that she produced a copy of a Rembrandt-type head study alongside a handful of still lifes in the tradition of Dutch seventeenth-century painting, all of which can be found in the collection of the Skagens Museum.[4] Still life would have been considered a highly appropriate subject for young women of the late nineteenth century, allowing them to hone their skills using objects within a domestic, interior setting. Under no circumstances would the women of Kyhn's school have drawn from a nude model, in the manner practised by their male peers at the Royal Danish Academy of Fine Art, which at that time still barred women from entry.[5]

Nearly all the works Ancher produced in her career depict scenes around her hometown of Skagen. She extolled the virtues of finding subjects from one's local area: 'I firmly believe that the very best thing is to go on small trips, but staying mainly at home and painting the people of one's own country'.[6] However, the artist's travels across Europe would have a profound impact on the direction of her work. For female artists, travel could also offer the possibility of freedom, since women could enjoy a degree of anonymity, and distance themselves from some of the social conventions that governed their lives at home.[7] Given that, after the birth of her first child, her teacher Kyhn had suggested she launch her painter's box out to sea, Ancher was certainly not isolated from such social pressures. Accompanied by her husband Michael (1849–1927), she went on her first journey abroad in 1882. Travelling south, they visited Berlin, Dresden, Munich and Vienna. It was in Vienna that the couple first met the artist Peder Severin Krøyer (1851–1909), who would later visit them in Skagen and soon after become a core member of the artist colony [fig. 8]. In 1885, the couple travelled again, this time to the Netherlands, Belgium and Paris.

Seeing historic artworks first-hand, and Dutch seventeenth-century painting in particular, was critical to these early journeys. In one letter, written from the Netherlands to her family in Skagen, she describes how Krøyer suggested staying an extra night in Amsterdam precisely for the sake of seeing Rembrandt's *The Night Watch*.[8] A large number of reproductions of Old Master paintings and drawings have also been found within the Anchers' photographic collection, pictures that may have been acquired either in Denmark or at the museums they visited.[9] Across Ancher's works there are subjects and motifs that were clearly absorbed from the Old Master paintings she saw. And while her fascination with Dutch painting was not unique amongst late-nineteenth-century artists, the distinctive way in which she selected and reworked these motifs, alongside more contemporary influences, is not seen elsewhere.

Ancher's debt to Dutch painting is witnessed foremost in her choice of subjects. In multiple works she concentrates on lone female figures within domestic spaces, a theme explored in the work of Pieter de Hooch (1629–1684) and Johannes Vermeer (1632–1675) among others. In *The Maid in the Kitchen* [cat. 4], we see a woman, standing alone, her back to the viewer, preparing food. Light enters through a window, filtered through a yellow-cream curtain, placing the figure almost in silhouette. The artist hints at a world beyond, through the window – where we see the rooftop of a nearby building – and the open door, at the right of the painting, which leads to another room. Her work recalls the interiors of De Hooch, who also depicted private spaces occupied by women. Often concentrating on just a corner of a room, De Hooch focused on the illumination of interior space and frequently included 'through-views': secondary, interior and exterior spaces, glimpsed through doorways. This device, also employed by Vermeer, has the effect of securing the realm of the domestic interior, by contrasting the sanctum of 'private' space with the outside 'public' space beyond.[10]

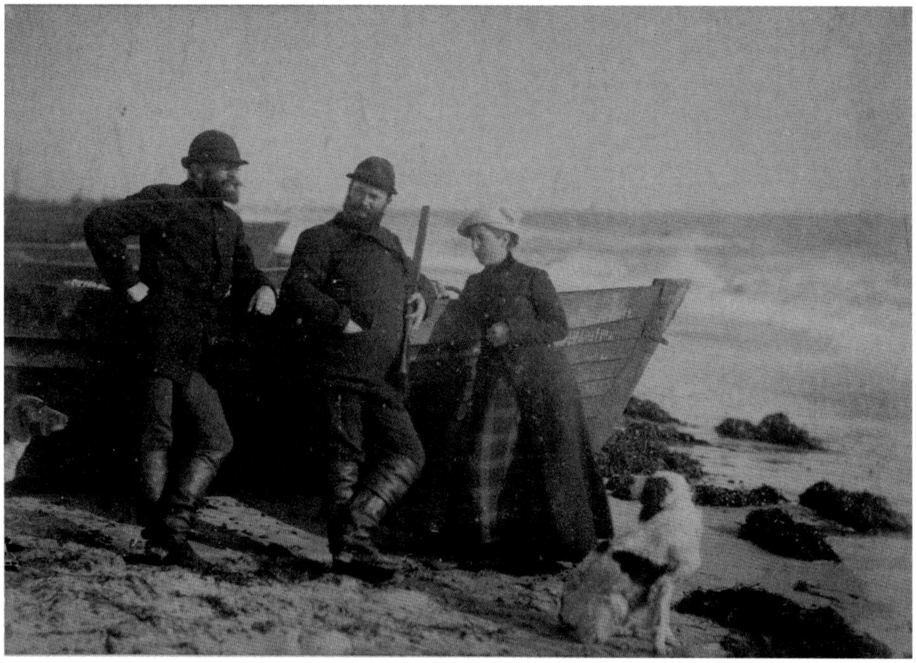

Another work that concentrates on a woman inhabiting a private space is Ancher's *Young Mother with Her Child* [cat. 26], a painting which can be likened to Vermeer's *The Milkmaid* [fig. 9]. As with *The Milkmaid*, Ancher places her figure against a white backdrop with a window to the left, allowing light to illuminate both the figure and the interior space. Both hint at the inner lives of the figures depicted, with the models wholly engrossed in their tasks – breastfeeding and pouring milk – seemingly unaware of the artists' presence. To a certain degree both scenes would have been staged but the viewer is given the impression that they are witnessing an intimate and unguarded moment. This is enhanced by the spontaneous, sketch-like quality of Ancher's painting which, in spite of its seemingly 'unfinished' state, was signed by the artist, suggesting she considered it more than a study, and that its quickly painted style was a key attribute of the work.

Fig. 8
Fritz Stoltenberg (photographer)
P.S Kroyer, Michael Ancher and Anna Ancher Beside a Boat at South Beach, c. 1884
Albumen print
118 × 170 mm
Skagens Museum

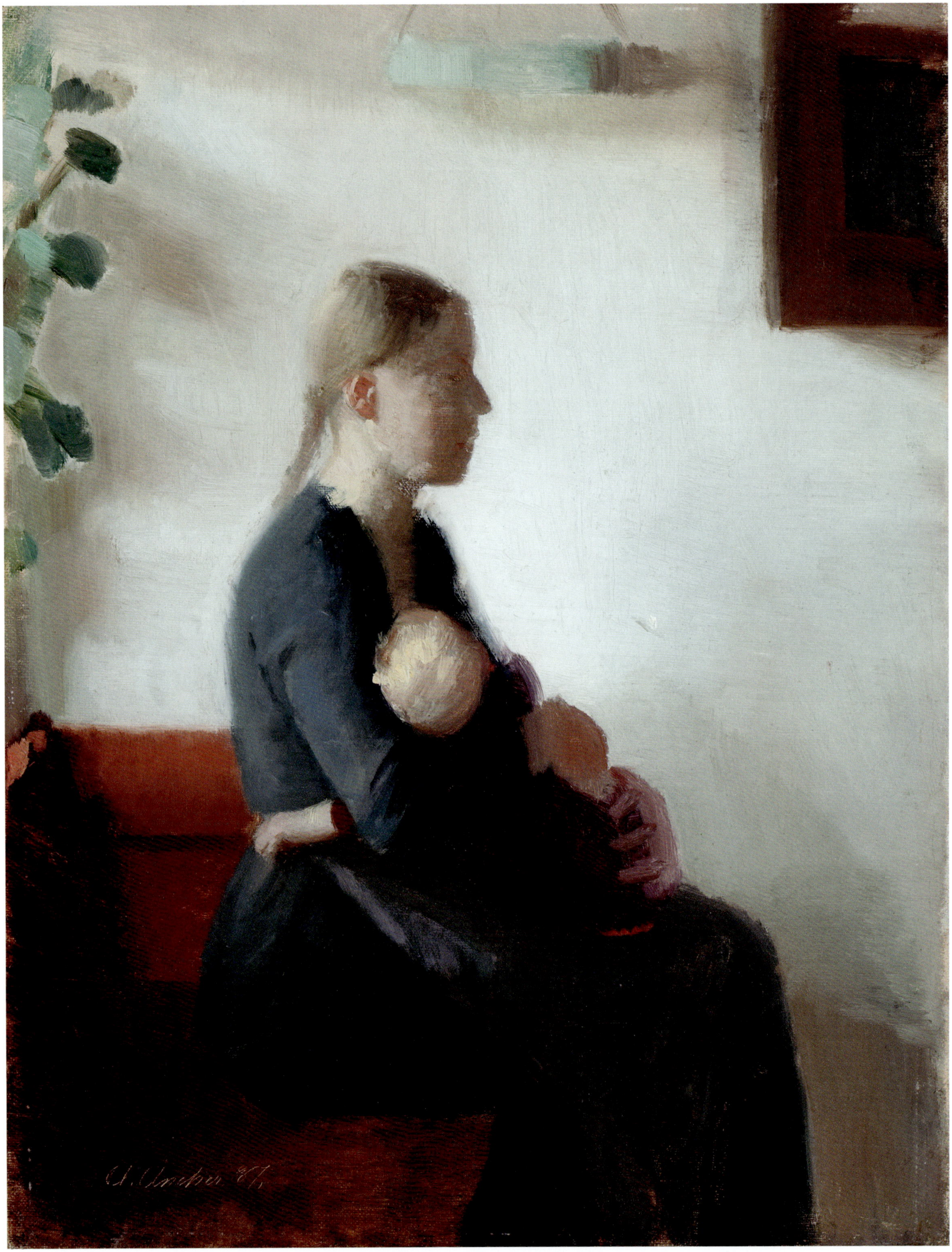

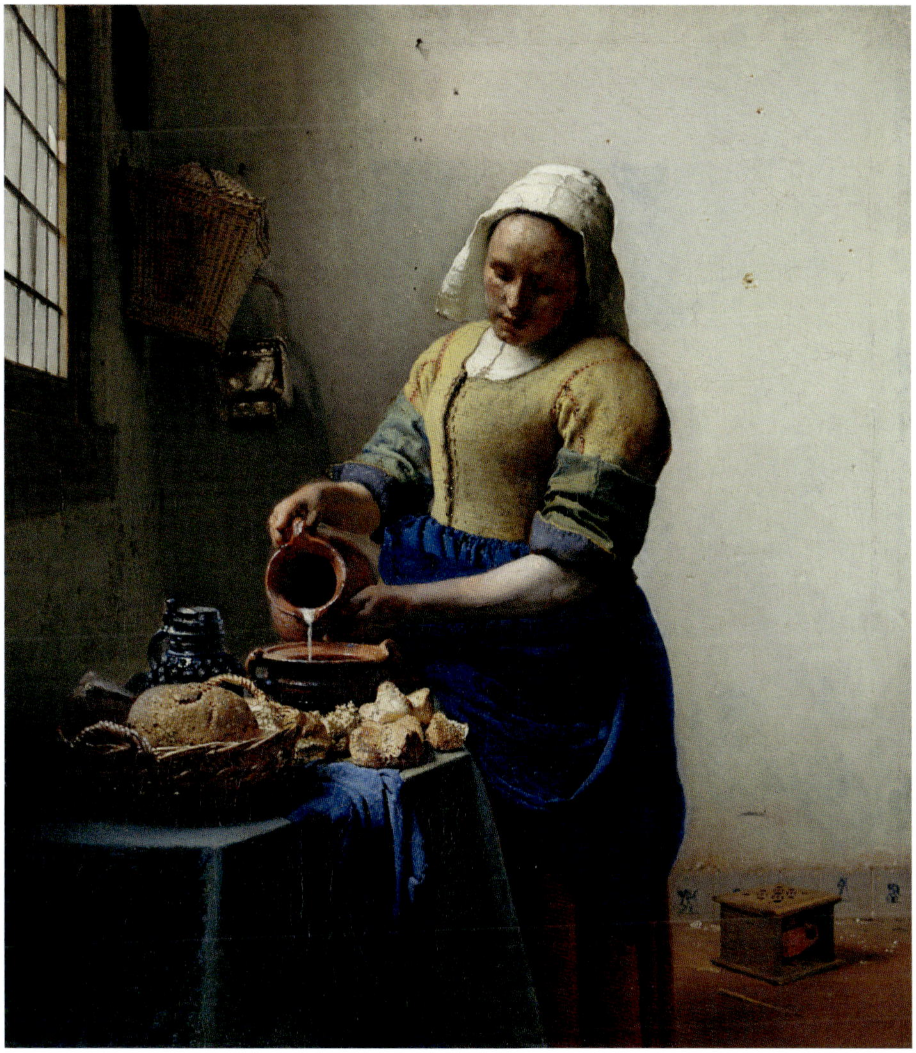

Depictions of women and girls sewing and knitting are another of Ancher's repeated motifs. Works like *Two Little Girls Being Taught How to Sew* [cat. 10] and *A Woman Knitting, Evening Light* [cat. 27] can be connected to images of spinning, sewing and lace-making by Dutch artists, including Nicolaes Maes (1634–1693) [fig. 10]. In *A Woman Knitting, Evening Light* an older woman is depicted front-on, dressed entirely in red against the backdrop of a blue wall. In Maes's scenes, the act of lace-making was associated with simple virtue and devout older people making themselves useful with household chores.[11] Although Ancher's works do not carry the same moralising undertones, she frequently shows the lives of the older people in her community, emphasising that their lives were not ones of leisure but continued hard work and activity. Ancher's use of vibrant reds to dress her figures – something which she does on multiple occasions – may also be borrowed from Maes. This choice serves to create a striking contrast, foregrounding the red-orange against the complementary tone of the blue-green.

As highlighted in the quote at the start of this essay, Ancher clearly admired Rembrandt. Her appreciation of the artist is communicated elsewhere in her letters too, including one where she described the artist affecting a 'glow' deep within her.[12] There are numerous works by Rembrandt catalogued amongst the photographic reproductions in the Anchers' collection, including the famous *Jewish Bride*, and artist Laurits Tuxen (1853–1927) even gifted Ancher his drawing after Rembrandt's *Self-Portrait at the Age of 63*, with the inscription 'To Anna from LT. An old friend!', implying that Ancher's 'old friend' was Rembrandt himself.[13] Both Ancher and Rembrandt shared a fascination with the effects of light, and a talent for manipulating the paint medium so as to make light feel tangible.

Cat. 26
Young Mother with Her Child,
1887
Oil on canvas
41 × 32 cm
Skagens Museum

Fig. 9
Johannes Vermeer,
The Milkmaid, c. 1658–1659
Oil on canvas
45.1 × 41 cm
Rijksmuseum, Amsterdam

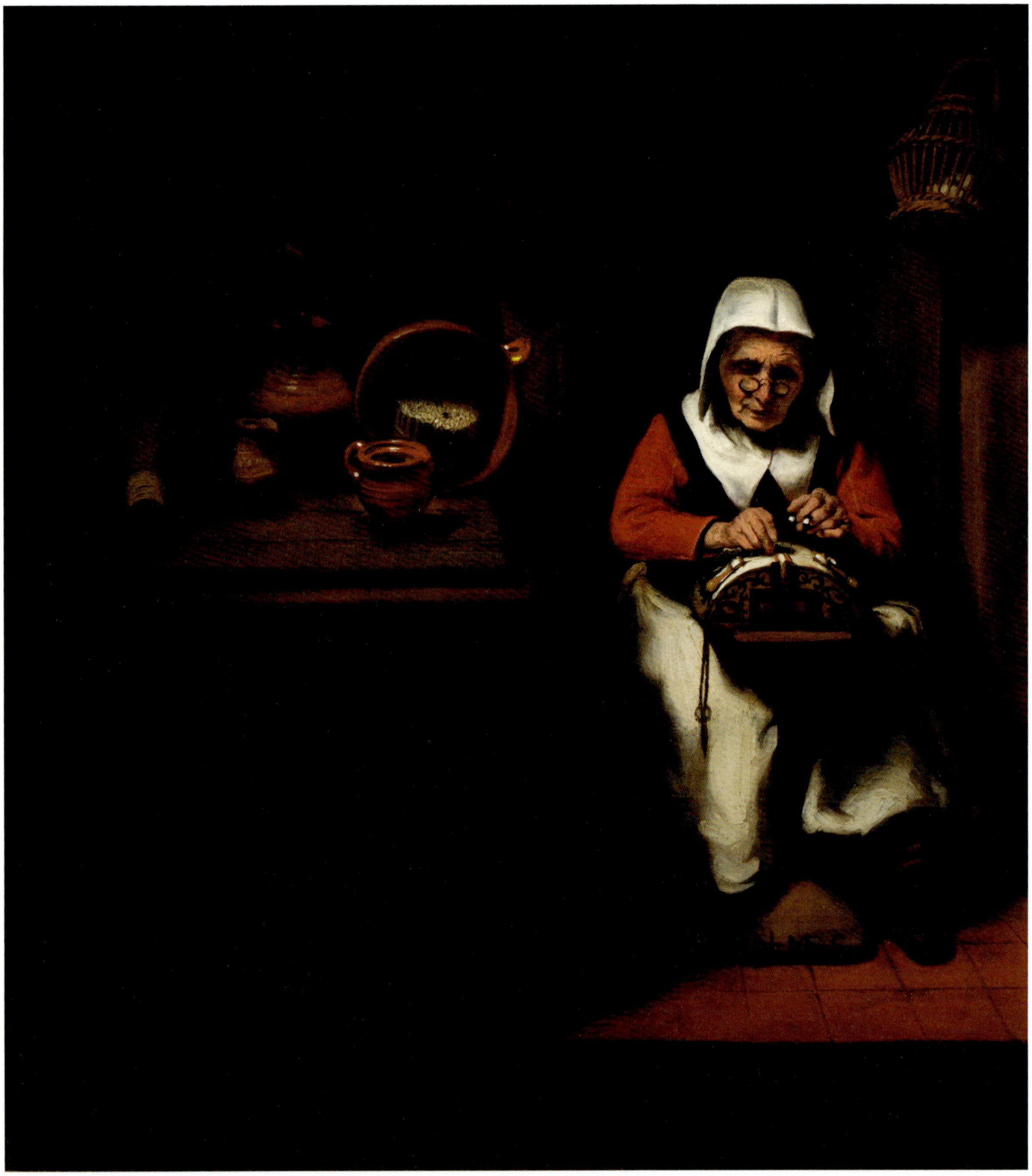

Fig. 10
Nicolaes Maes
The Old Lacemaker, c. 1656
Oil on panel,
37.5 × 35 cm
Mauritshuis, The Hague

Cat. 27
A Woman Knitting. Evening Light,
1919
Oil on canvas
82.5 × 64.5 cm
Skagens Museum

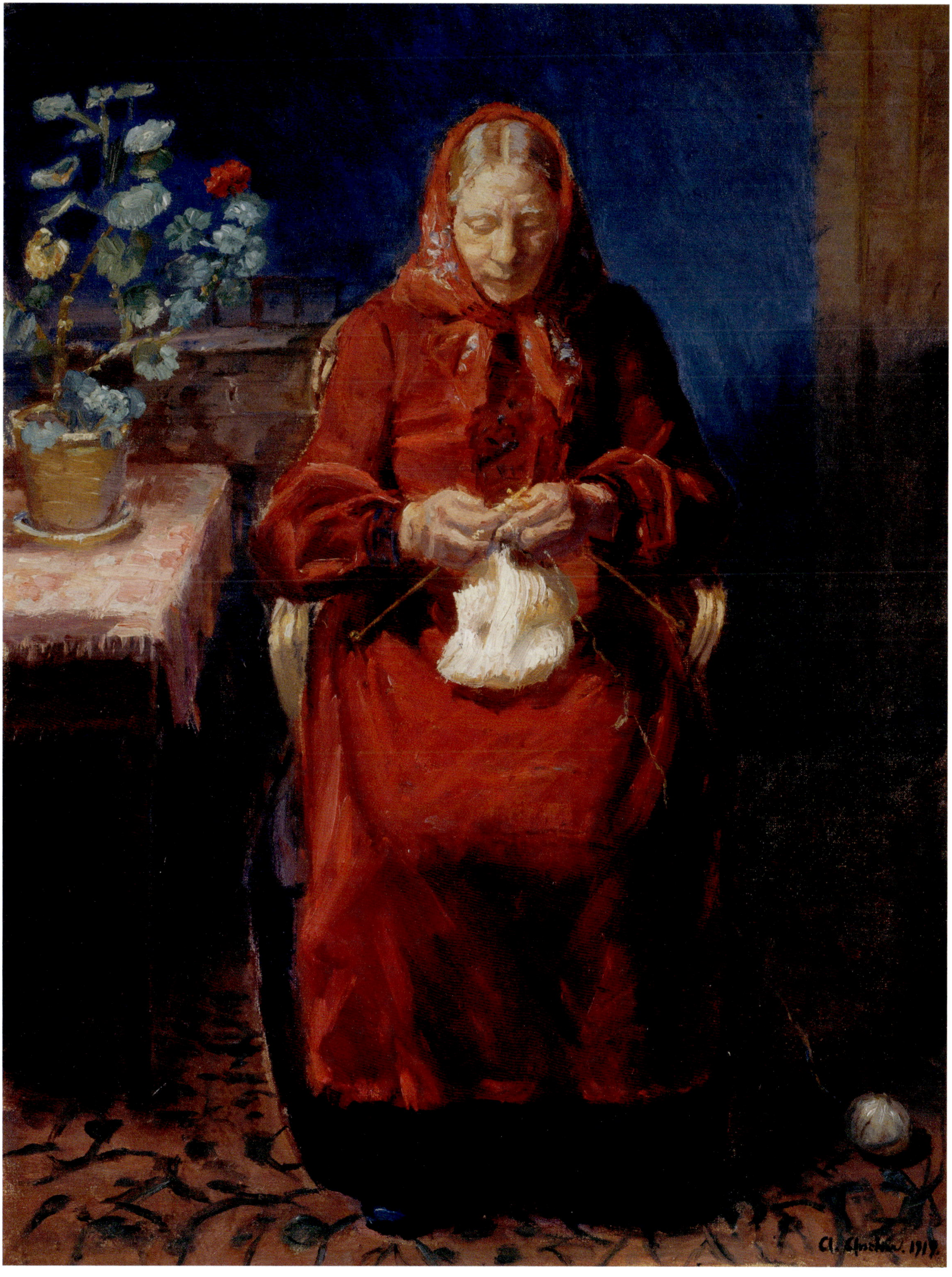

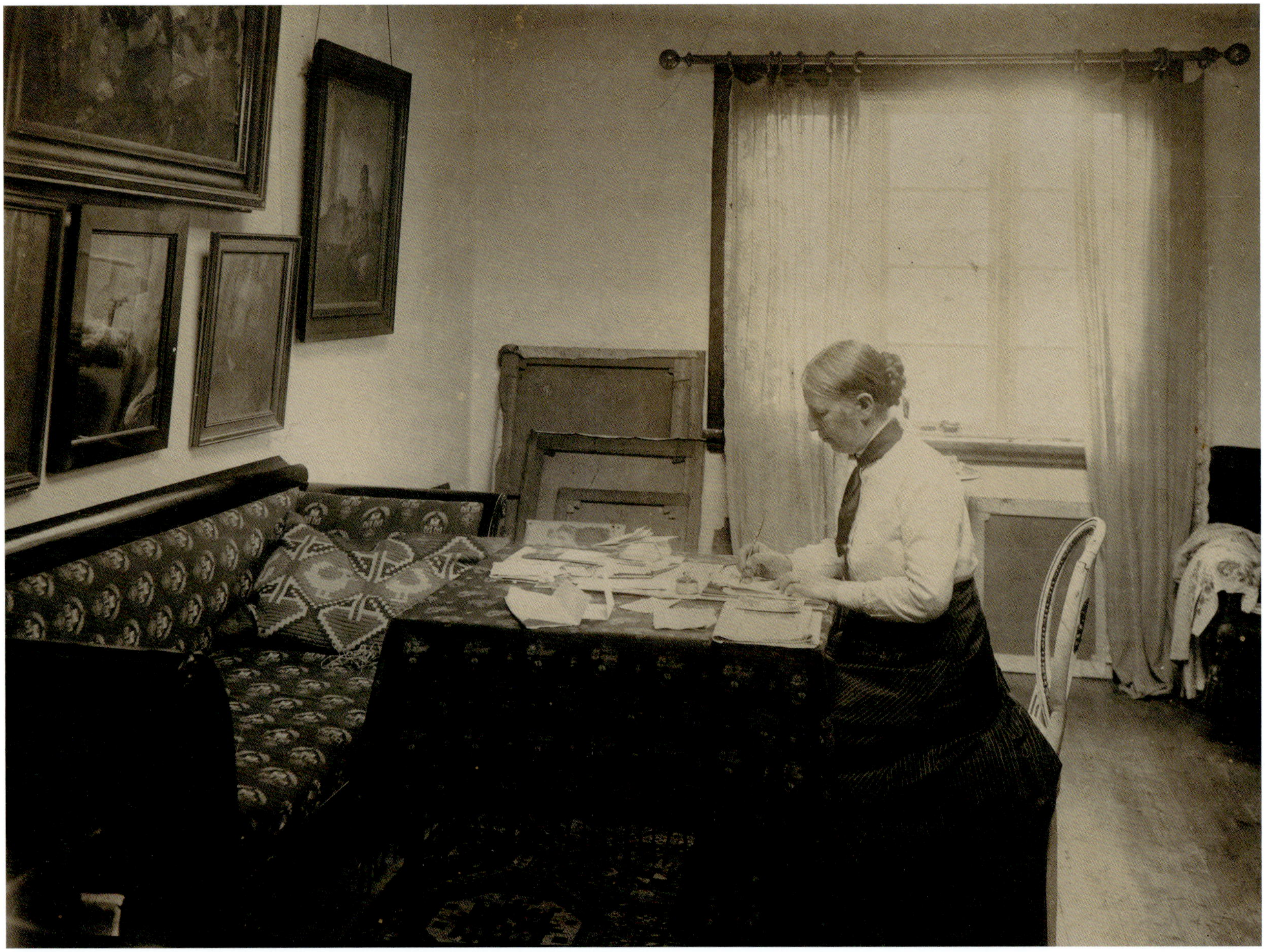

Rembrandt purchased his house on the Breestraat in Amsterdam (today the Rembrandthuis Museum) precisely for the access it gave him to the cool northerly light, which was considered ideal for painting.[14] Surrounded by two seas – the Skagerrak and the Kattegat – Skagen was renowned for its unique light. And, when Ancher finally got her own studio in 1913, after the house on Markvej was extended, her new space was illuminated with two windows facing north and east, in addition to a skylight above [fig. 11].[15]

In Ancher's sketch *At the Meal* [cat. 28], the artist uses light and shadow to elevate a simple supper, in a manner reminiscent of Rembrandt's *Supper at Emmaus* [fig. 12].[16] In Rembrandt's painting, light seems to emanate from somewhere behind Christ, who is thrown into silhouette. A similar, albeit less extreme, version of this technique is offered in Ancher's painting. There, light falls from somewhere in the upper right. The effect is to illuminate the face of the female figure and the food laid on the table, while the seated man, with his back to the viewer, is in almost-silhouette. Through this, she imparts dramatic potential to what is an otherwise ordinary scene, lending a sense of heroism to the everyday. In her rendering of light, Ancher may also have been inspired by Rembrandt's distinctive use of impasto. This is especially evident in Rembrandt's *Jewish Bride*, where thickly applied paint is used to create texture and 'catch' the light falling on a painting surface, emphasising sections of highlight. This ability is seen foremost in *Sunlight in the Blue Room* [cat. 8] where she illustrates a patch of light on the back wall of the room, filtered through the window to the right, describing it with expressive, loosely applied brushstrokes.

Fig. 11
Morten Johannes Knudstrup (photographer)
Anna Ancher Writing Letters in Her Studio, undated
Gelatin silver print
119 × 165 mm
Skagens Museum

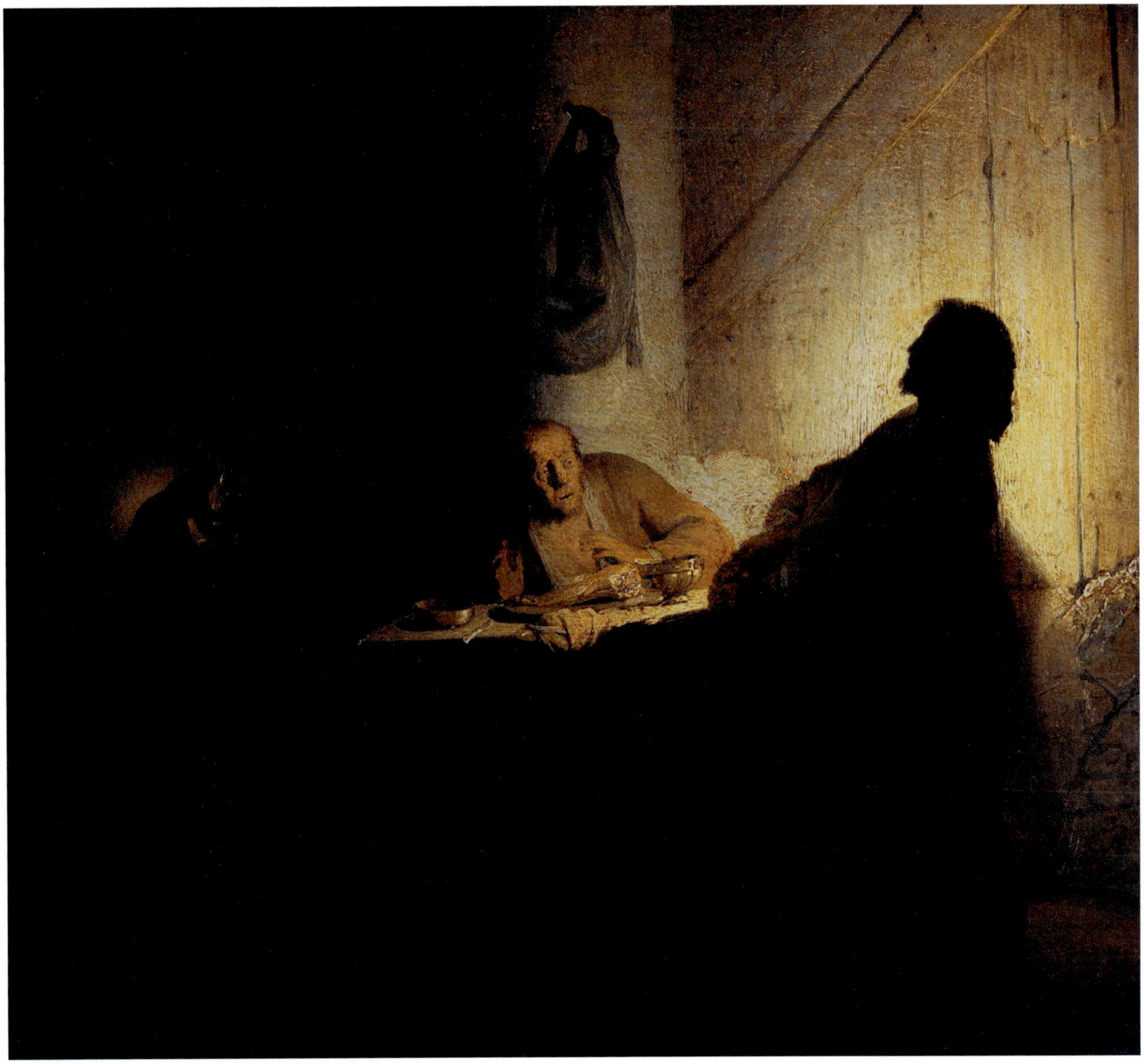

Fig. 12
Rembrandt van Rijn
The Supper at Emmaus, 1628
Oil on panel,
39 × 42 cm
Musée Jacquemart-André, Paris

Cat. 28
At the Meal, 1880s
Oil on card
21.4 × 27 cm
Skagens Museum

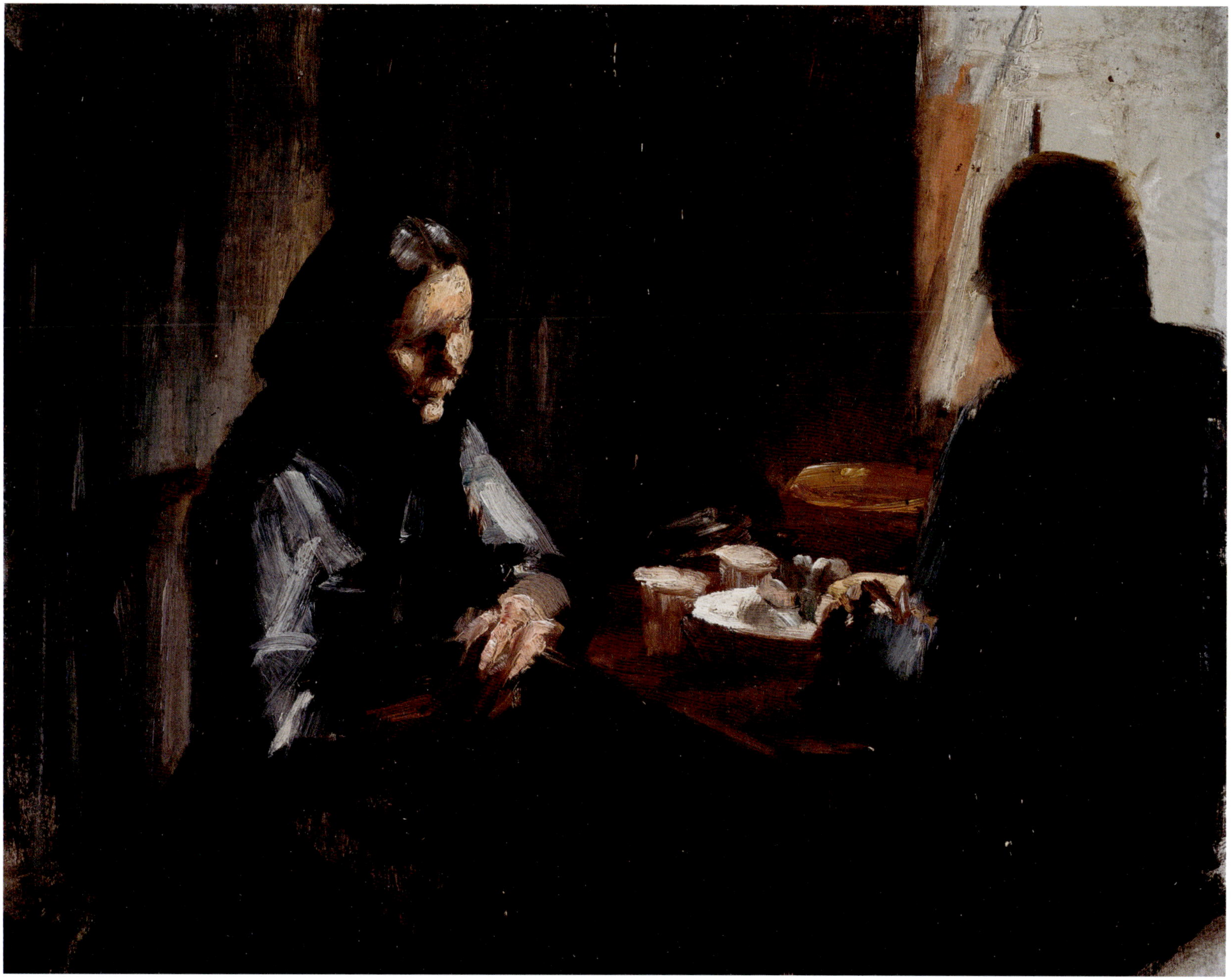

With these two side-on views, Anna Ancher may also have been exploring the type of composition popularised by Italian artists like Leonardo da Vinci and Raphael during the Renaissance.

Cat. 29
A Young Girl from Skagen, c.1900
Oil on canvas
32.2 × 23.5 cm
Skagens Museum

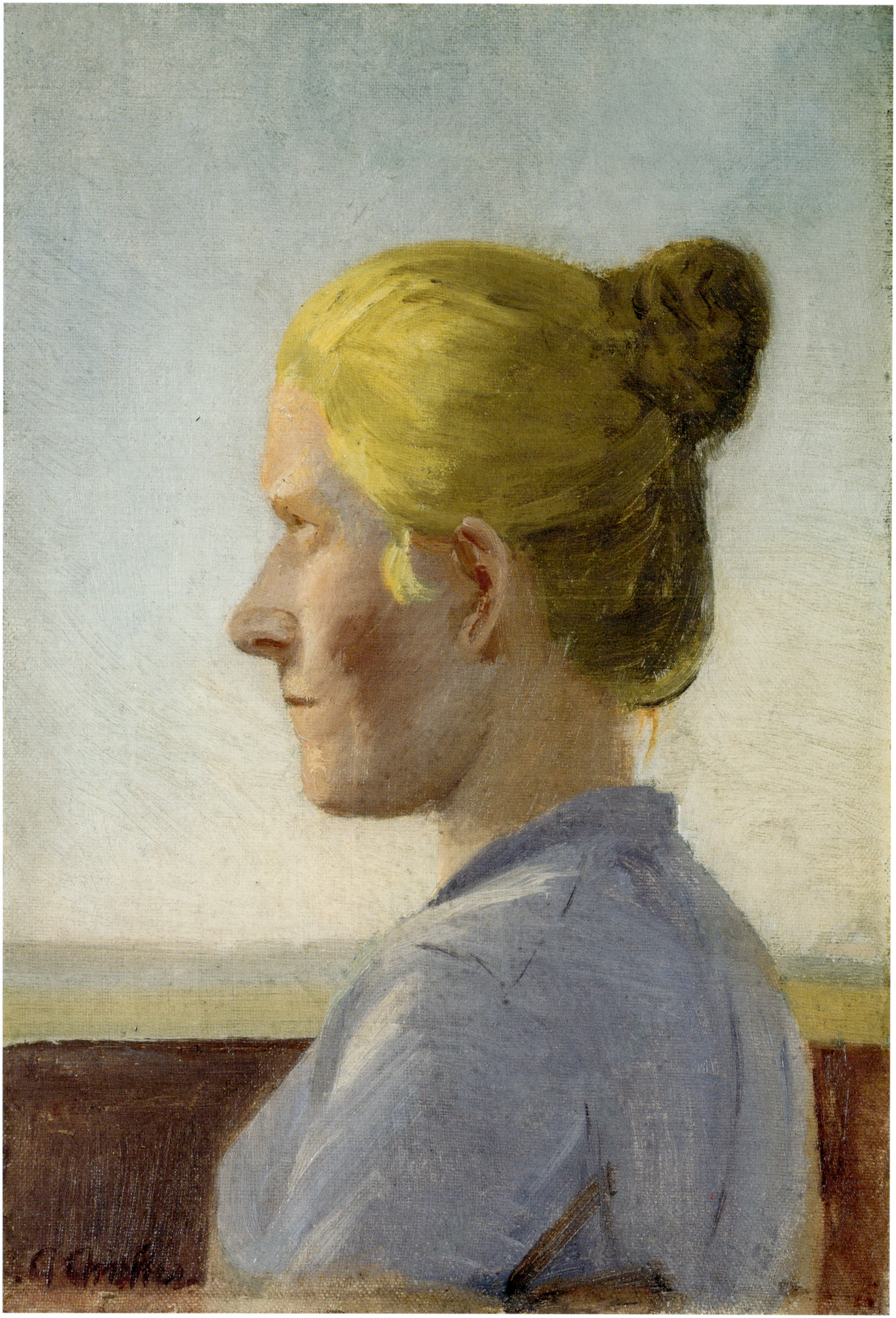

Cat. 30
Profile Portrait of a Woman from Skagen, c. 1905
Oil on panel
23.5 × 19.5 cm
Skagens Museum

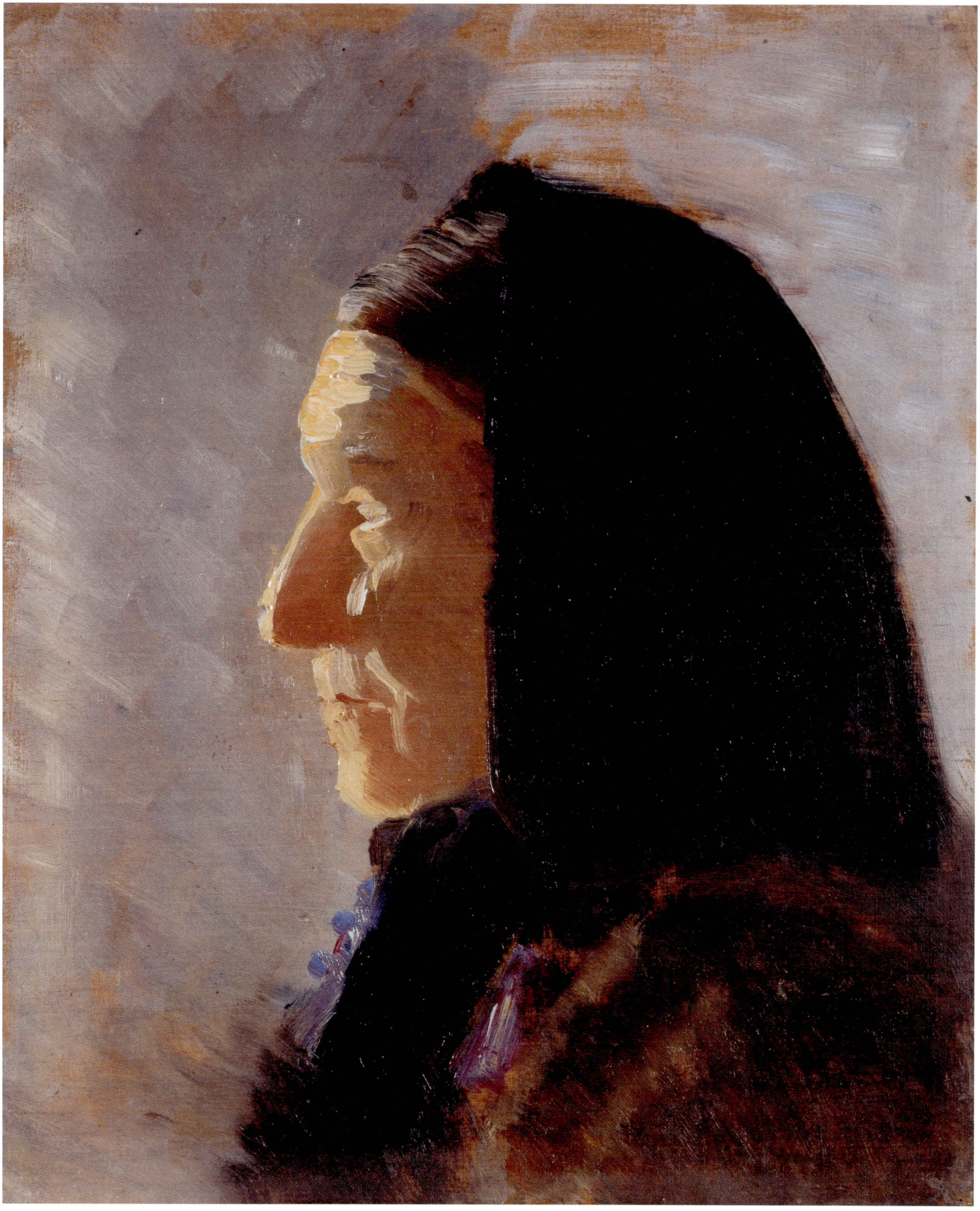

Ancher's numerous head studies depicting individuals from Skagen can be related to the Dutch *tronie*, a type of head study practised by Rembrandt and his contemporaries. Unlike portraits, these studies typically depict unnamed or even imaginary figures. These works concentrated on the face, usually just head and shoulders, with little in the way of costume or accessories. For Rembrandt, such studies were a means to experiment with different types of expression, as well as the way in which light falls across a person's facial features.[17] In a similar manner, *A Young Girl from Skagen* [cat. 29] and *Profile Portrait of a Woman from Skagen* [cat. 30] offered the artist opportunity for characterful studies of local people, while also allowing her to address questions of form and colour. With both works, we get the impression that she was working quickly, exploring her medium in a spontaneous way, rather than producing precise and highly finished paintings. With these two side-on views, Ancher may also have been exploring the type of composition popularised by Italian artists like Leonardo da Vinci and Raphael during the Renaissance.[18] Her husband also made numerous works within this genre and the fact that – in paintings by both Ancher and Michael – most of their sitters are unnamed, supports the idea that they cannot be considered portraits in the traditional sense. For both Ancher and the Dutch masters, it was often older faces that offered the most interesting opportunities. The artist's *Fisherman with Red Scarf* [cat. 31] would have been an ideal subject in this regard. The fisherman's face is redolent of his age and experience. Although his social status may have been considered lower than Ancher's, he is presented with compassion and dignity regardless. The decision to depict people's faces as they truly were, unvarnished and with an emphasis on truth to nature, was shared by both Rembrandt and the Skagen painters. Their focus on the, often harsh, reality of working life stood in contrast with the more romanticised attitude of the previous generation of Danish artists, the painters of the so-called Danish Golden Age (c. 1815–1850).[19]

A lesser explored aspect of Ancher's art is her death scenes, including *The Artist's Dead Mother* [cat. 32] and *Mrs Brøndum at the Bed of her Daughter Agnes* [cat. 33]. These are amongst the artist's most personal works; with these paintings, the artist draws on a long tradition of deathbed portraiture. Alongside plaster casts of faces and cuttings of hair, deathbed portraits could serve as mementos of a person, long after they had died. This type of portraiture was not intended to be macabre, and typically showed individuals as they would have appeared in life. *The Artist's Dead Mother* might be compared to *Venetia, Lady Digby, on her Deathbed* by Anthony van Dyck (1599–1641) [fig. 13]. After Venetia Stanley, Lady Digby (1600–1633) died unexpectedly, her grieving husband commissioned Van Dyck to record her likeness and, in doing so, create a permanent memorial. Lady Digby is shown in bed, as if she has simply fallen asleep. Ancher's portrait of her mother is especially moving, given how frequently Mrs Brøndum featured as a subject in her daughter's art. In life, she had visited her mother practically every day, bringing her canvas and paints in order to paint her in the blue or red rooms of Brøndum's Hotel. Following the death of her mother, she wrote: 'now, unfortunately we no longer have Mother among us; the rooms are so empty, and the gentle face framed by the white cloak is missed immeasurably'.[20] The painting of the artist's mother on her deathbed presents a powerful meditation on the transience of life, while also bringing to a close one of the most important chapters within Ancher's art.

Cat. 31
Fisherman with Red Scarf, 1880s
Oil on canvas
31.1 × 25.8 cm
Skagens Museum

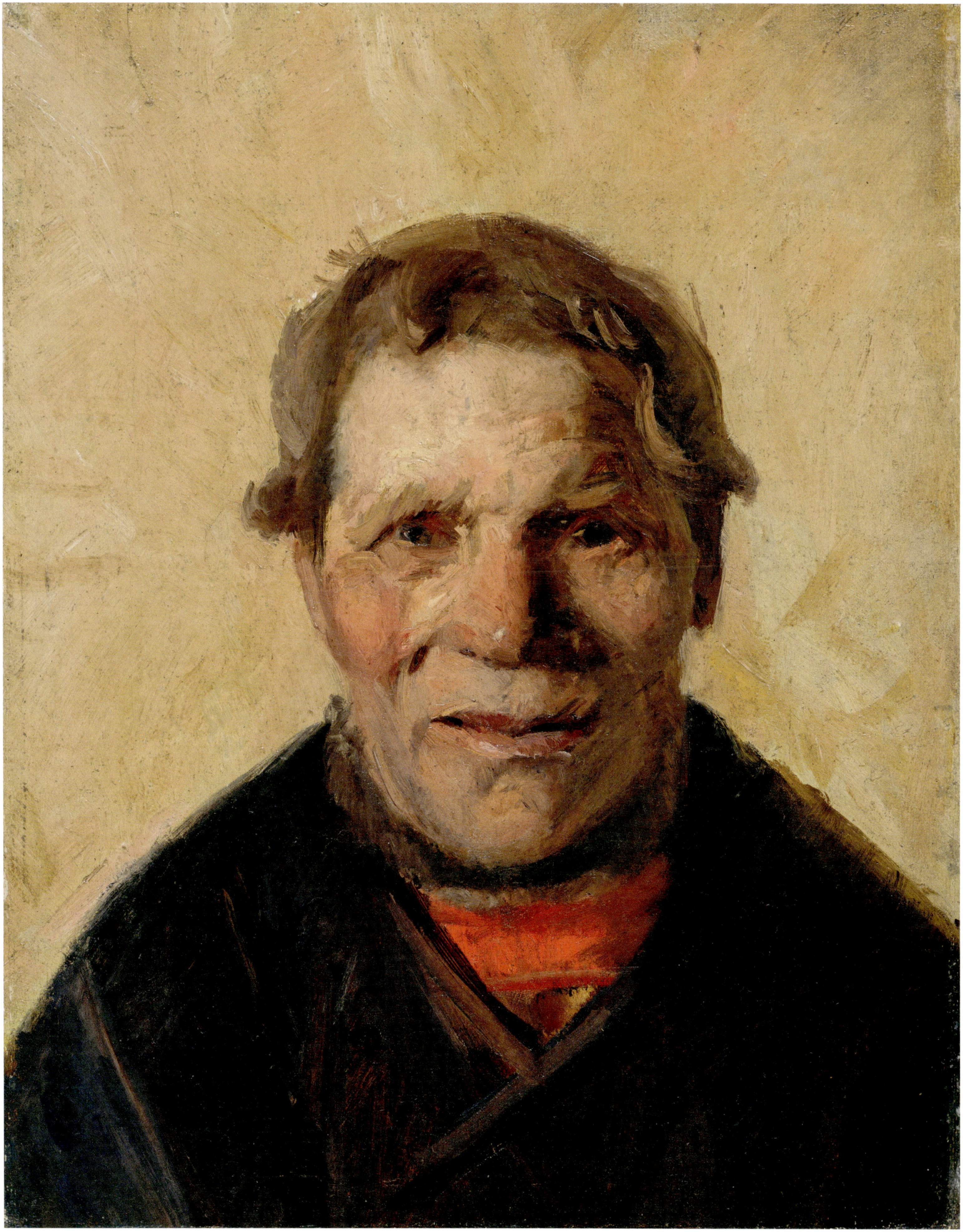

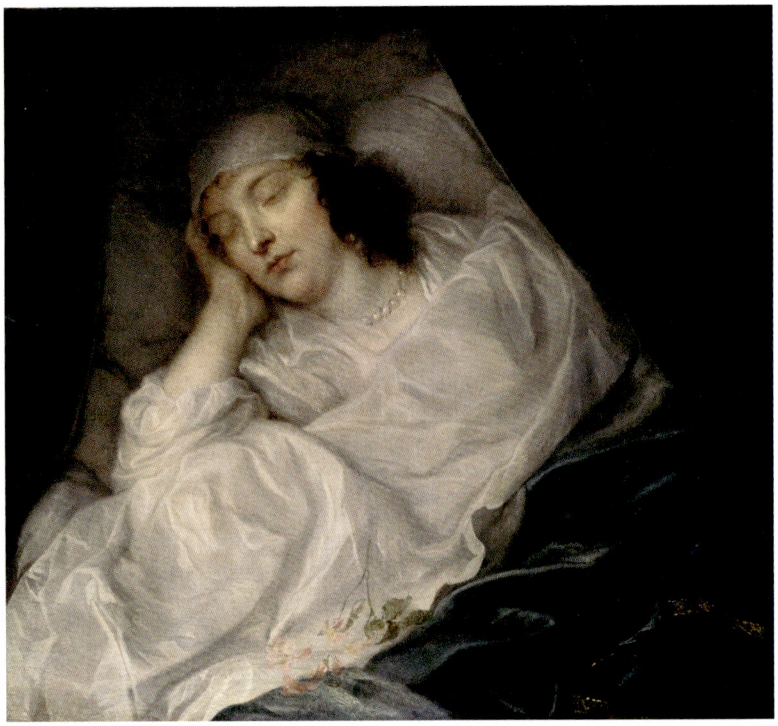

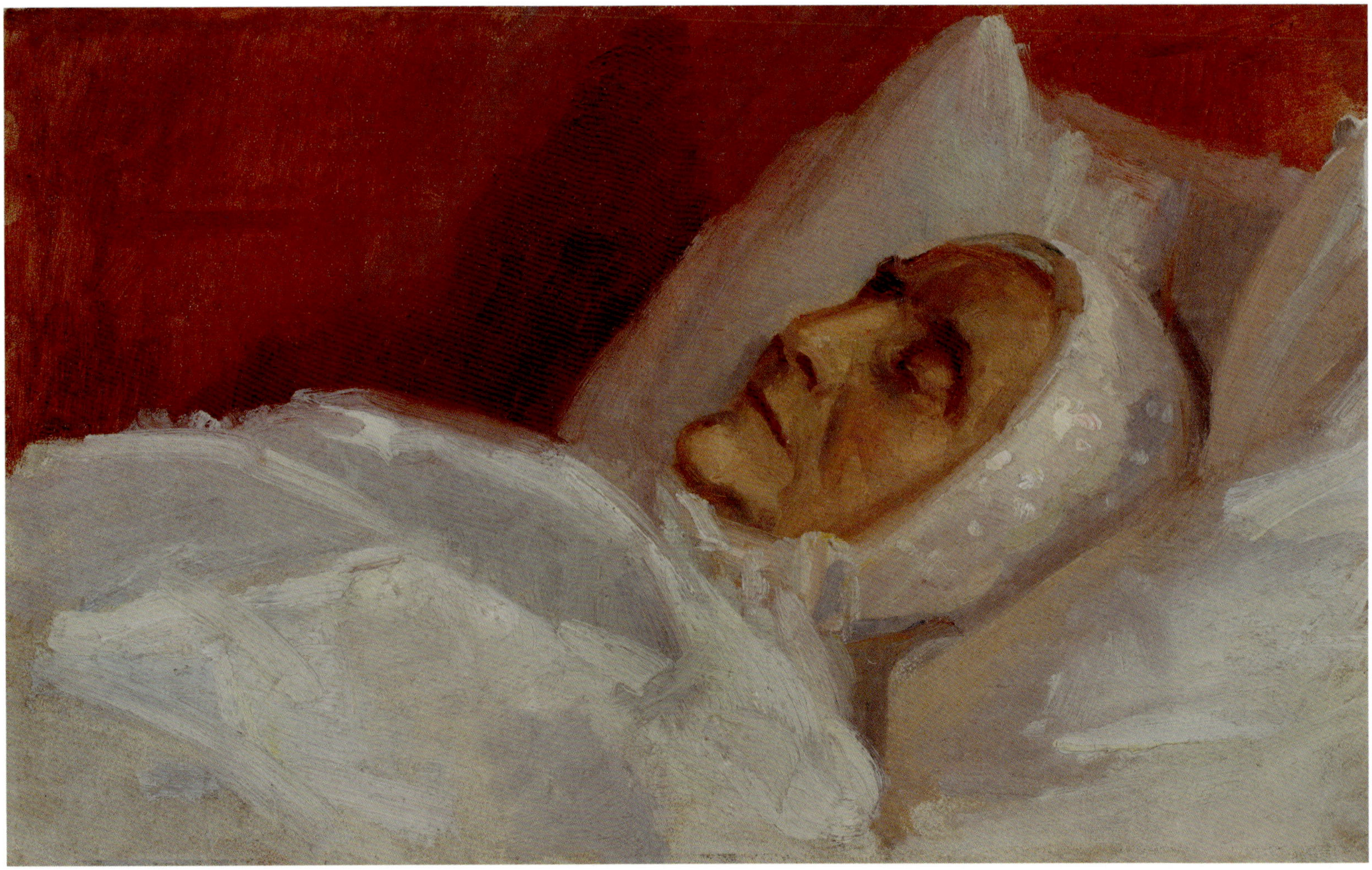

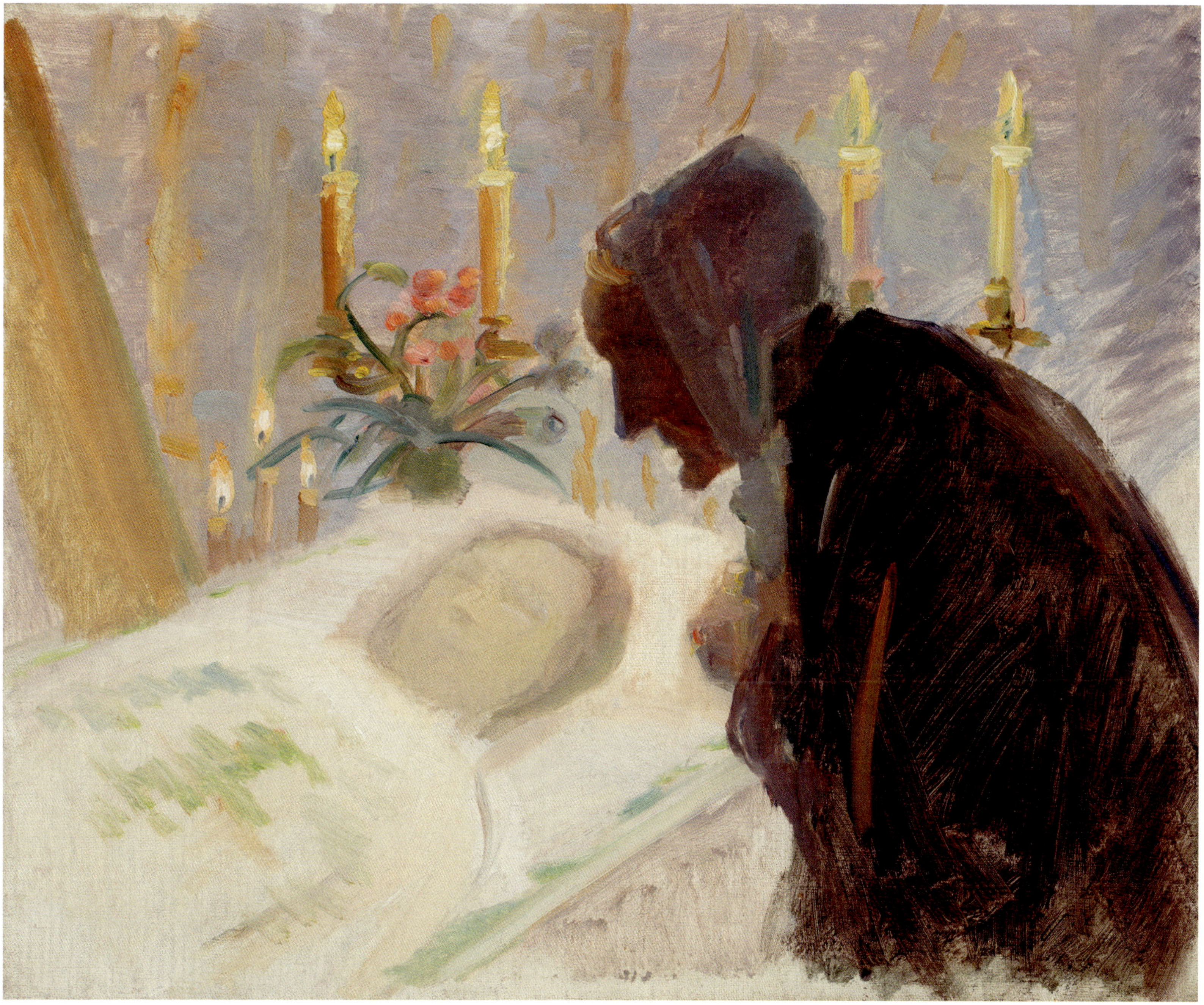

Fig. 13
Anthony van Dyck
Venetia, Lady Digby, on Her Deathbed, 1633
Oil on canvas
74.3 × 81.8 cm
Dulwich Picture Gallery, London

Cat. 32
The Artist's Dead Mother, 1916
Oil on card
24.7 × 39.7 cm
Skagens Museum

Cat. 33
Mrs Brøndum at the Bed of Her Daughter Agnes, 1910
Oil on canvas
42.3 × 52.4 cm
Skagens Museum

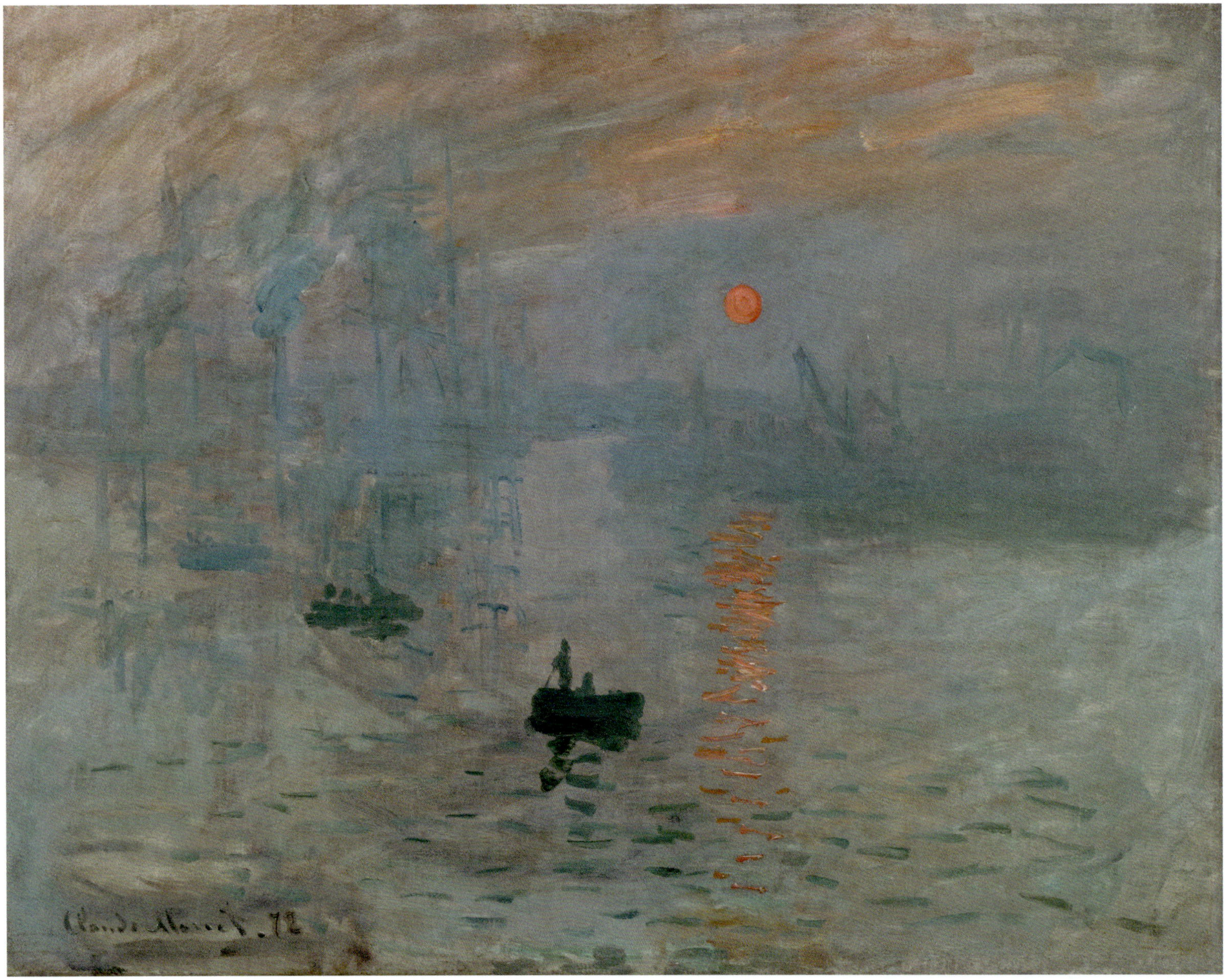

The Lure of Paris

Ancher, along with many of the other artists of the Skagen colony, can be counted as part of the 'Modern Breakthrough' in Denmark. The term was coined by the Danish art scholar Georg Brandes (1842–1927) in his lecture series 'Main Currents in Nineteenth Century Literature', delivered at the University of Copenhagen in 1871. Brandes was a major influence on the Skagen painters. He kept regular correspondence with Michael Ancher and spent significant time in Skagen, to the extent that his portrait is featured among those in the Brøndum's dining room [fig. 4]. For artists, the new 'currents' Brandes described translated into a focus on contemporary life and truth to nature. They reacted against the classicising art of the Danish Golden Age and the teaching of the Academy, which was increasingly considered outdated. The Skagen artists wanted to depict modern life in all its glory, looking to France, and Paris in particular, as their guiding light.

The artist and her husband made multiple trips to Paris. They had first travelled to the city in 1885, as part of an extended journey across Europe, but returned again in 1889, settling there for six months. In Paris, Ancher attended an art school where she studied under Pierre Puvis de Chavannes (1824–1898), and both she and Michael exhibited work as part of the Exposition Universelle. The Exposition Universelle undoubtedly counted among the most important cultural events of the age, with the 1889 Exposition drawing 32 million visitors to the city.[21] The couple fell into a network of Scandinavian artists drawn to Paris, with no fewer than 50 Nordic artists working in France during the 1880s, including many female painters.[22] Ancher took lessons alongside Marie Triepcke (1867–1940), who would later marry Skagen artist Peder Severin Krøyer, and one of Ancher's only surviving works from her time in Paris is a portrait of Norwegian artist Kitty Kielland (1843–1914).

In Paris, Ancher had the opportunity to visit numerous exhibitions and immerse herself in the art of the impressionists. In doing so, she built upon her previous experiences of seeing modern French art in Copenhagen.[23] On her first visit to Paris in 1885, she was able to see paintings by Claude Monet (1840–1926) as part of a show arranged by the art dealer Georges Petit (1856–1920). At the Exposition Universelle in 1889, she would also have seen work by Monet, as well as Camille Pissarro (1830–1903) and Paul Cezanne (1839–1906). Although few of Ancher's letters from her time in Paris survive, her work demonstrates how formative this period was. While she chose not to depict the scenes of 'modern life' typically associated with the impressionists – such as cafe scenes, transport hubs or street life – her approach to light and colour was undoubtedly guided by the impressionists.[24] Works like *Sunlight in the Blue Room* [cat. 8] and *Evening Sun in the Artist's Studio at Markvej* [cat. 7] could not have been created without the benefit of her experience in Paris. For *Evening Sun in the Artist's Studio at Markvej*, the artist uses blue as the dominant colour, pairing this with a vibrant orange to describe the squares of light filtered through an unseen window. It is hard not to make a connection to Monet's use of colour to convey atmospheric effects, for example, in *Impression, Sunrise* – the work that gave its name to the impressionist movement – where an orange-pink sun is outlined against a blue background and reflected in the water below [fig. 14]. The pictorial device of the orange-pink sun was one favoured by Monet and frequently placed at the top of his compositions as a unifying element.[25] Monet's obviously loose brushstrokes and dissolution of form likewise became an important aspect of Ancher's style and this technique is apparent to a greater degree in her work than that of any other Skagen painter.

Fig. 14
Claude Monet
Impression, Sunrise, 1872
Oil on canvas
48 cm × 63 cm
Musée Marmottan Monet, Paris

A Tapestry of Influences

Ancher was influenced by post-impressionism too, seemingly to a far greater degree than any of the other artists of the Skagen circle. Although the term 'post-impressionist' was not used until 1906, it has subsequently been used to define a group of artists who began to move beyond naturalism, seeing art not simply as a representation of the external world but rather allowing deeper ideas and emotions to be expressed by colour and form.[26] Paul Gauguin (1848–1943) was a key figure in these new advances and was well known to Danish artists, having lived in Copenhagen for a period with his Danish wife, Mette (1850–1920). Ancher's use of colour, and the use of yellow in particular, may have been inspired by the artist. His Volpini Suite, which consisted of black prints on yellow paper, was likely a key influence in this regard.[27] The Volpini Suite was named after Cafe Volpini, where the works were first exhibited in June 1889 and where Ancher likely saw them. A similar yellow is used in the background of *Study of a Seamstress in Blue* [cat. 9].[28] Yet, whilst she may have borrowed from the post-impressionist palette, her choice of subjects largely remained rooted in realism and the citizens and environs of Skagen. The exception to this is *Grief* [cat. 34] a work where the artist experimented with the creative possibilities of symbolism.

Grief and its preparatory study [cat. 35] are amongst Ancher's most moving works. The finished painting depicts an older woman cloaked in black, opposite a younger woman, naked, her face shielded by her hair. Both figures kneel by a grave marker, set within the distinctive heathland of Skagen. It is unclear what the relationship between the two women is, whether they are mother and daughter, or perhaps the same woman depicted at different stages of life. The subject is unusual for Ancher and has no comparison within her oeuvre. It is the artist's only work to depict nudity, and one of few works to move away from the naturalism that dominated the rest of her practice.[29] She described how the subject for *Grief* came to her in a dream: 'The other night I dreamed that I saw a picture vividly before me, something I had never thought of or seen before'.[30] In terms of visual inspiration, the crouching nude figure has been connected to Paul Gauguin's *Étude de nu*, 1880, which had been part of Mette Gauguin's collection in Copenhagen and with which she would have been familiar.[31] It has also been connected to Vincent van Gogh's *Sorrow* [fig. 15], a drawing by the artist that was later reproduced as a lithograph.[32] *Sorrow* depicts Clasina Maria Hoornik, a sex worker who, together with her children, lived with Van Gogh between 1882 and 1883, during which time Hoornik modelled for the artist. Both *Sorrow* and *Grief* share symbolist overtones, offering visual representations of complex emotional states. And yet, if Ancher was inspired by Van Gogh, she also made the subject of the nude entirely her own, since *Grief* represents the first time in Danish art that the female nude was considered from a woman's perspective.[33] It addresses female pain, both embodied and shared. The concept of grief is shown to be both generational while also deeply isolating, emphasised by the younger woman's nakedness. With *Grief*, Ancher showed that she was not afraid to delve into matters of the subconscious, even though this was potentially at odds with the naturalism that had previously shaped her career.

Like Van Gogh and other post-impressionists, Ancher also looked to Japanese visual culture for inspiration. European artists had been fascinated with Japanese art, following the opening up of the country in the 1850s. The Anchers would have had access to Japanese art as part of the Exposition Universelle, an event which 'democratised' access to Japanese

Cat. 34
Grief, 1902
Oil on canvas
86.5 × 73.8 cm
Skagens Museum

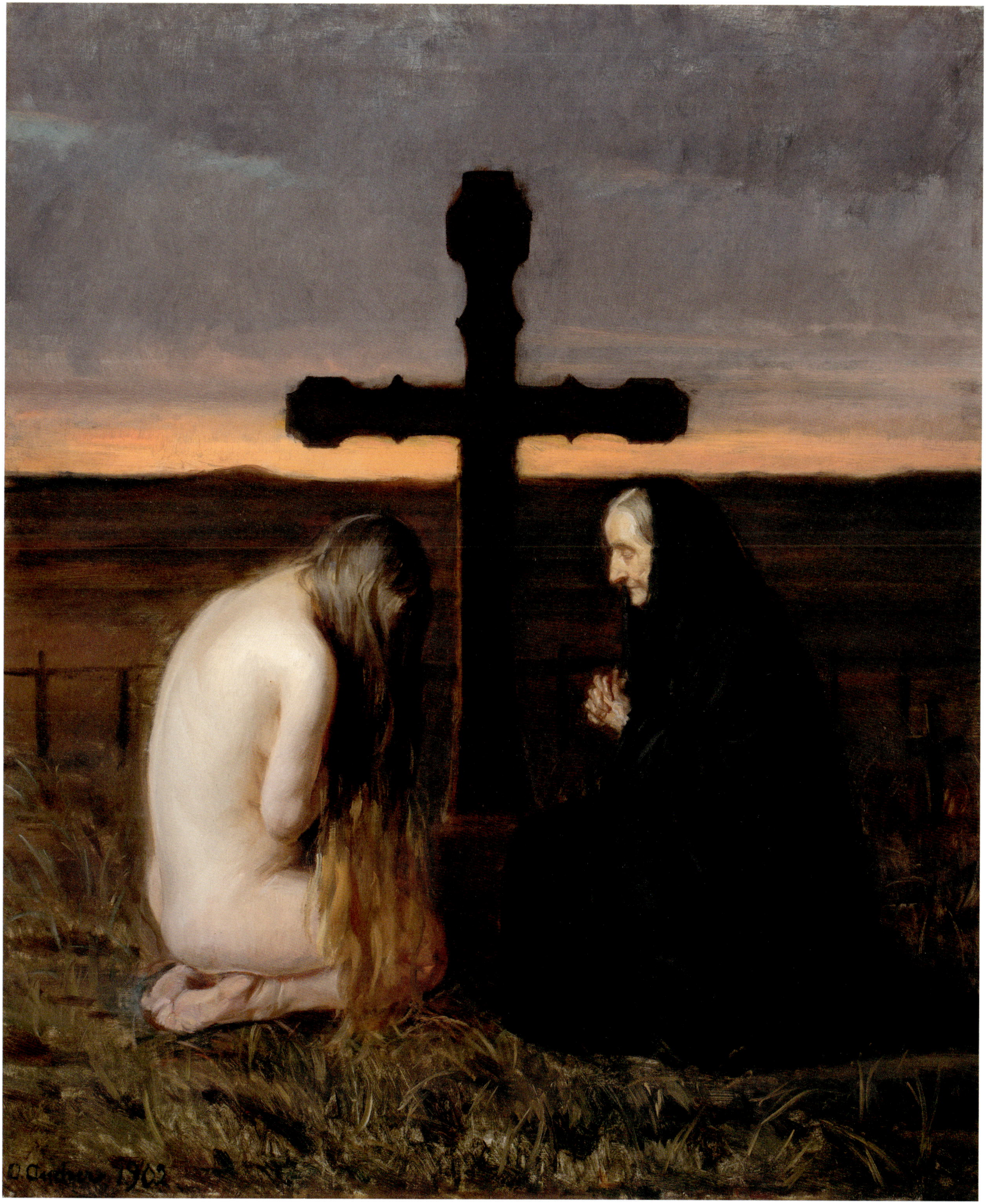

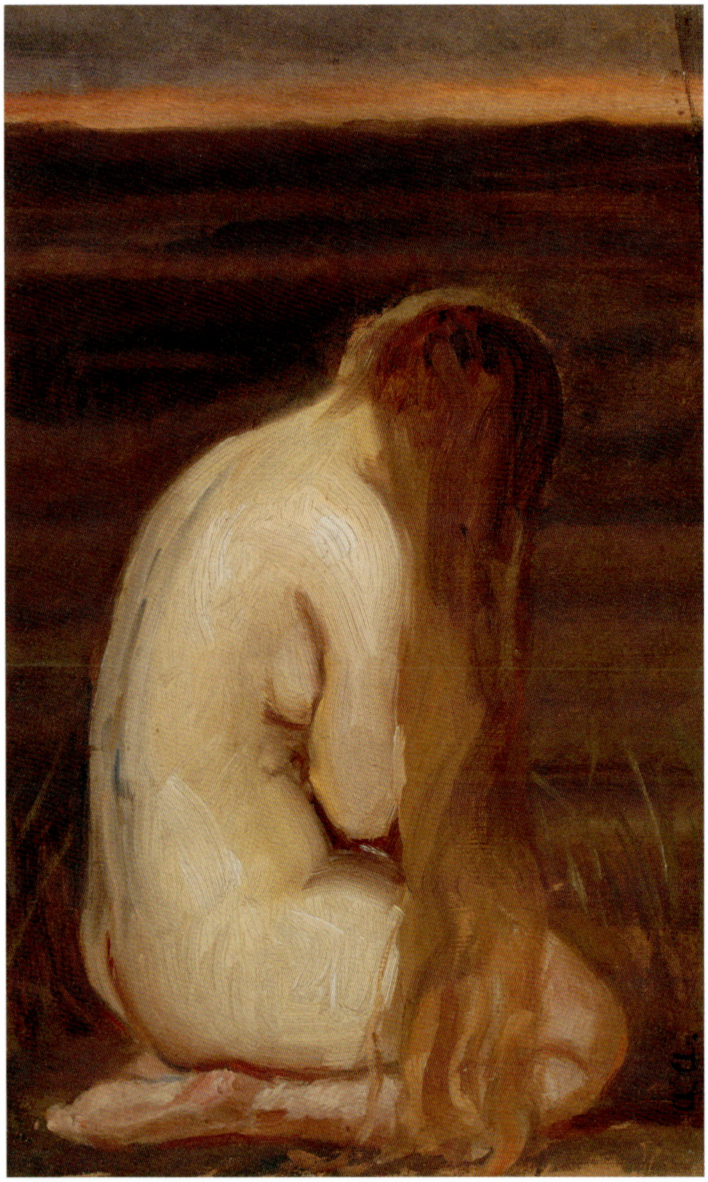

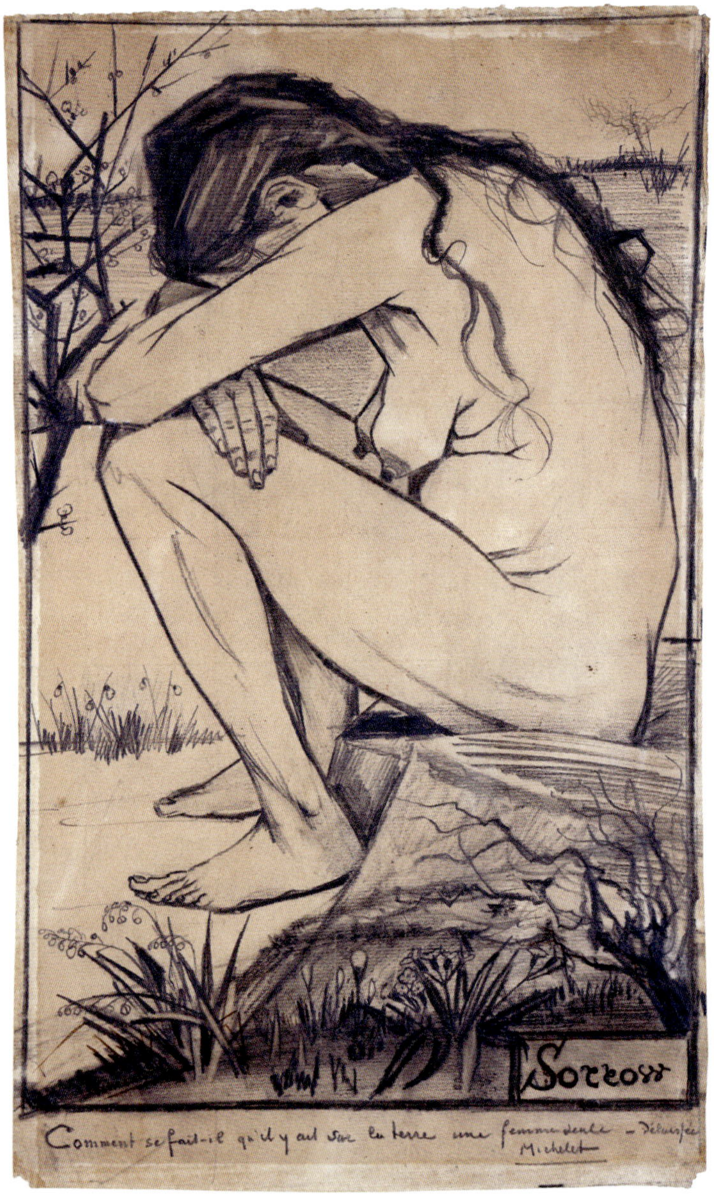

Cat. 35
Grief. Study, c. 1902
Oil on canvas
41.6 × 28.8
Skagens Museum

Fig. 15
Vincent van Gogh
Sorrow
Lithograph on paper
49.9 cm × 38.8 cm
Van Gogh Museum, Amsterdam

art, making it accessible to collectors at all levels.[34] The Anchers owned a complete edition of Katsushika Hokusai's manga books, and also acquired Japanese objects from the Magasin du Nord in Copenhagen. Only rarely do these objects make an appearance in Ancher's paintings; one notable example is *Mrs Ancher by the Desk* painted by both Anna and Michael Ancher, which depicts the silk hangings owned by the couple.[35] However, there are other instances where the compositional devices of Japanese art crept into her work;[36] for example, the strong diagonals that dominate a work like *Sunlight in the Blue Room*, or the close cropping of interior spaces, might be compared with the interiors of Suzuki Harunobu (1724–1770).[37] In these interiors, natural elements also play a strong role. In this regard, *Interior with Red Poppies* [cat. 42] is especially evocative of Ukiyo-e prints.

In her adoption of newer tendencies within art – including symbolism, impressionism, post-impressionism and Japonisme – it could be argued that Ancher was more open to adapting and changing her art practice than any of her peers. She is often perceived as a more 'modern' contributor than other artists of the Skagen colony, including her husband.[38] Elsewhere in this volume, Mette Harbo Lehmann highlights how, for some critics, Ancher was even considered 'too modern' (see p. 45). And while, with her early works at least, Ancher was influenced by her husband's style, it is likely that she was the one who pushed him to be more radical with his painting, introducing more light and colour into his work. However, this was evidently something her husband struggled with.[39] It was only at the very end of Michael's career – and even then, only occasionally – in a work like *The Red Room* of 1914 (today at Ribe Kunstmuseum) that we see a work remotely comparable in terms of its approach.[40]

One of Ancher's greatest strengths was the way in which she was able to combine visual influences from both past and present, weaving them together, while also pulling on certain threads, to create work that was entirely original. Through this, she was able to create fresh interpretations of historic themes, riffing on Old Masters while incorporating the colour, light and atmospheric effects being pushed in French art of the period. At the same time, works like *Grief* show her practice cannot be easily categorised or defined. She was able to deviate from the 'expected', introducing radically new subjects into her practice, even as a mature artist. Across her works we see a painter capable of producing beautiful art who was also not afraid to tackle personal or emotionally raw subjects, such as grief, death and loss. Even today, Ancher's works still feel immediate and powerful. It is surely this ability to hold all these strands simultaneously – past and present, aesthetic and personal – which has cemented her enduring legacy.

'THE DESERT BETWEEN TWO ROARING SEAS':

Helen Hillyard

ANNA ANCHER AND SKAGEN

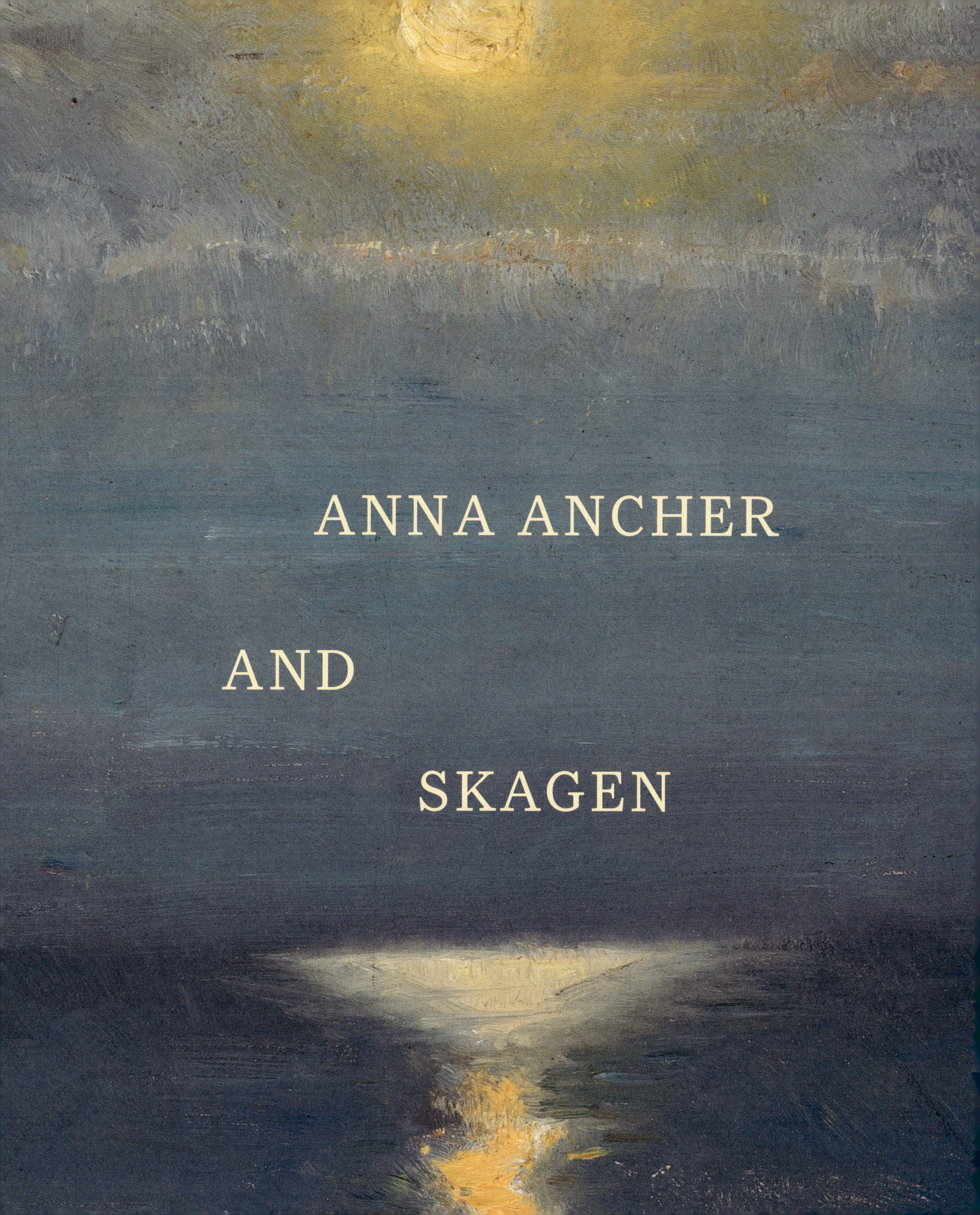

We wanted to visit 'Denmark's remote corner', the desert between two roaring seas, the town, which has no paved streets or alleys, to hear the magpies and the wild geese fill the air with their cries over the shifting sand dunes and the buried church. If you are a painter, then follow us up here, here there are subjects for you, here there is scenery for poetry; here in the Danish country will you find a nature, which gives you a picture from the African desert, from Pompei's ash hills and from the birds, which glide over the sand banks in the world's sea. Skagen is well worth a visit.[1]

Hans Christian Andersen
on Skagen, 1859

When Danish author Hans Christian Andersen (1805–1875) described Skagen in his travelogue of 1859, it was as an exotic, wild place. He captured the essence of this fishing town, located at Denmark's northernmost point – 'the desert' situated between the two seas of the Skagerrak and the Kattegat. Today, tourists still travel to the beach at Grenen to witness the natural phenomena, where the seas meet, merge and break [fig. 16]. While Ancher's Skagen could be perceived as a remote, faraway place, it was also a site of confluence and intersection.

Skagen was the ideal location to stage the great social and artistic experiment that was the Skagen artist colony. Responding to Andersen's call to 'follow us up here', the town drew artists from across Scandinavia, France, Germany and even Britain and the US. Through their migration, these artists created a modern, bohemian community within a traditional fishing town. Skagen became the improbable place where old and new collided. Ancher was the only member of the Skagen artist colony native to the town. She was a product of both worlds and her relationship to the town was different from others of the group. Her unique position enabled her to depict this special place through the lens of a modern artist, offering a radical re-interpretation of the people and places she knew well. While this had its benefits, Ancher's position was also a difficult one to occupy. There are moments when we, perhaps, see her struggling to align the conflicting values of her conservative upbringing with her role as a progressive female painter.

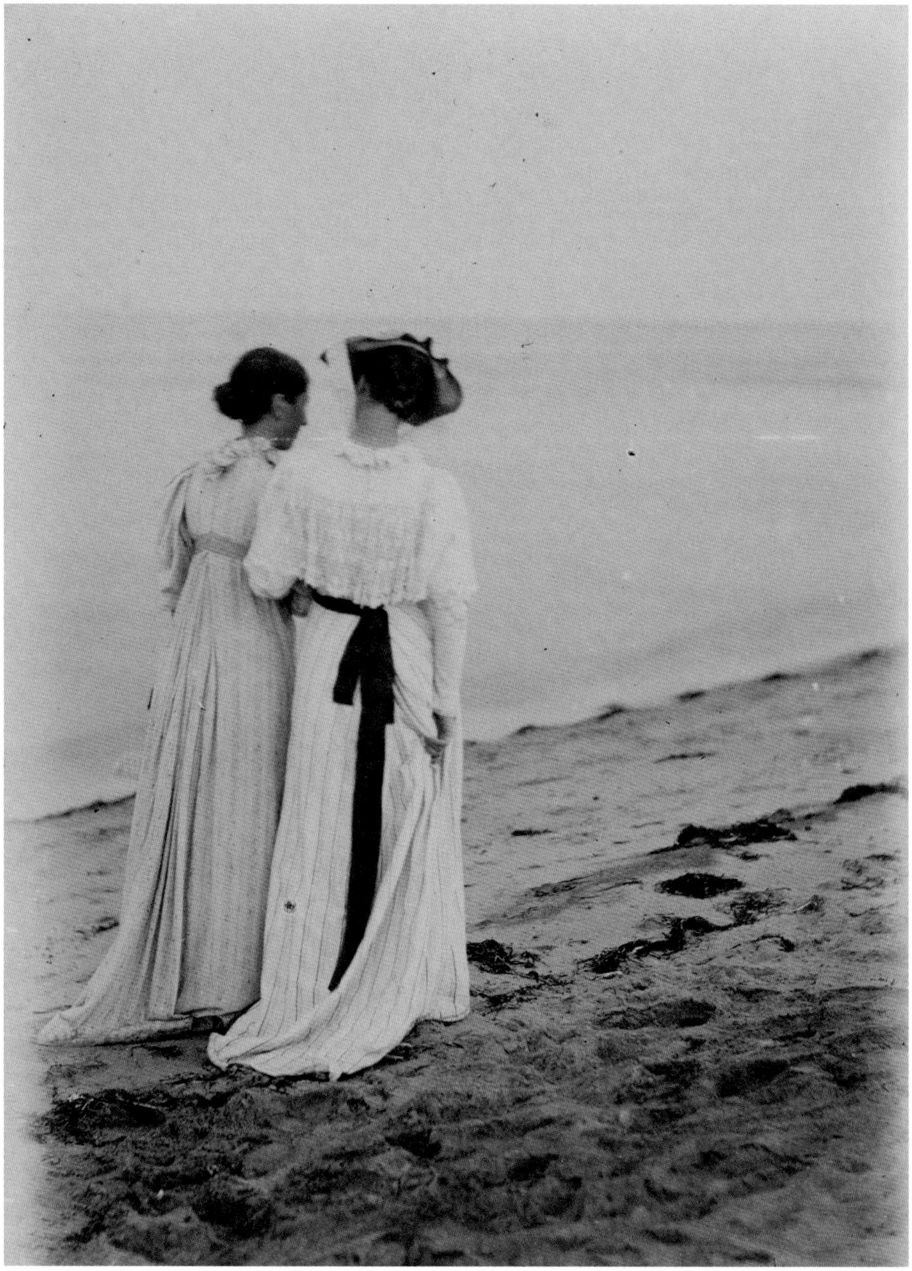

Fig. 16
Peder Severin Krøyer (photographer)
Anna Ancher and Marie Krøyer on Skagen Sønderstrand, c. 1893
Collodion print
17.5 × 13 cm
Skagens Museum

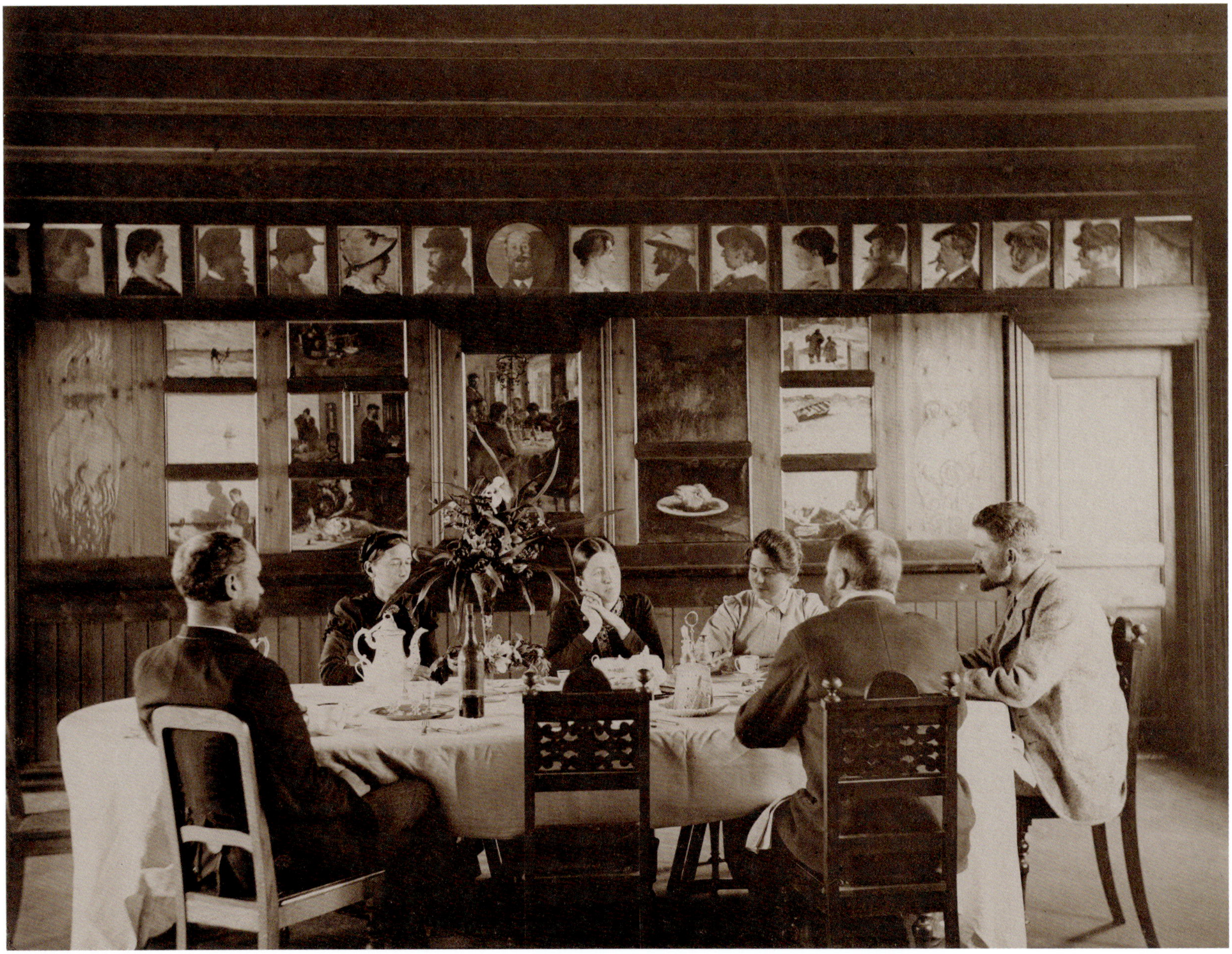

A Wilderness on Denmark's Doorstep

Anna Ancher, née Brøndum, was the beating heart of the Skagen artist colony and, in many regards, it was a community that built itself around her. The first painters of this group to arrive were the Norwegian painter Frits Thaulow (1847–1906) and the Dane Holger Drachmann (1846–1908) in 1872.[2] When these artists arrived in Skagen, Brøndum's Hotel – which was run by Ancher's parents – was practically the only place where visitors to Skagen could stay.[3] They were soon followed by other artists, including her future husband Michael, and it was within this fertile environment that she learned how to draw and paint. As more artists came to Skagen – including those who chose to settle in the town long-term – this informal collective of painters grew into the 'colony' we recognise today and by about 1880 it was firmly established. In 1883 a project was started to decorate the dining room of Brøndum's Hotel with paintings by, and portraits of, its members, immortalising the Skagen artists. Pictures of Ancher and her husband were placed at the centre of the dining room, in close proximity to a circular portrait of the artist's brother Degn Brøndum (1856–1932), by that point proprietor of the hotel [fig. 17].

But why Skagen? In selecting the fishing town as the base for their activities, the painters were inspired by the French landscape artists of the Barbizon School. The School had centred their work around the village of Barbizon, located at the edge of the Forest of Fontainebleau, to the southeast of Paris and, with the rise of *plein air* painting, numerous 'artist colonies' emerged in France including those at Cernay-la-Ville, Grez-sur-Loing, Pont-Aven and Concarneau.[4] Like the French artist colonies, Skagen had a dramatic and varied landscape that was ideal for *plein air* painting. Additionally, the town's location, sandwiched between two seas, was thought to give the area a unique light not found elsewhere. The town may also have enticed artists, precisely because it was so difficult to reach. When the first painters arrived in 1872, it would have taken four days to reach Skagen from Copenhagen. The railway line, which ran from Frederikshavn to Skagen, effectively connecting Skagen to the rest of Denmark, did not open until 1890. Before this, the journey from Frederikshavn – the nearest major port town, almost 40 kilometres south – was usually made by horse-drawn carriage along the shore. The journey could also be made by boat but this was less preferable, since Skagen had no harbour before 1907. Skagen was simultaneously remote, yet local. A wilderness on Denmark's doorstep.

Despite its distance from Copenhagen, in Skagen Ancher was certainly not isolated. Her formidable mother, Ane Brøndum (1826–1916), championed her daughter's creative career. Ane Brøndum's support is all the more remarkable, and perhaps surprising, given the religious, conservative context in which she herself had been raised.[5] In 1875, aged 15 and with her mother's blessing, Ancher would travel to the Danish capital for teaching under the artist Vilhelm Kyhn (1819–1903), where she would be surrounded by other gifted female painters. After her marriage in 1880, Ancher travelled extensively throughout Europe, and elsewhere in this volume it has been highlighted how influential these travels were for her art. In Paris, she was once again able to train with talented female artists, as well as being part of a larger community of Scandinavian painters in the French capital.[6] She travelled throughout Europe well into her sixties and, in this regard, although Ancher made her hometown the focus for her art, she was certainly never cut off from the wider world. Yet, her rural background also

Fig. 17
Hans Peter Ferdinand Lundsteen (photographer)
Brøndum's Dining Room, Skagen, 1891
Gelatin silver print
16.8 × 22.3 cm
Skagens Museum

set her apart from other artists in her circle, which is apparent in her approach to religious themes.

Matters of Faith

For many artists of the 'Modern Breakthrough' – the conceptual framework with which many of the Skagen painters aligned – God had no part in the modern world. This was reflected in their art, which tended to focus on earthly rather than spiritual concerns. Photographs of the group reveal their bohemian, hedonistic lifestyle [fig. 18][7] and some of the Skagen painters, such as Holger Drachmann, were declared atheists.[8] The location of the colony may have appealed because of its pagan character, untamed and at the edge of civilised society. This is conveyed in Ancher's *Fireworks on Fyrbakken* [cat. 36]. The artist most likely depicts a Midsummer's Eve celebration on the beach at Skagen with the lighthouse (*fyr*) in the distance. These celebrations, which are still held across Denmark, represent a melding of pre-Christian and Christian traditions, marking both the summer solstice and Saint John's Eve on 23 June.[9]

The lives of most Skagen citizens were guided by religious faith, and this had been core to Ancher's upbringing. Ancher recounted how, during childhood, her mother would regularly take her to church and Bible classes.[10] Faith was, understandably, of importance to a fishing community whose day-to-day existence was governed by the sea and for whom risk of death was an occupational hazard. In 1862, when Ancher was just three years old, Skagen had been the site of a terrible shipwreck, where eight Skagen fishermen had drowned attempting to save the crew of the *Daphne*. Later, in a letter of 1909, the artist herself recounted another tragic event when, due to bad weather, lifeboats had been unable to reach the victims of a ship run aground; she had been haunted by their screams.[11] The potentially fatal toll of life at sea was illustrated in Michael Ancher's powerful and unsettling painting *The Drowned Fisherman*.[12] It was in this context that the Home Mission (*Indre Mission*) thrived. Originating in the 1860s, the Home Mission was a conservative Lutheran revival movement, emphasising biblical doctrine and personal piety. It found a large and receptive audience amongst poor, rural communities. Ancher's mother, along with her sisters, all became part of the movement when it first arrived in Skagen in the 1870s;[13] in Ancher's portraits of her mother, we frequently see her wearing a black headscarf, an item typically adopted by its members.[14]

Ancher pictured the powerful hold the Home Mission had over her community in her masterwork *A Field Sermon* [cat. 37]. The artist shows a preacher of the Home Mission giving a sermon amidst the distinctive topography of Skagen, the shoreline visible in the distance. Such sermons would have been regular occurrences in this part of Denmark but Ancher presents the event through a modernist lens. She does not offer a critical view of the scene; rather she unites the religious experience with her distinct approach to depicting the natural world. We have a sense of the wind blowing across the dunes, both the preacher and crowd withstanding the elements. It is almost as if the figures are about to be absorbed within the grassy mound, the loose brushstrokes appearing to envelop them. The artist made multiple sketches in preparation for this work and, with her finished piece, Ancher shows herself to be wholly capable of producing the type of multi-figure painting practiced by her male counterparts.

Fig. 18
Unknown Photographer
The Drachmann Party on the Occasion of the Poet's 60th Birthday at Tuxen's Villa, 1906
Gelatin silver print
11.7 × 17 cm
Skagens Museum

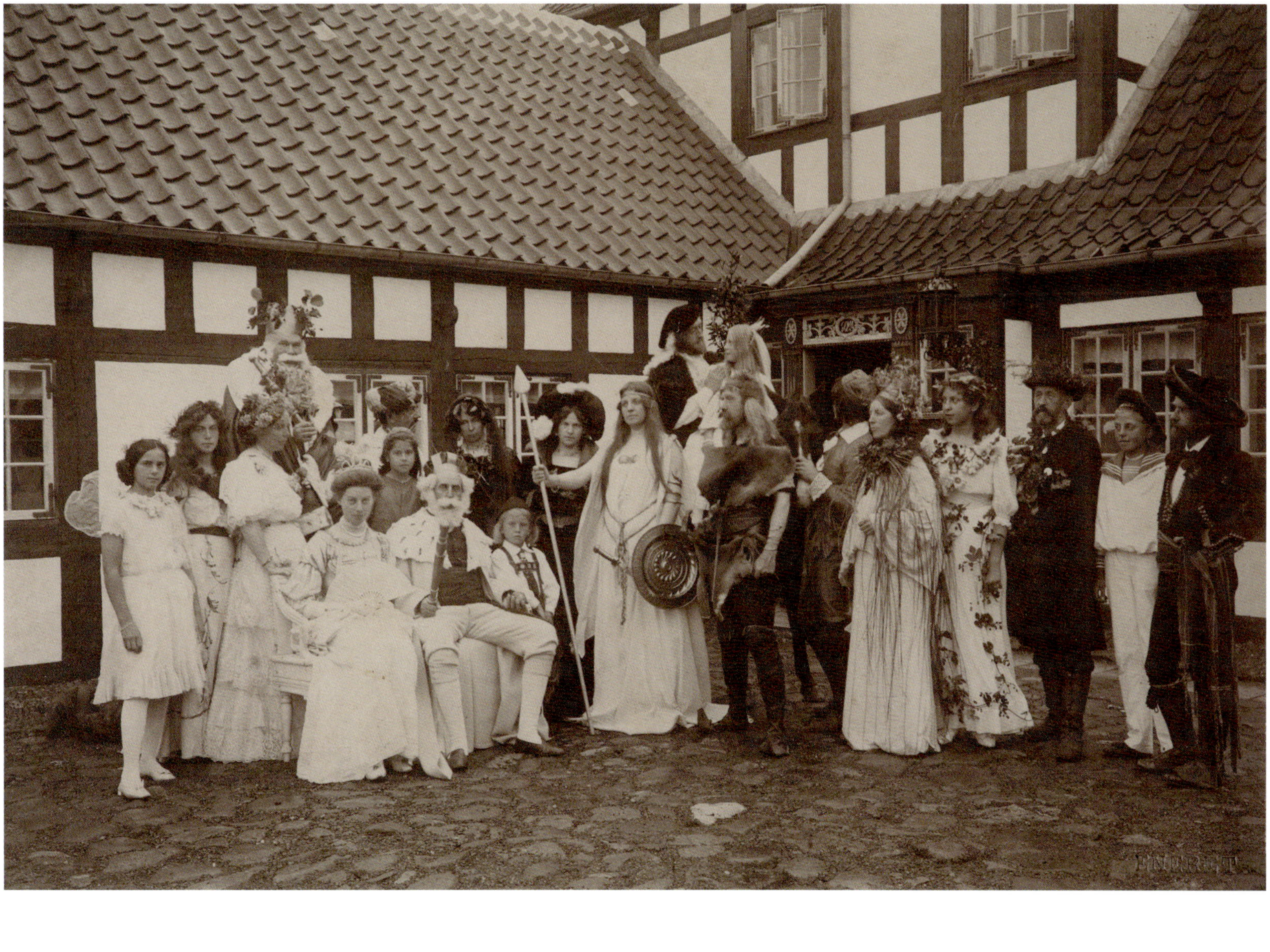

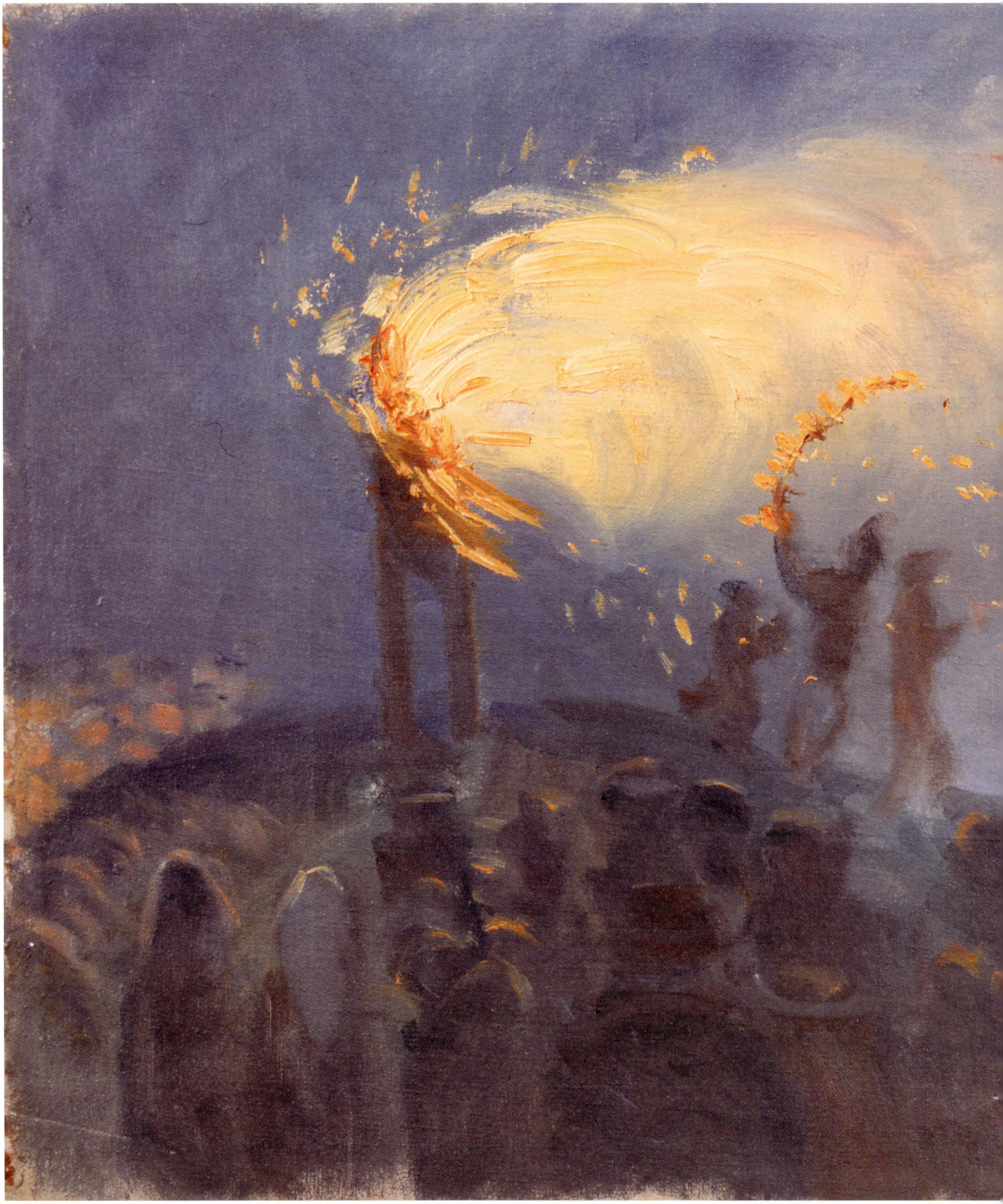

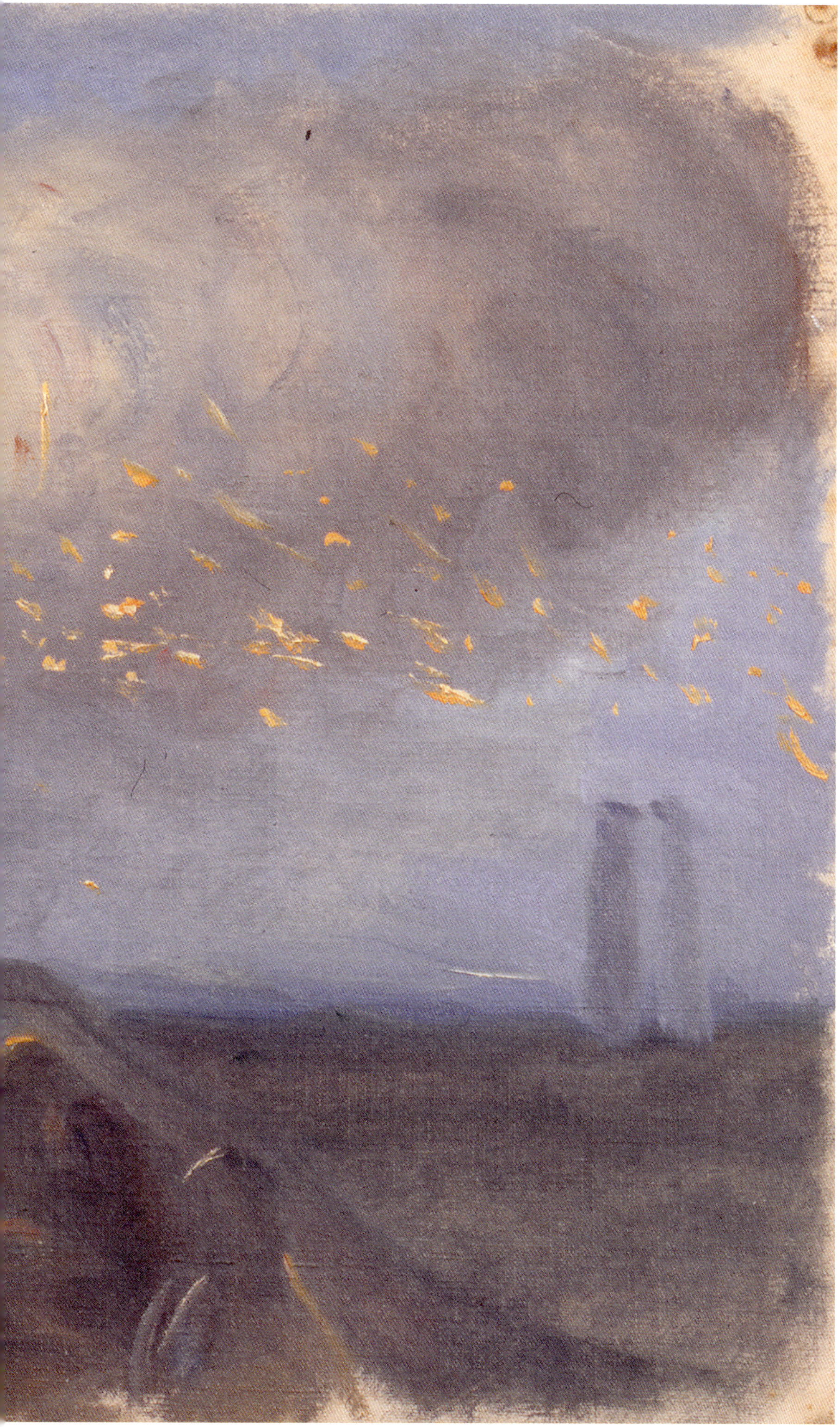

Cat. 36
Fireworks on Fyrbakken, undated
Oil on canvas
38.8 × 57.5 cm
Skagens Museum

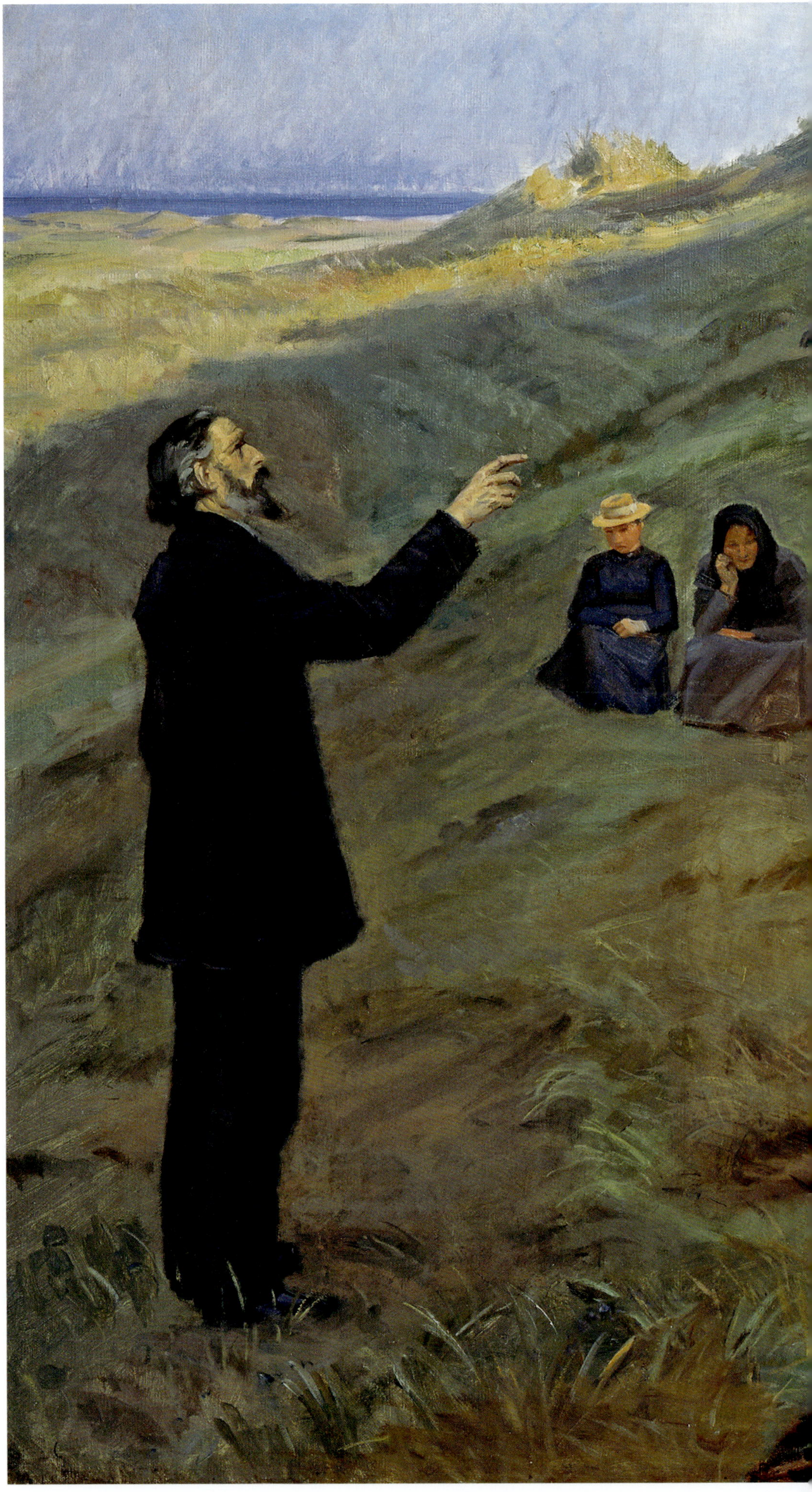

Cat. 37
A Field Sermon, 1903
Oil on canvas
100.5 × 145 cm
Skagens Museum

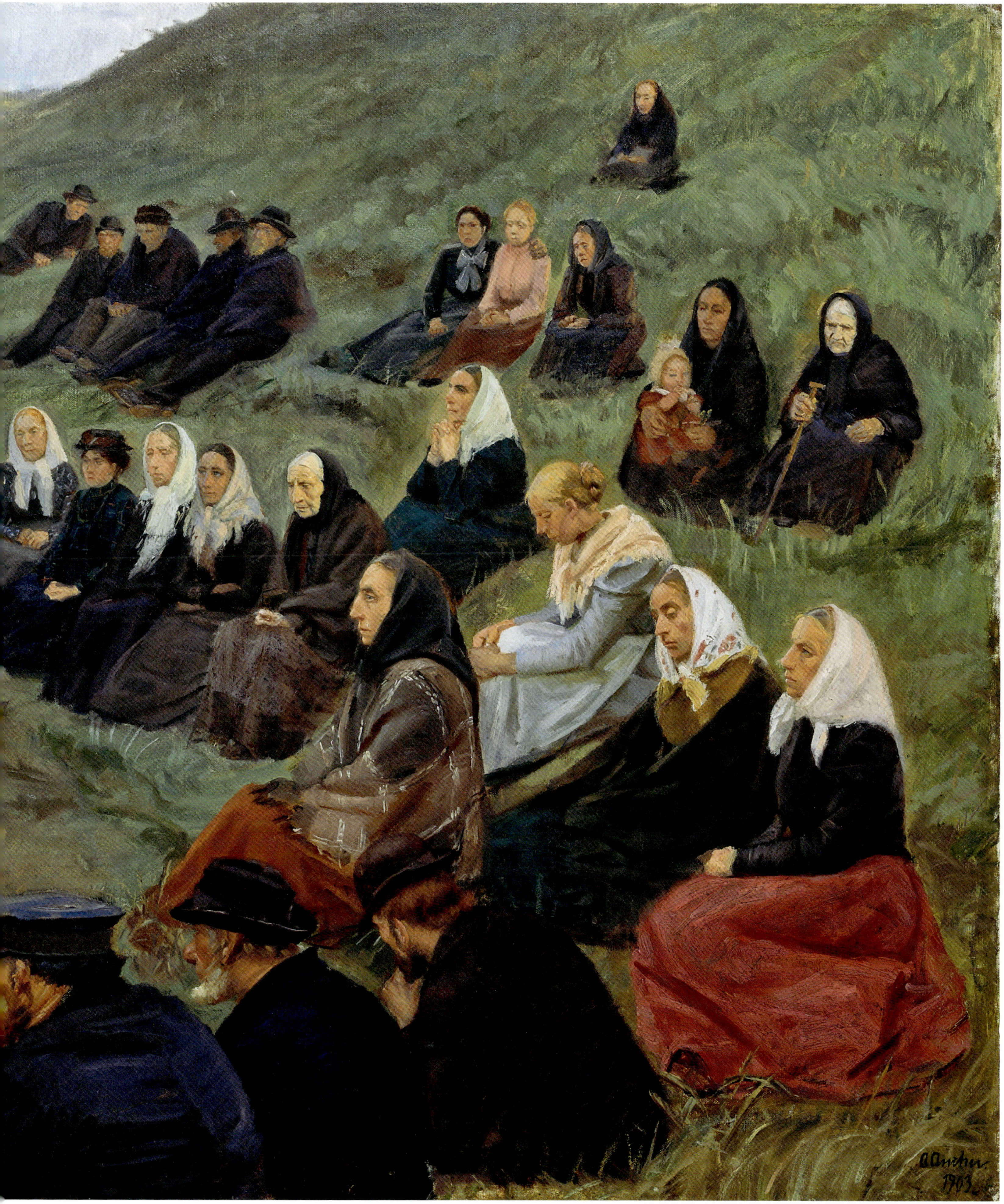
A Ancher
1903

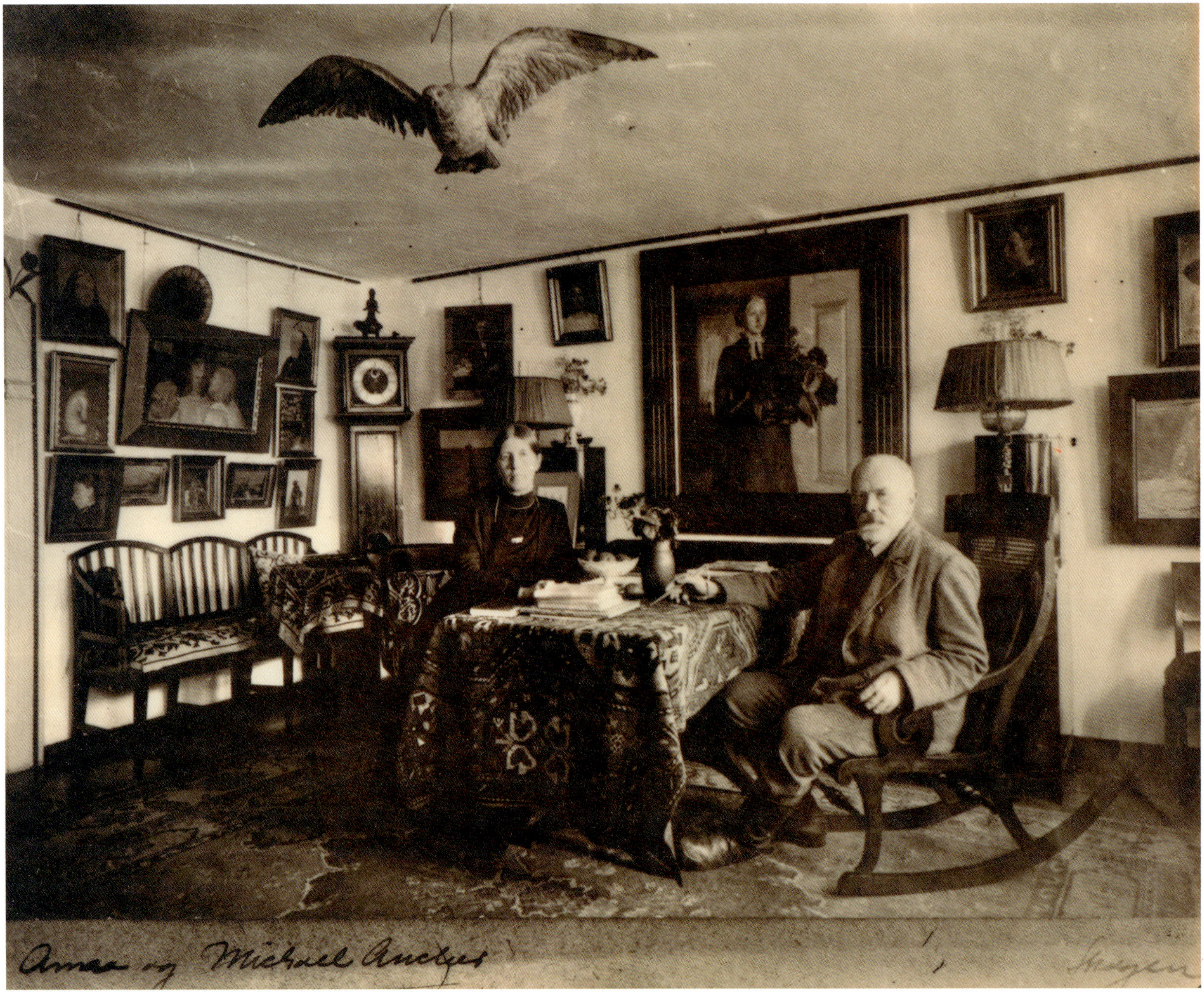
Anna og Michael Ancher

Religious themes were a relatively rare subject in the work of the Skagen artists, and Ancher was one of the few artists to consider such themes within her work.[15] It was perhaps her upbringing that gave her the impetus, and the confidence, to tackle such subjects. Balancing her artistic and spiritual values cannot have been an easy task. *Grief* [cat. 34] can be interpreted as Ancher questioning her religious beliefs, illustrating the confrontation between tradition and modernity.[16] The younger, naked woman, tormented and in pain, faces a representative of the older generation, her black attire symbolic of her piety and religious conservatism. Produced at the turn of the twentieth century, *Grief* is one of Ancher's most provocative works. In it, she makes visible her internal struggle as a modern artist coming to terms with the context and the values with which she was raised.

Home Is a Radical Place

Throughout her career, Ancher concentrated on depicting the sights and settings familiar to her. Her family and friends were frequently the subject of her work, as was her own home [fig. 19]. As a result, previous generations of art historians have sometimes devalued her work, framing it within categories of 'domestic' and 'feminine' in contrast to the large-scale narrative paintings of her male peers. Such a view overlooks Ancher's multi-figure compositions, such as *A Field Sermon*, and also fails to observe Ancher's innate capacity for experimentation. It was precisely because she concentrated on subjects that were familiar to her, that she could pursue more radical approaches to the depiction of everyday life.[17] Far from being 'safe', in the work of Ancher we see home as a radical place.

If we are to consider the Skagen colony as a sort of social and artistic experiment – one which provided the opportunity for artists to pursue the purest form of naturalism, by allowing artists to live and work amongst their subjects – then Ancher was its ideal agent. As the only member native to the town, she had known many of her sitters since childhood and could thus claim a different relationship with them. While she did not share their working-class background – as the daughter of local hotel owners, she would have been considered middle class – her family was well known and respected. Unlike other artists of the group, many of whom were from Copenhagen, Ancher could also speak and understand the heavily accented Danish dialect characteristic of rural Jutland.[18]

There are certain subjects that Ancher repeats within her work. Such repetition suggests that such scenes were part of everyday life in Skagen but, in reusing these themes, Ancher also had a sort of 'scientific control' for experimenting with different artistic approaches. In this regard, she operated in a similar manner to Claude Monet (1840–1926) who had produced works in series, depicting the same subject at different times of day, or under changing atmospheric conditions. This method allowed her to concentrate on a narrow range of effects, sometimes with only slight variation between works.[19] *Women Plucking Chickens* [cat. 38] and *Plucking the Geese* [cat. 39] provide an illustration of this practice. Both works are in horizontal format, each showing a group plucking birds, collecting the feathers in baskets. Made just two years apart, they demonstrate a clear difference of approach. In *Women Plucking Chickens*, the earlier of the two works, she adopts a darker, richer palette, with a greater focus on the contrast

Fig. 19
Edith and John Larsen (photographers)
Anna and Michael Ancher in the West Room in the Anchers' House, c. 1915
Gelatin silver print
16.9 × 20.8 cm
Skagens Museum

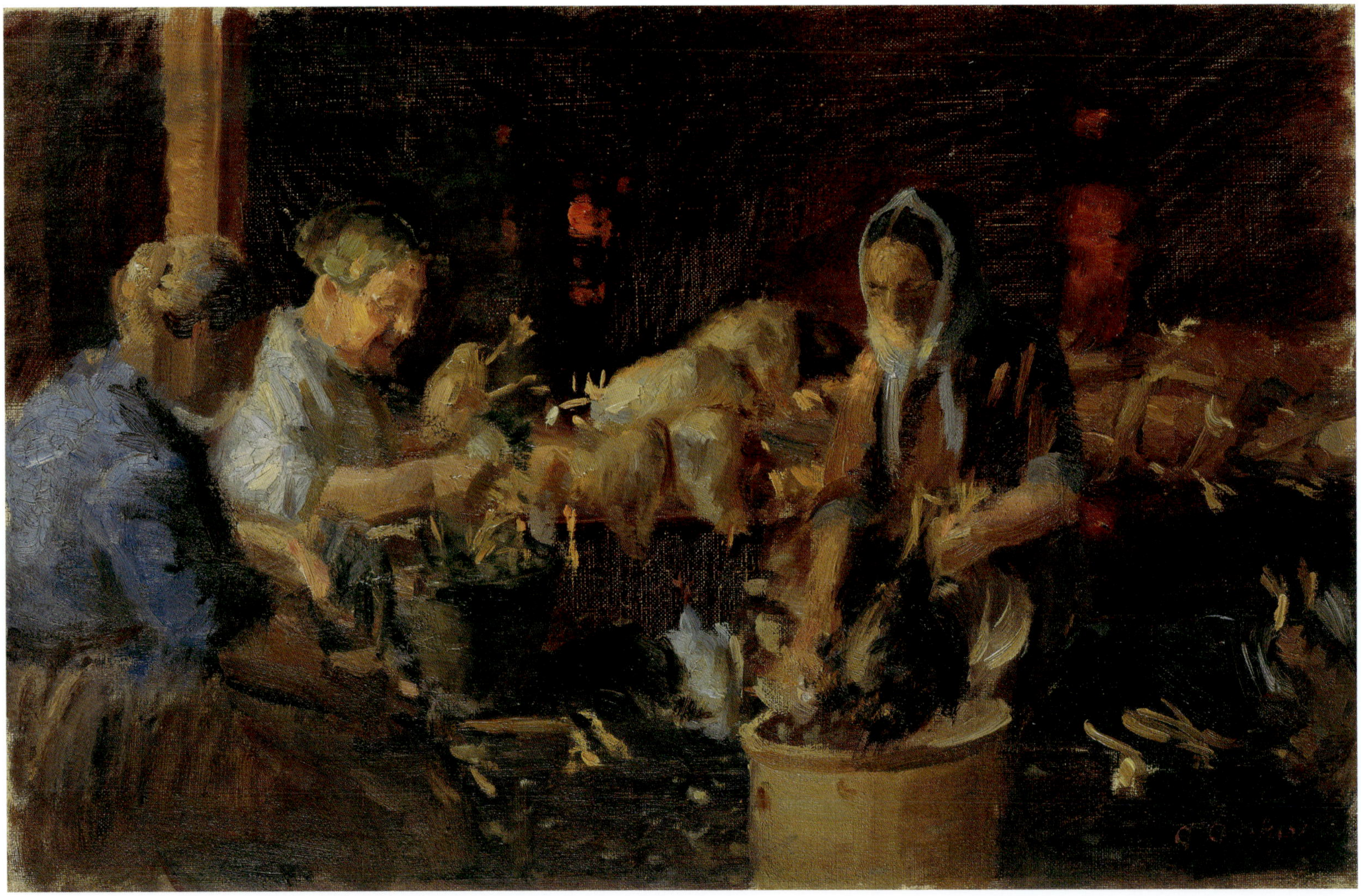

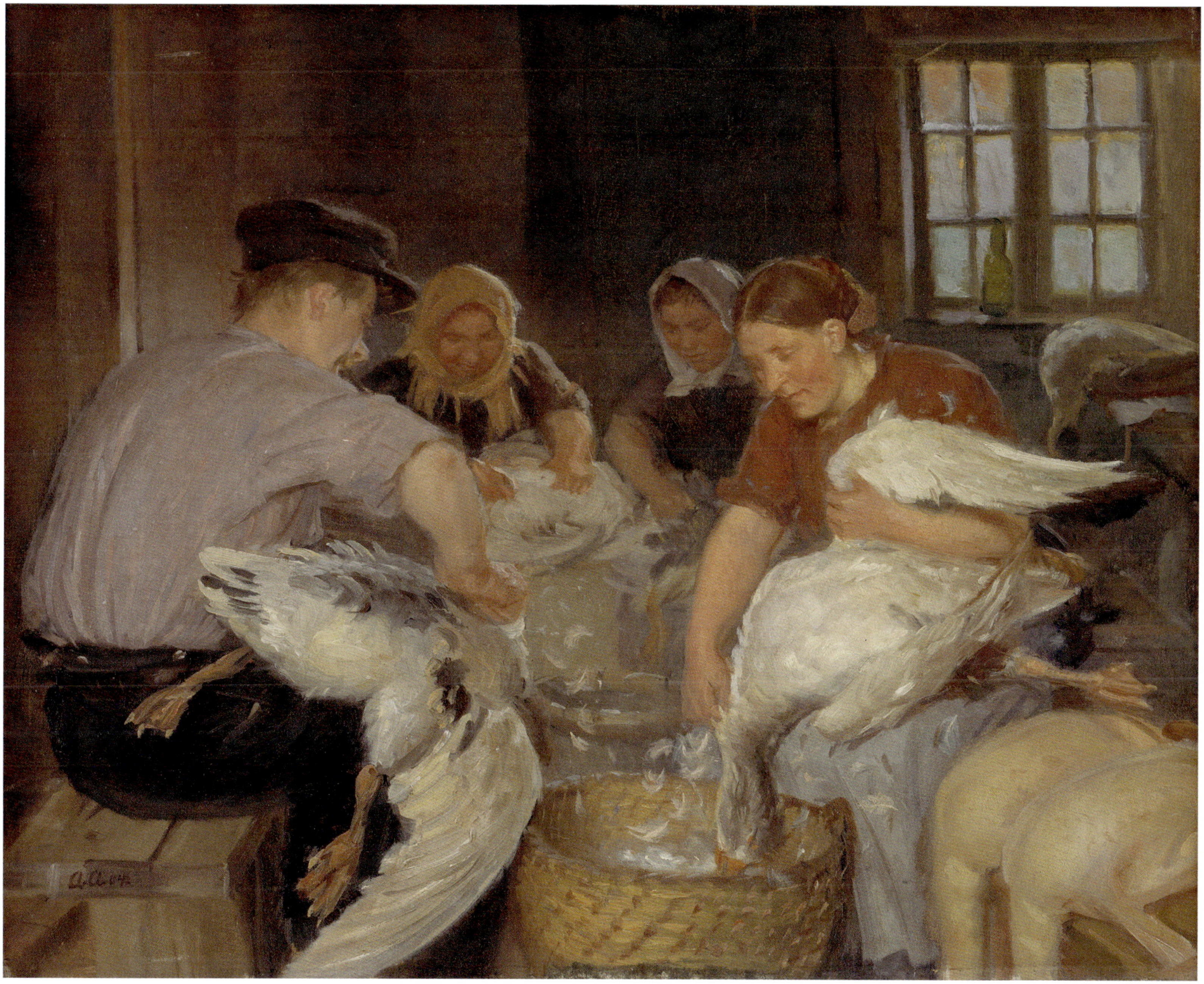

Cat. 38
Women Plucking Chickens, 1902
Oil on canvas
32.3 × 50.4 cm
Skagens Museum

Cat. 39
Plucking the Geese, 1904
Oil on canvas
55 × 67 cm
SMK, National Gallery of Denmark

of light and shade. In this regard, the work is perhaps more reminiscent of a Dutch genre scene. In *Plucking the Geese*, Ancher was able to refine her approach. Although the figure arrangement is similar, the scene is altogether lighter and airier. Light enters the space through a window at the right background, while the white feathers of the geese provide a tonal contrast and a focal point for the picture.

All of the Skagen painters looked to the local community for their subjects, yet Ancher, far more than the others, connected the artistic with the personal by finding subjects within her own home and family [fig. 20]. Ancher's mother and sisters were clearly supportive of her career as a painter, in spite of their religious commitments and more traditional outlook. This is demonstrated by the frequency with which they appear as sitters in her works. The artist painted her mother, Ane, on multiple occasions in various rooms of Brøndum's Hotel, which can be identified by their distinct colours. Her painting *Mrs Brøndum in the Red Room* [cat. 40] is amongst the most artistically radical of these works. More than any other of her figurative works, this painting can be read as a pure study in colour, red-on-red, not so far away from *Combing the Hair* by Edgar Degas (1834–1917).[20] Ancher's sisters, Marie and Hulda, also worked with their mother at Brøndum's Hotel, and in *After the Labours of the Day* [cat. 41], the artist paints them within the 'blue room'. One of the sisters leans back against the wall, while the other rests her head on a table, both with their eyes closed. The scene depicts their exhaustion following a day's hard work. The image is charming and suggests an intimate, unguarded moment, without pretence. The work is demonstrative of Ancher's close relationship with her family, the trust they shared and how this, in turn, opened new avenues for her work.

While Ancher was born and raised at Brøndum's Hotel, even when she left to begin her married life with Michael, she kept within its periphery. Their first house as a couple, Havehuset, was situated next to the family hotel. Later, their house on Markvej was still only a stone's throw away. And, despite having a house of her own, she naturally continued to spend significant time at the hotel. In this regard, we must consider Ancher's art within an expanded concept of 'house' and 'home'. She had multiple places where she would have been 'at home'. The Markvej house features frequently as a subject within her art. In some instances, Ancher offers vignettes set within specific rooms of the house, for example *Lunch Before the Hunt* [cat. 5], which shows Michael seated for lunch at the table in the front room of the house; or *Interior with Red Poppies* [cat. 42], which depicts the artist's friend, the pianist Lizzy Hohlenberg, reading at the same table. The distinctive couch, upholstered with chartreuse-coloured fabric, can be seen in both paintings, and Ancher's painting of her mother is displayed on the wall behind Hohlenberg.[21] In a work like *The Old Window* [cat. 43], however, Ancher offers just a snapshot of her home, focusing on details of the house, without figures. In *The Old Window*, plant life frames one of the windows at the front of the artist's house, overwhelming and completely covering the house's exterior walls. With little offered by way of context, the painting becomes an almost abstract study of colour and form. With this work and others, such as *Evening Sun in the Artist's Studio at Markvej* [cat. 7], we see Ancher's extremely close observation of the environment around her. These constitute some of Ancher's most progressive works, yet their creation was only possible because they were drawn from the settings with which she was most familiar.

Fig. 20
Frederik Andreas Hollesen (photographer)
The Families Brøndum and Ancher by Brøndums Hotel, 1890s
Gelatin silver print
16.8 × 23 cm
Skagens Museum

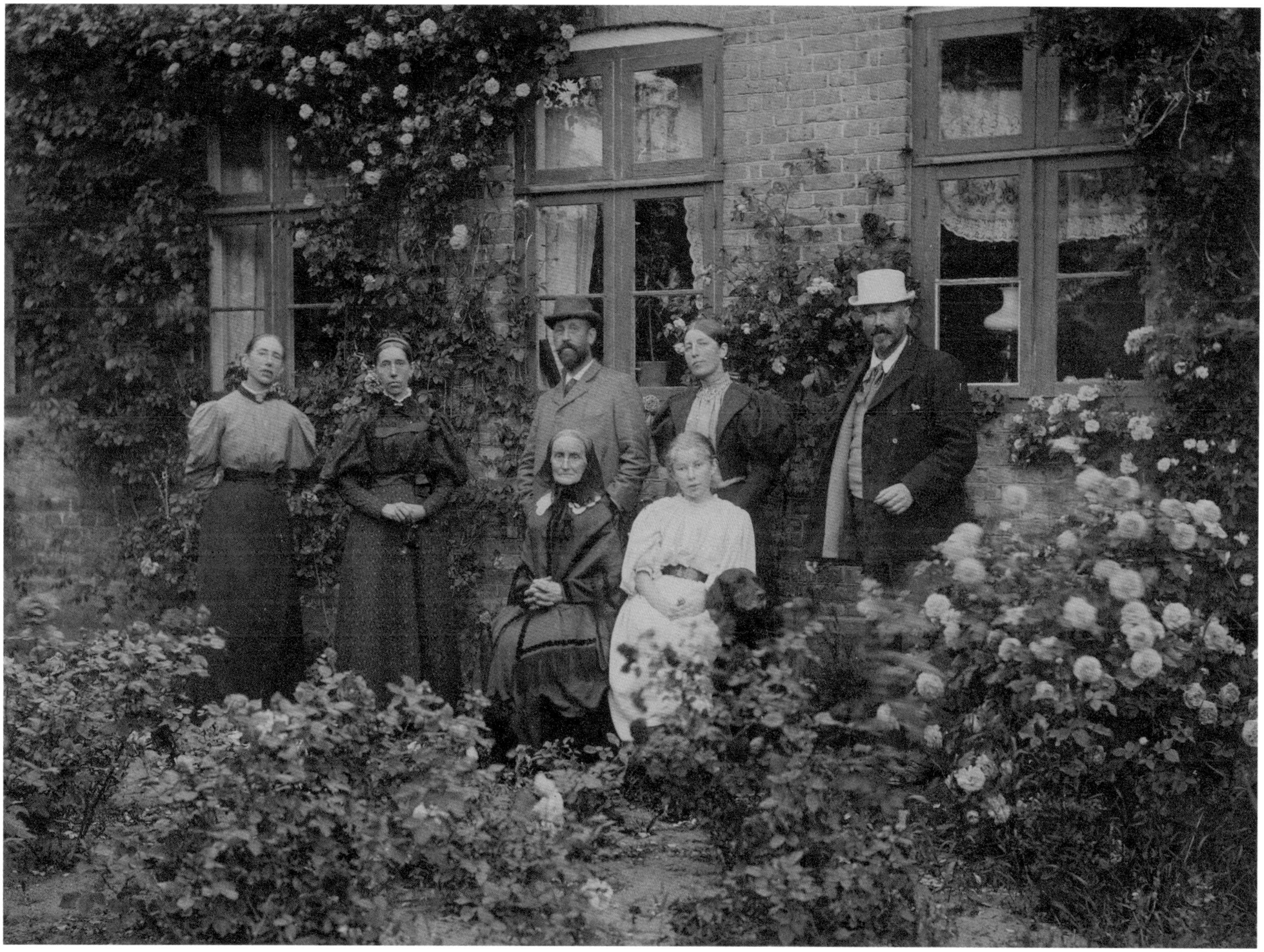

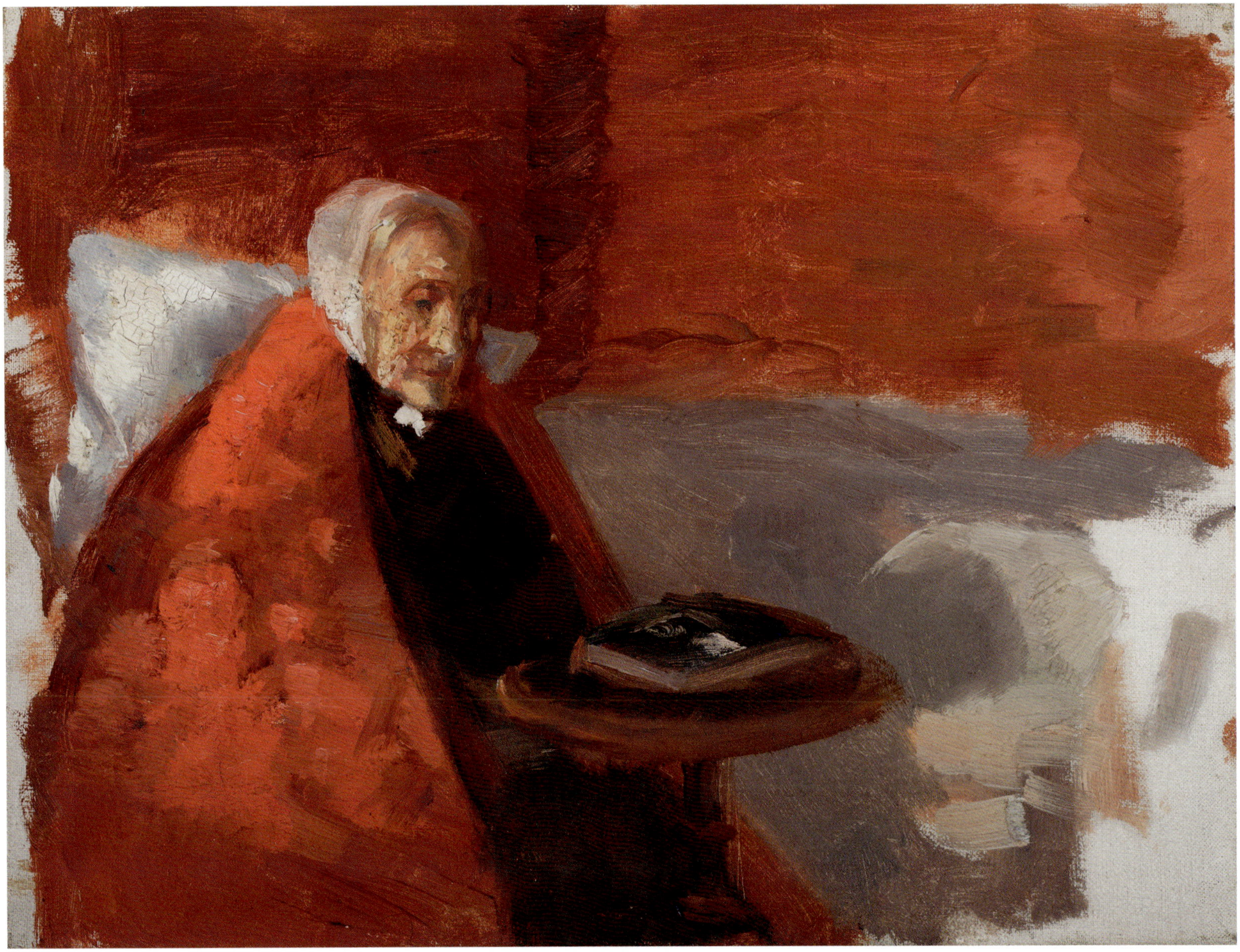

Cat. 40
Mrs Brøndum in the Red Room, c. 1910
Oil on canvas
23.6 × 31.8 cm
Skagens Museum

Cat. 41
After the Labours of the Day, 1917
Oil on canvas
52 × 64 cm
Skagens Museum

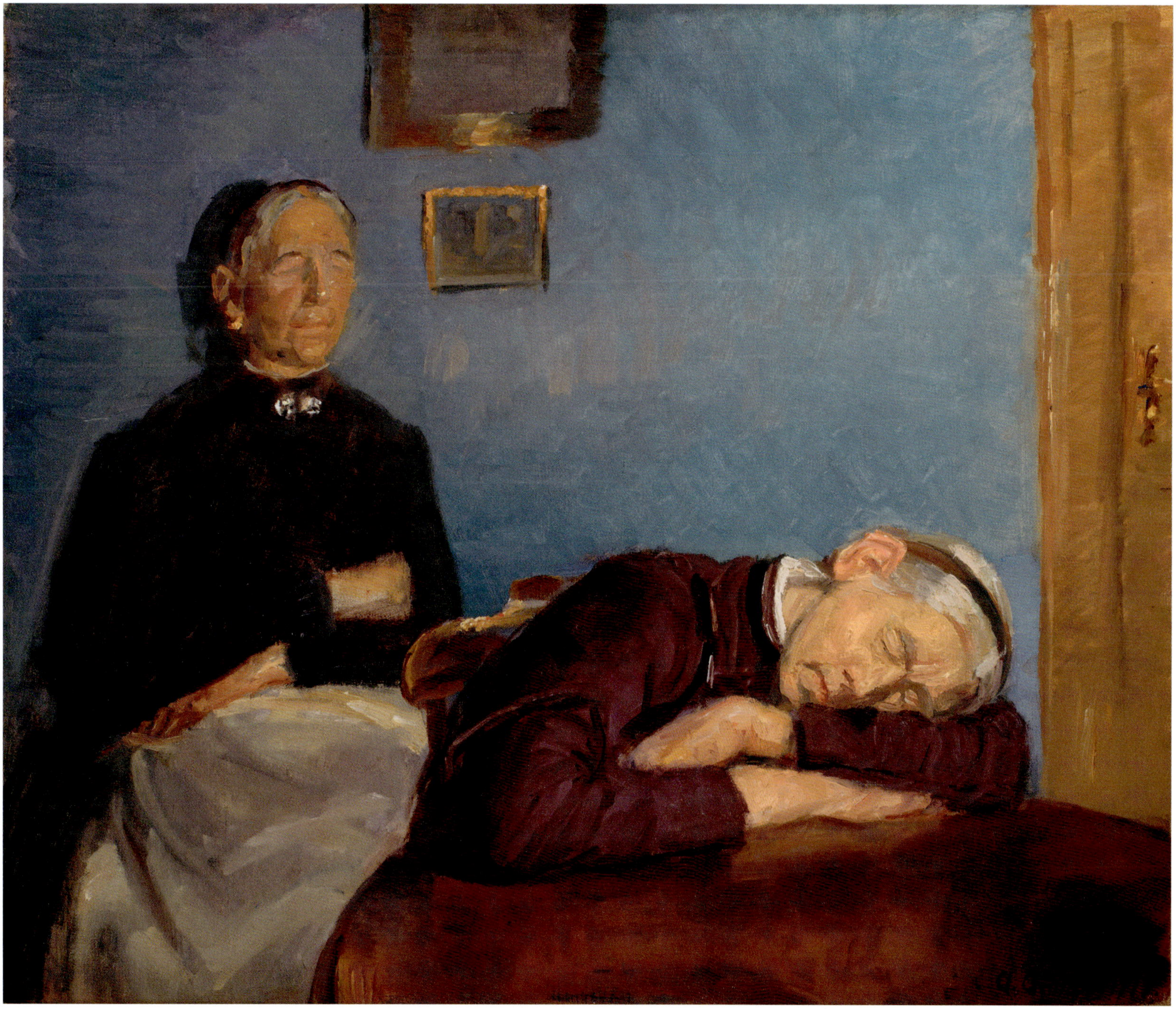

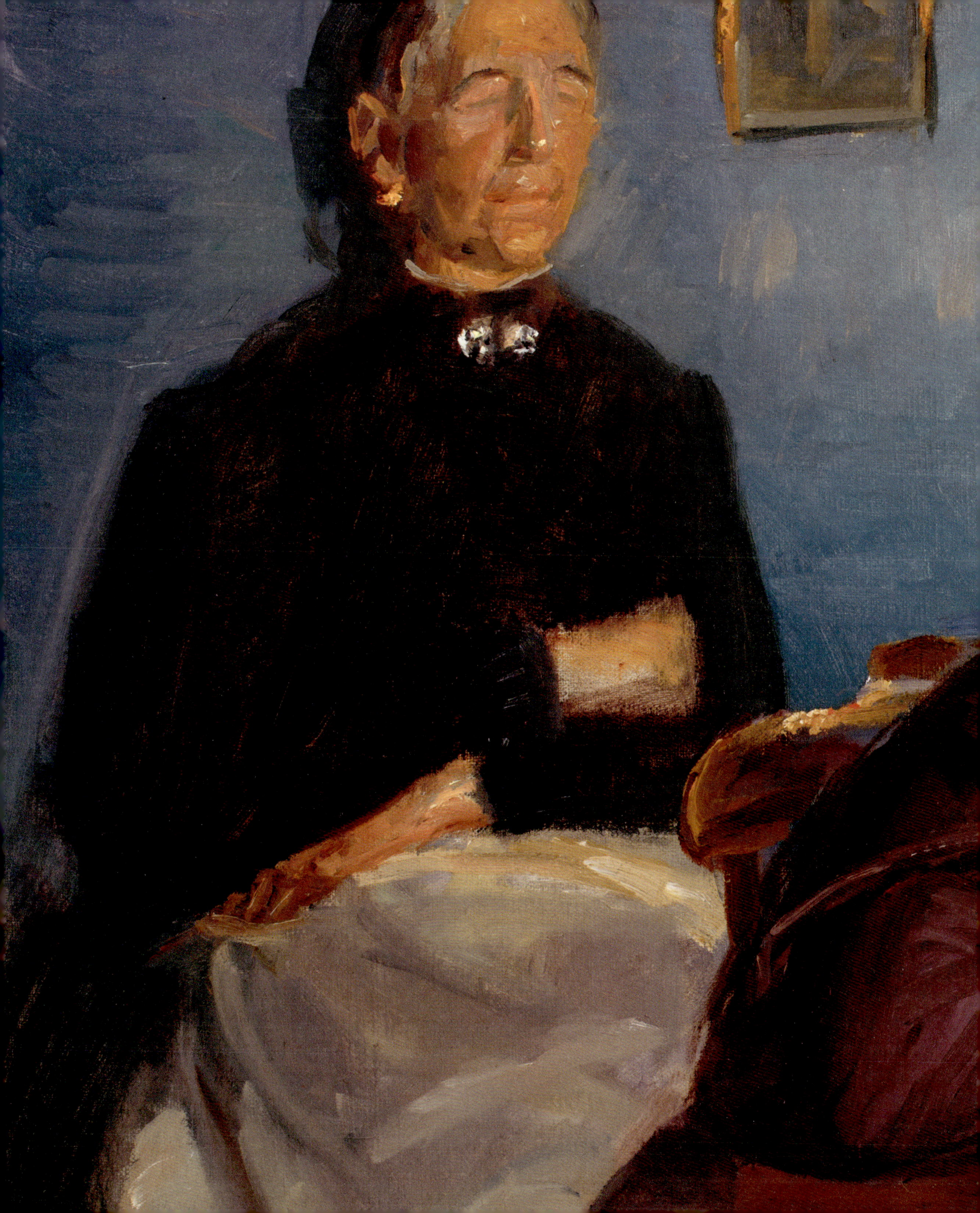

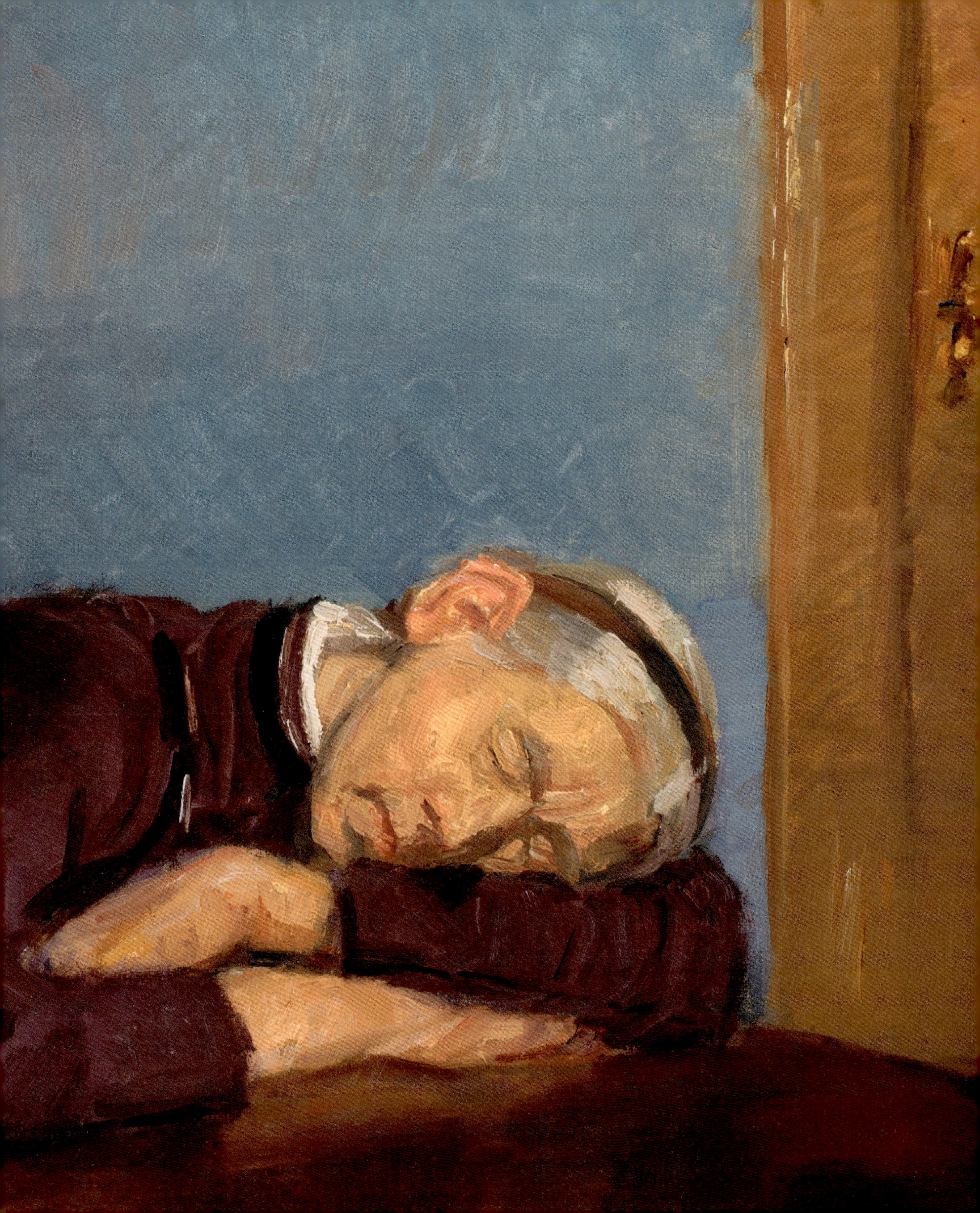

She had multiple places where she would have been 'at home'.

Cat. 42
Interior with Red Poppies, 1905
Oil on canvas
52 × 64 cm
Skagens Museum

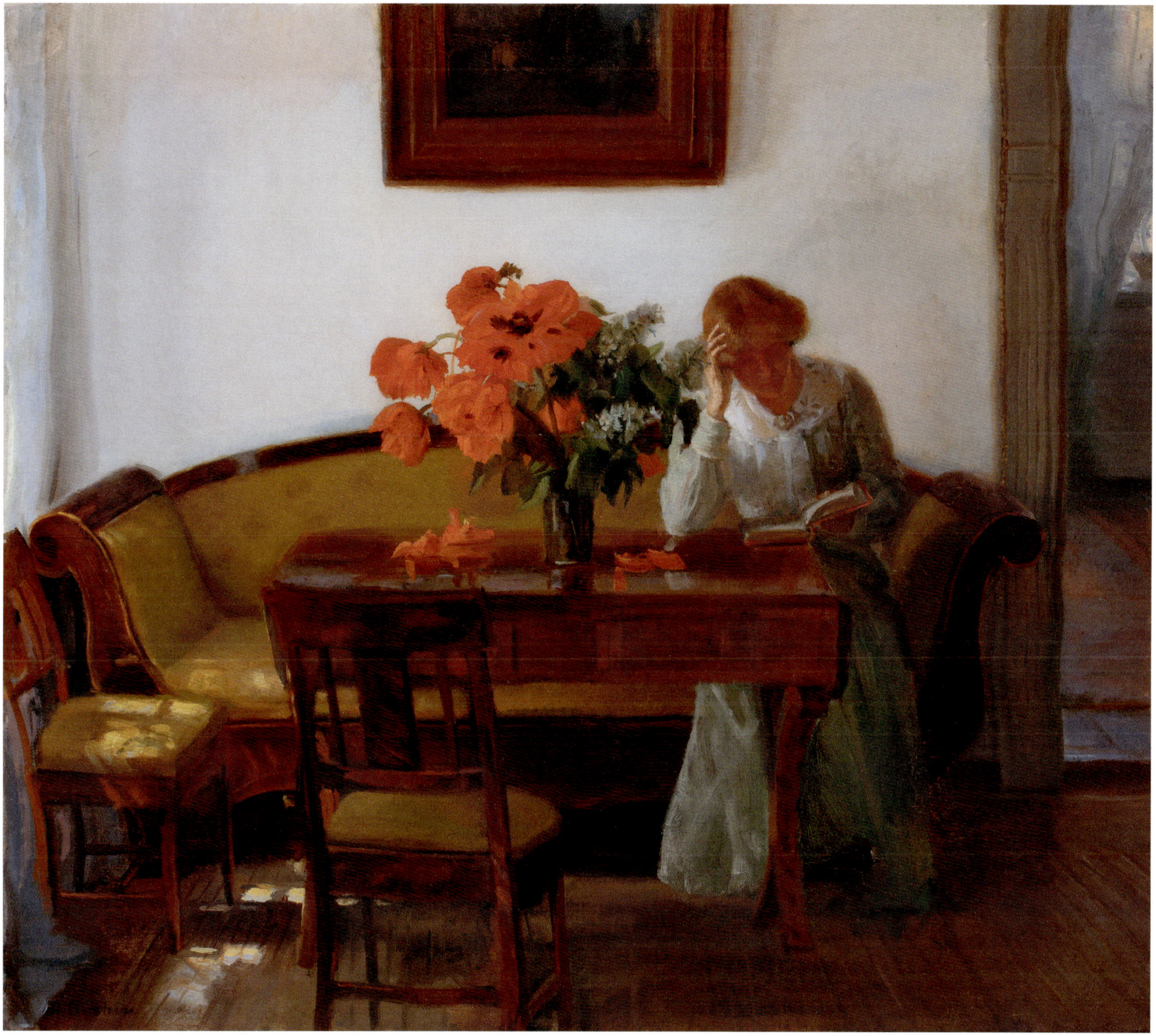

Cat. 43
The Old Window, 1914
Oil on canvas
44 × 40.4 cm
Skagens Museum

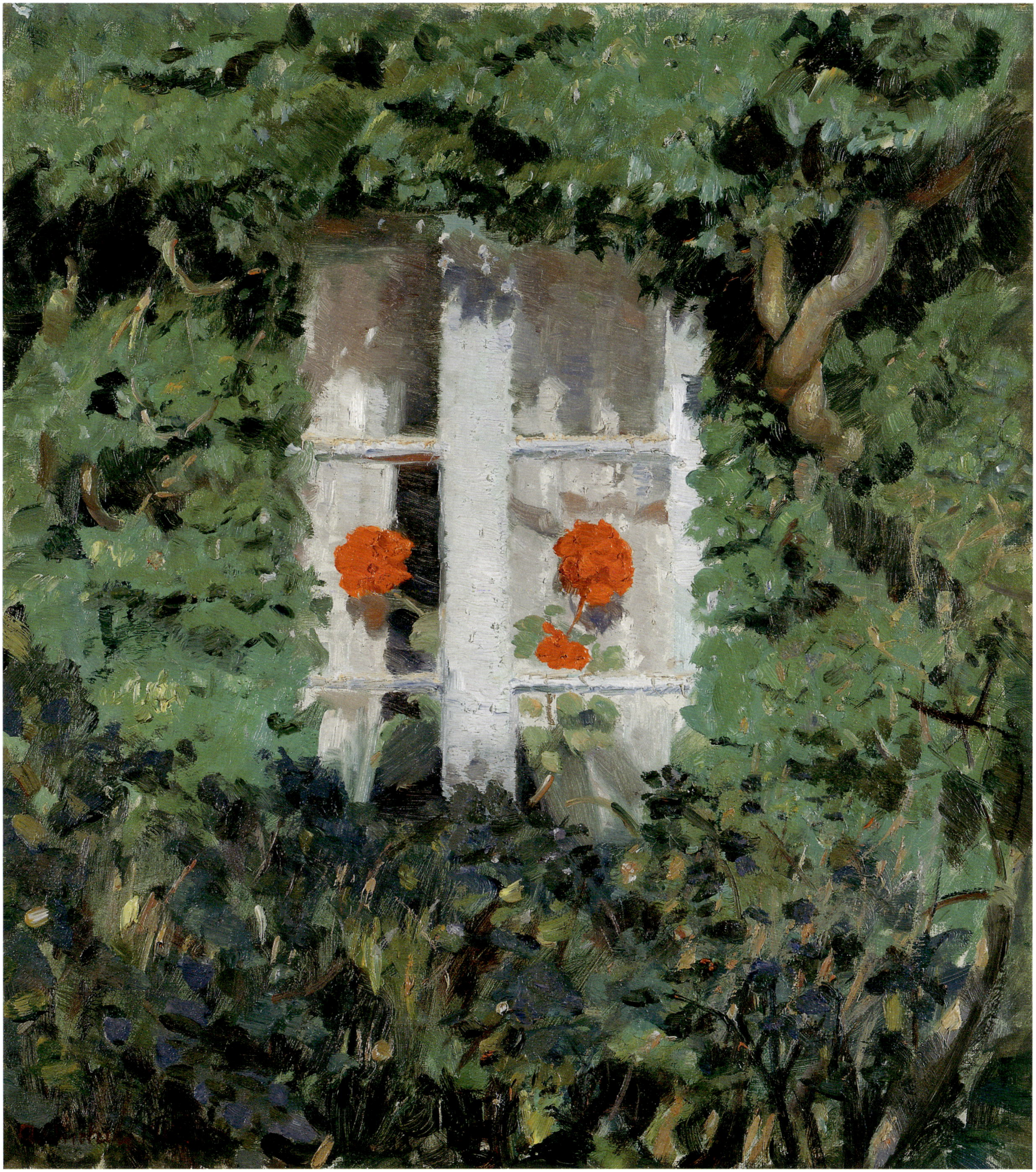

Ancher's home on Markvej was a work of art in itself, and its distinctive decorative scheme makes it readily identifiable within her pictures. This can still be witnessed when visiting the house-museum today, which is open to visitors and remains largely unchanged since Ancher's time.[22] In the house, works by Anna and Michael are displayed together alongside antiques and decorative works of art, while door panels are decorated with various wading birds, including herons, ducks and lapwings [fig. 22].[23] We know that the idea of an 'open' home was important to Ancher. She would often play host, welcoming visitors and holding parties. One such celebration is illustrated in Krøyer's painting *Hip, Hip, Hurrah!* [fig. 23] which depicts a lively party in the couple's garden, with other Skagen artists in attendance. A recent project to catalogue the 5,000 photographs taken by and of the Skagen painters – held in the collection of Skagens Museum – likewise highlights the many celebrations that took place within the Anchers' home [fig. 21].[24] Through her role as host, Ancher became the de facto matriarch of the Skagen painters, building an artistic community with her home at the centre.

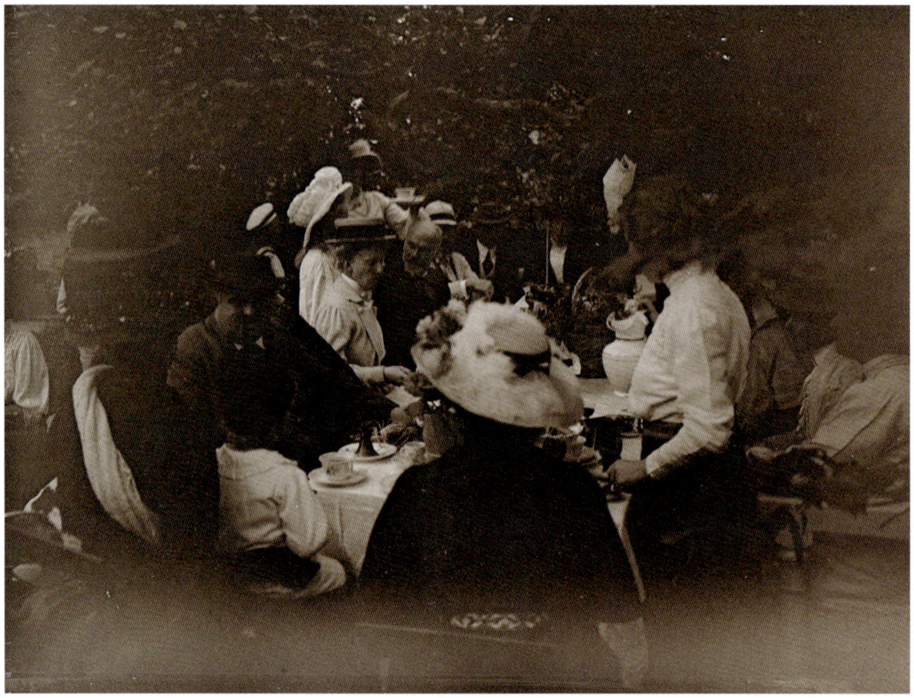

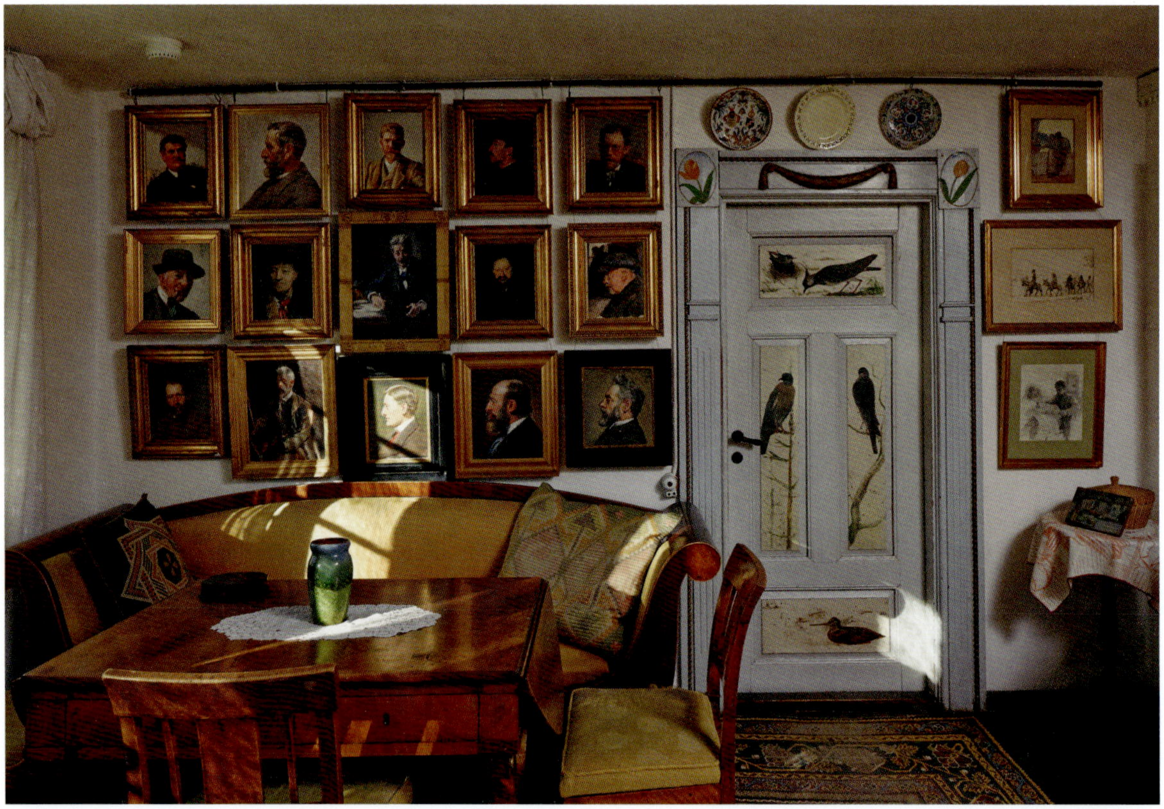

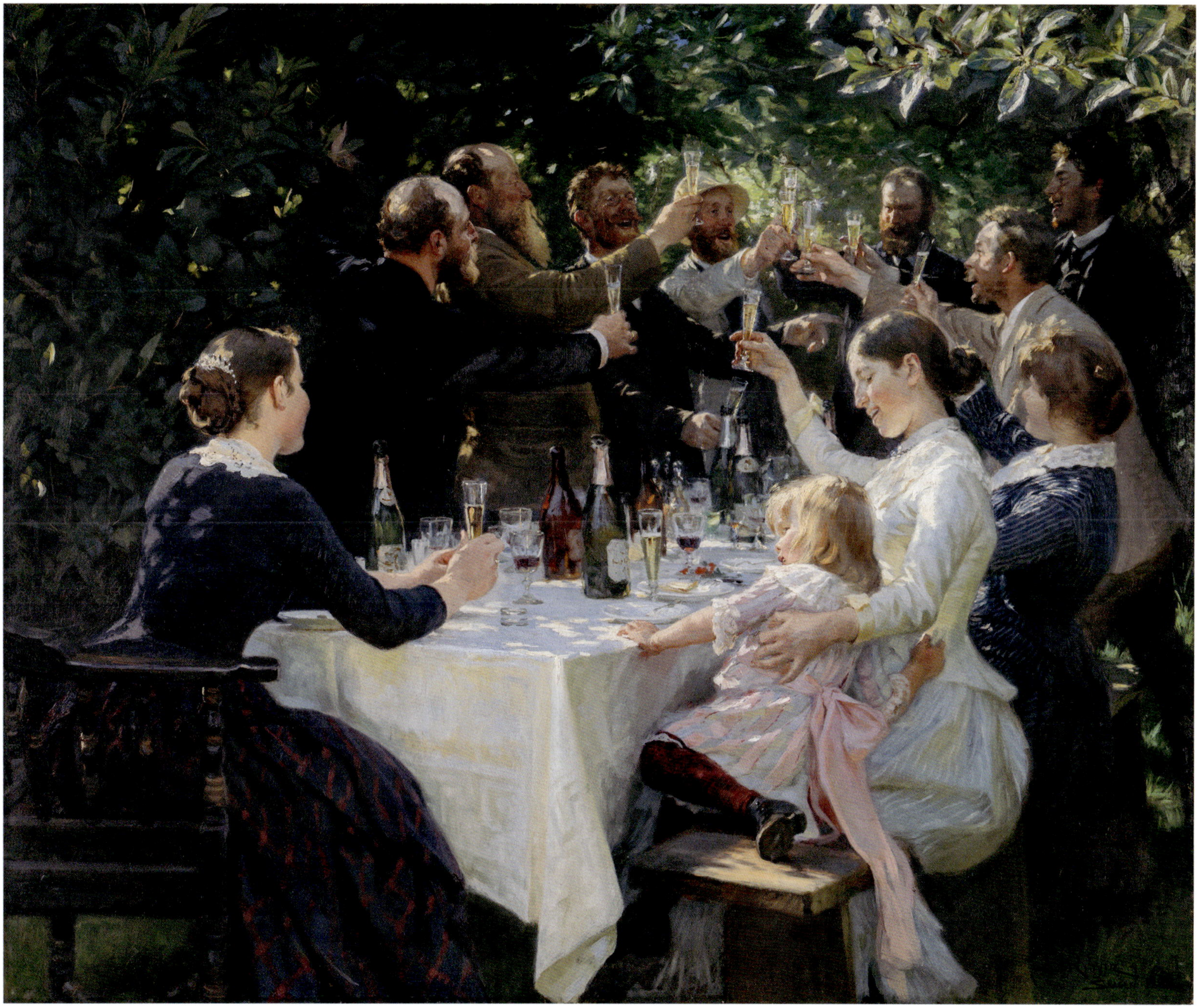

Fig. 21
Unknown Photographer
Anna Ancher's 50th Birthday, 1909
Skagens Museum

Fig. 22
South Living Room, the Anchers' House
Skagens Museum

Fig. 23
Peder Severin Krøyer
Hip, Hip, Hurrah!, 1888
Oil on canvas
134.5 cm × 165.5 cm
Gothenburg Museum of Art

A Room of One's Own

In Virginia Woolf's 'A Room of One's Own', originally published in 1929, the writer argued that a woman must have a space of their own, both literal and metaphorical, in order to produce creative work.[25] Such a construct would offer safety, security and the freedom necessary for a woman to create on her own terms. In Skagen, Ancher possessed such a 'room'. She had multiple spaces in which she could work, financial security, a loving and supportive family, and peers who respected and encouraged her. This essay has highlighted how Ancher's unique position between two worlds, gave her intimate insight into the rural community in which she had been raised, while also connecting her to Europe's cultural scene. Yet, it can also be argued that Ancher operated in something of a bubble, one in which she deliberately disconnected herself from some of the major political debates of her period. If we are to take Woolf's thesis to heart, it may be because Ancher was able to create a room 'of her own' – sometimes choosing to isolate herself when it suited her – that she was able to thrive at a time when so many other female painters struggled. Ancher's fame was established in her lifetime and at no point has she been forgotten by history. By contrast, many of her female peers are only now being acknowledged.

Ancher had a complicated relationship to the women's movement, which gained momentum in Denmark at the end of the nineteenth century. That Ancher was able to pursue a profession as a painter, especially after her marriage and the birth of her daughter, was remarkable and subverted the gendered expectations of the period. Many would have regarded her life amongst the Skagen painters as bohemian, and even scandalous. Previously in this volume, Mette Harbo Lehmann highlighted how Michael's picture of

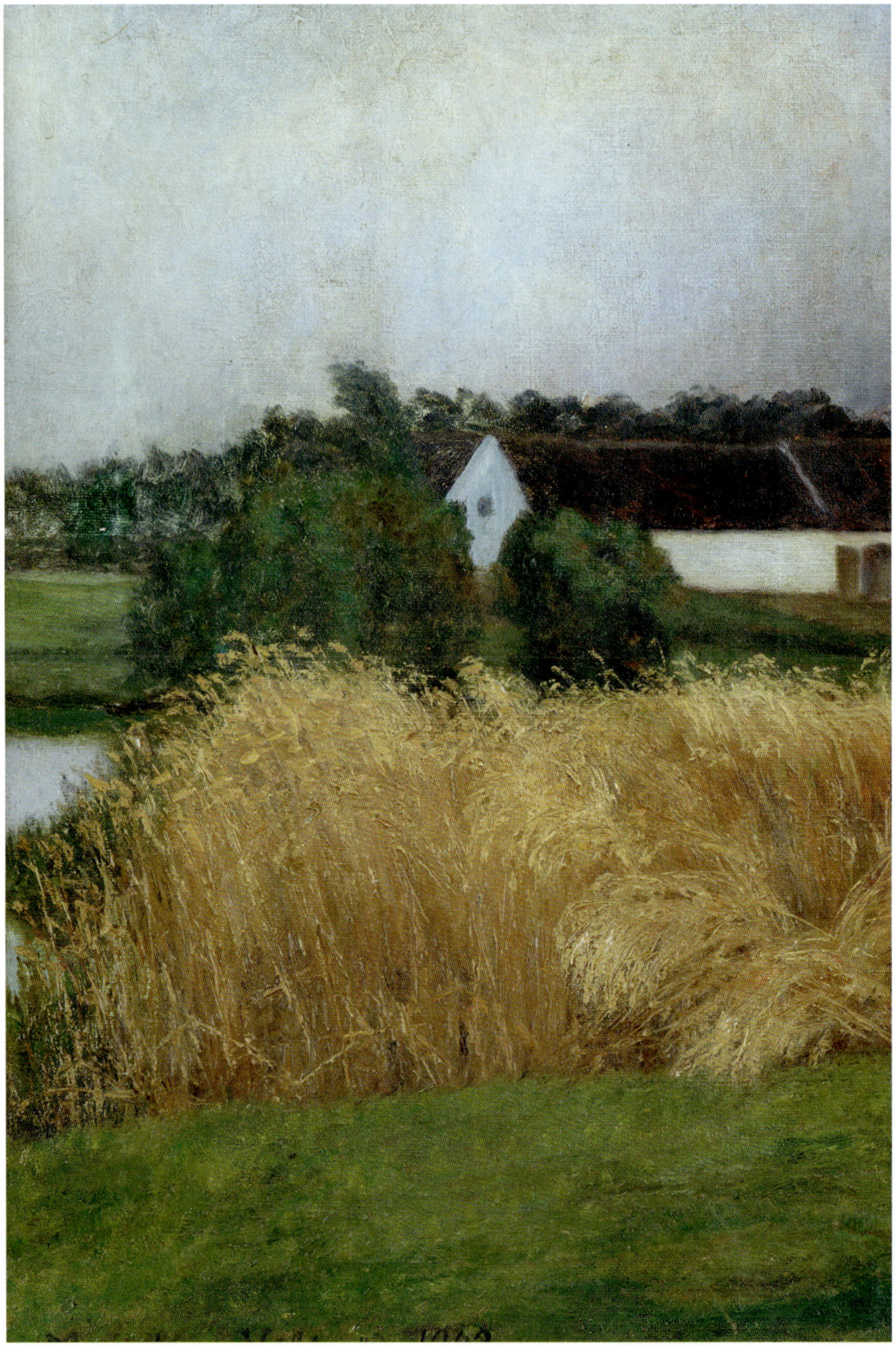

Cat. 44
Marie Luplau
Landscape from Vallerød with a Rye Field, 1903
Oil on canvas
42 × 29 cm
Collection of Sandi Toksvig

Cat. 45
Emilie Mundt
Woman Reading by the Window, 1914
Oil on canvas
61 × 52 cm
Collection of Sandi Toksvig

a pregnant Ancher caused a considerable stir when it was exhibited for the first time at the Copenhagen salon (see p. 24). Yet, although Ancher may have pioneered greater gender parity in her personal life, she sometimes showed reluctance to become involved in wider debates. In a letter to her cousin Martha Johansen (1861–1929) discussing the creation of a new art school for women, attached to the Royal Danish Academy of Fine Art, Ancher was somewhat dismissive. She described the debate over the new school as 'the women's nonsense'. The artist suggested that she no longer wished to be involved and had, to some degree, been coerced into lending her support in the first place. It is unclear as to whether she felt this way because the cause was not worthwhile or whether she felt she was too far away to be of use.[26] In any case, in her words and actions, Ancher comes across as less 'activist' than some of her peers.[27]

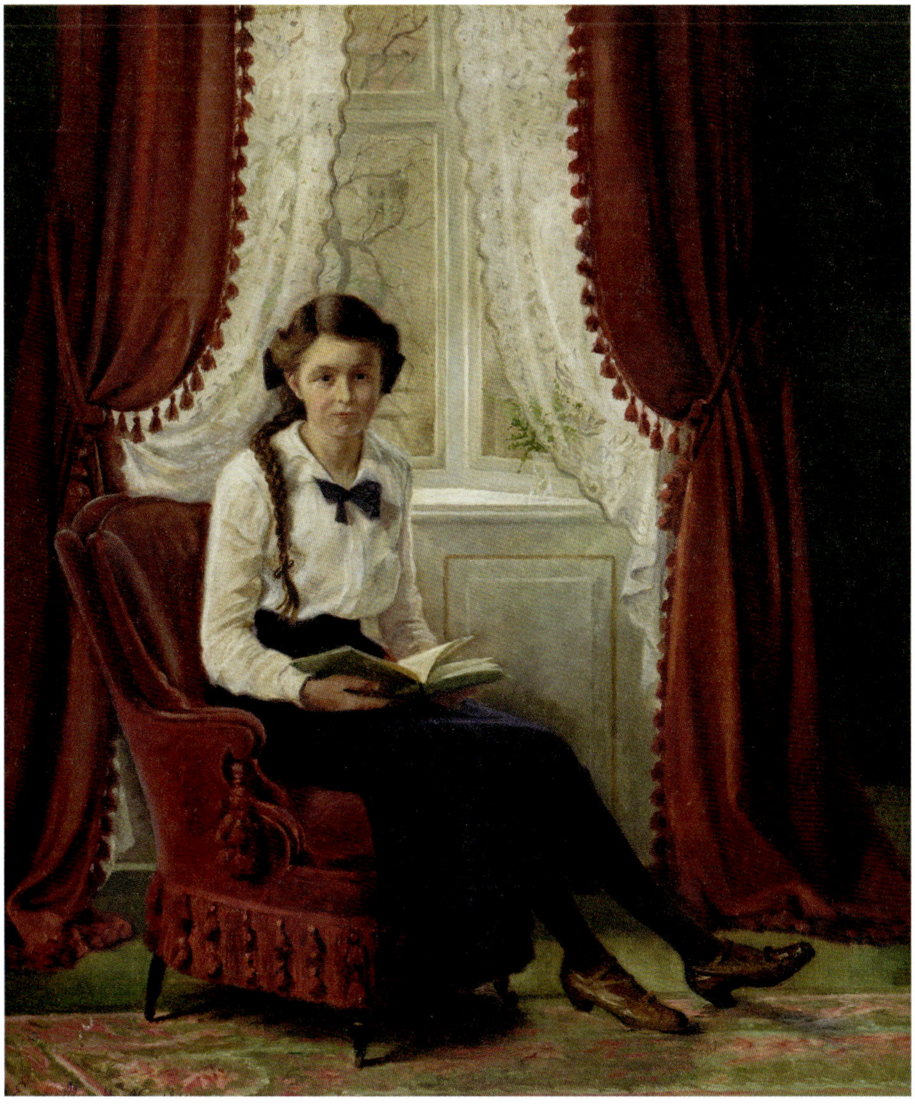

The landscape artist Marie Luplau (1848–1925) [cat. 44] and her partner Emilie Mundt (1842–1922) [cat. 45] were at the forefront of the women's movement. Luplau and Mundt both attended Vilhelm Kyhn's drawing school for women, where Ancher also studied (albeit probably not at the same time).[28] Luplau's mother, Nicoline Christine Luplau, was a co-founder of the women's suffrage association in Denmark, and both artists were politically active from early in their careers.[29] Later, recognising the dearth of opportunities available to female artists, the couple would establish and run their own drawing school for women. Ancher, Mundt and Luplau had participated in an exhibition of female artists organised by artist Viggo Johansen (1851–1935) in 1891.[30] Later, in 1895, they would again participate in the famous Women's Exhibition in Copenhagen, inspired by the exhibition held at the World's Fair in Chicago and intended to show the diversity of production by women across arts and crafts. Marie Sandholdt [cat. 47] and marine painter Louise Bonfils [cat. 46] also showed works in this exhibition.

Ancher sat on the visual arts jury for the 1895 exhibition. However, a contingent of artists, led by Luplau, questioned the jury's methodology for selection. They argued that the jury was employing the same methods as male committees had done previously and, in doing so, privileged the few women artists who were already well recognised.[31] This pointed criticism may have been a barb directed at Ancher who, by that date, had enjoyed national and international acclaim. Rather than engage with the protesting artists, Ancher removed herself from the jury. Later, she joined a smaller committee, to continue the selection once the protest had passed. To an extent, Luplau and her circle may have been right: Ancher had gained respect and

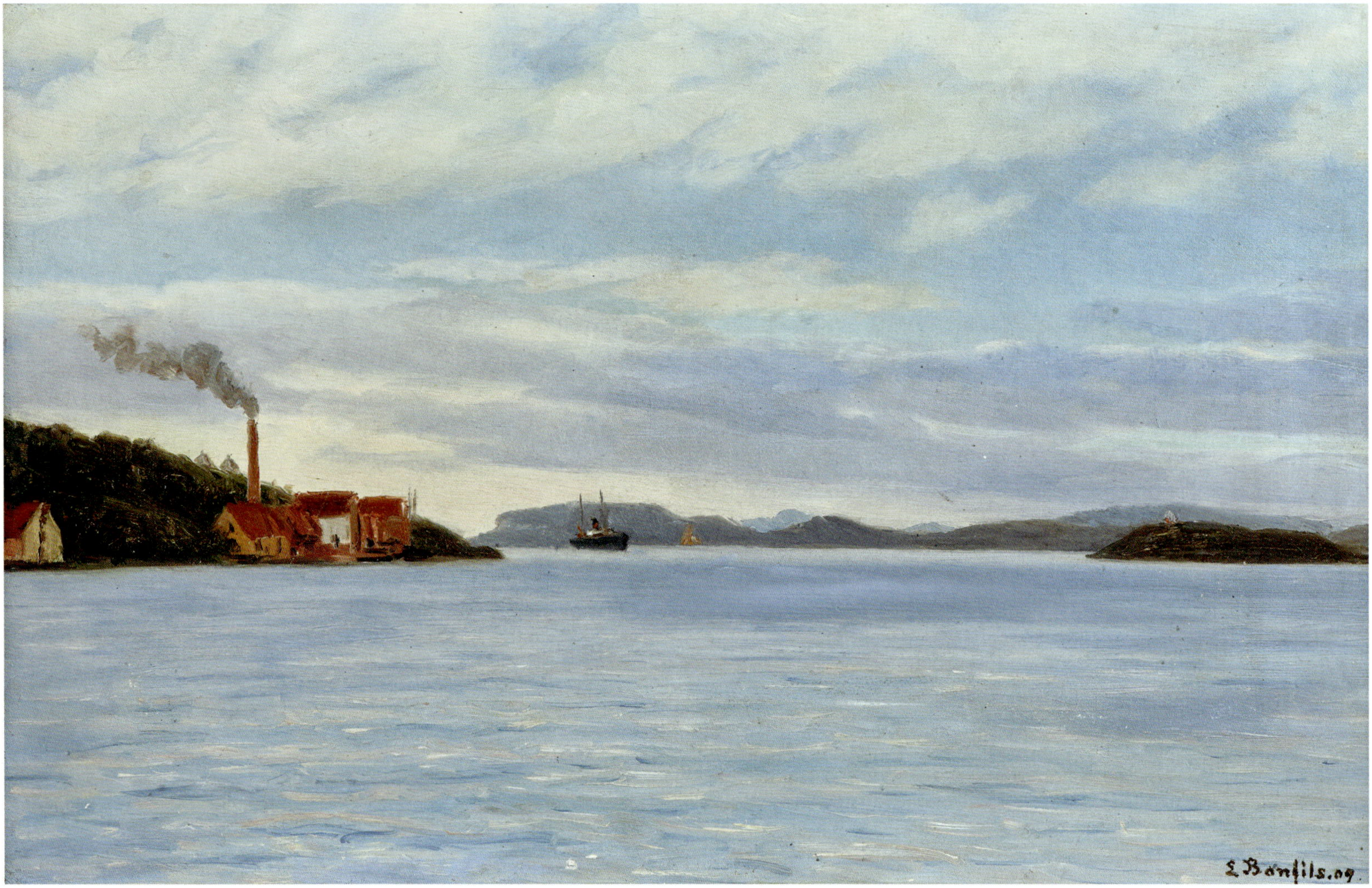
E. Bonfils.09

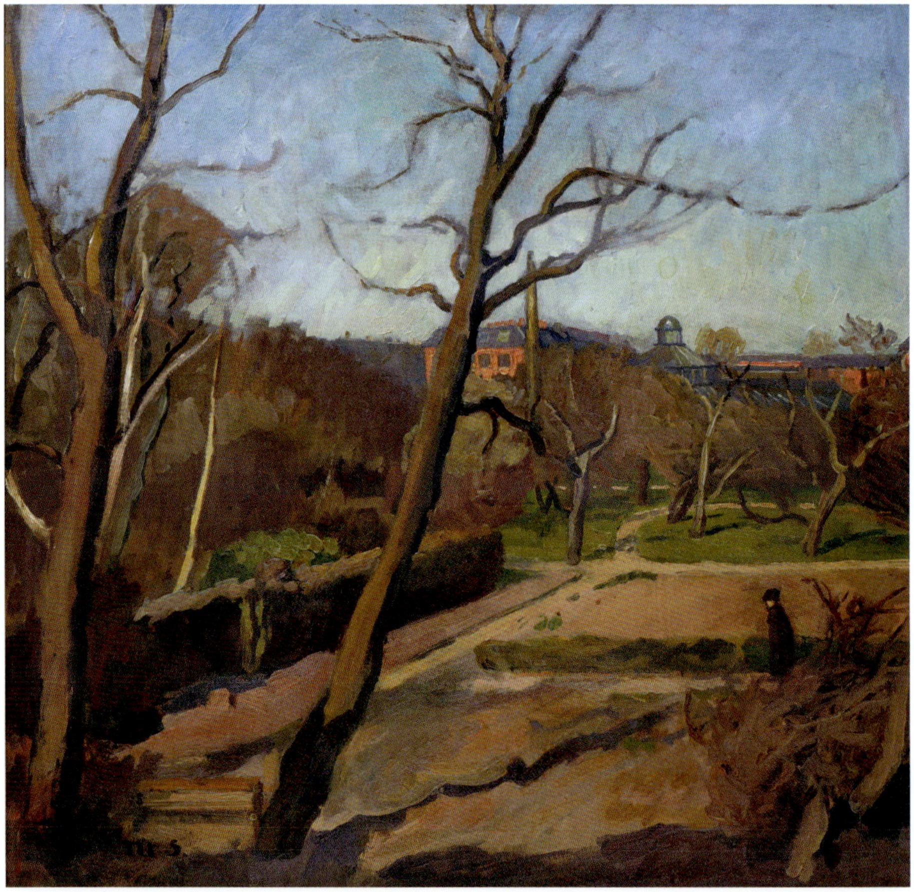

reputation within a community of largely male artists, operating on their terms. In working from Skagen, Ancher may have had the option to tactically withdraw, both literally and metaphorically. This position might make her seem unsympathetic, and yet, it may also have been the very thing that enabled her success at a time when it was hugely difficult for women to forge professional artistic careers. It may also have allowed her to enjoy greater artistic freedoms than her female peers, a fact witnessed in her artworks, which are far more ambitious in their technique, composition and colouring than other artists of her time.

Where the Waves Meet

Studying Ancher and her works from a contemporary standpoint we see a woman contending with external change: the major social, cultural and intellectual developments taking place at the turn of the century. At the same time, we see her reckoning with internal conflicts: her ties to the traditional values with which she had been raised and the liberated perspectives she encountered as part of her artistic community. In Skagen, Ancher was simultaneously connected to and set apart from the world at large [fig. 24]. This position enabled her to depict the subjects and themes closest to her, while also presenting them through a detached, modernist lens, exploring new approaches to colour and form.

In Skagen, where the two seas meet at Grenen, they break and crash together, forming tempestuous waves. If we extend this metaphor to consider Ancher's artistic output, it was precisely through this confrontation, the meeting of opposites, that she was able to produce some of the most radical work to come out of the Skagen artist colony.

Cat. 46
Louise Bonfils
Evening light from Stavanger Fjord, 1910
Oil on canvas
102.2 × 99 cm
Collection of Sandi Toksvig

Cat. 47
Marie Sandholt
A view from Gothersgade Towards the Botanical Gardens of Copenhagen, undated
Oil on canvas
46 × 66 cm
Collection of Sandi Toksvig

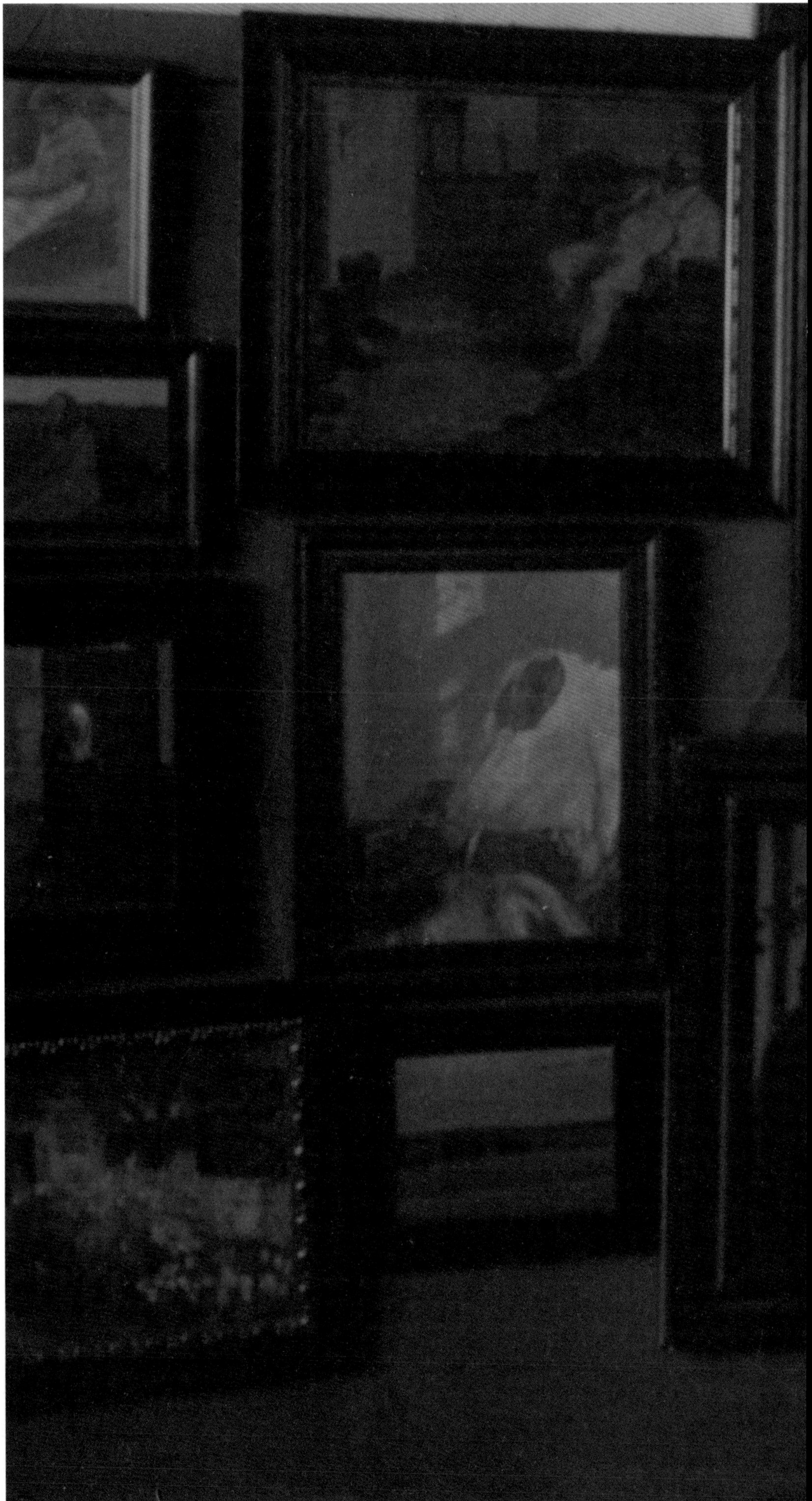

Fig. 24
Unknown photographer
Anna Ancher in Front of a Wall with Her Own Paintings, after 1913
Photograph
Skagens Museum

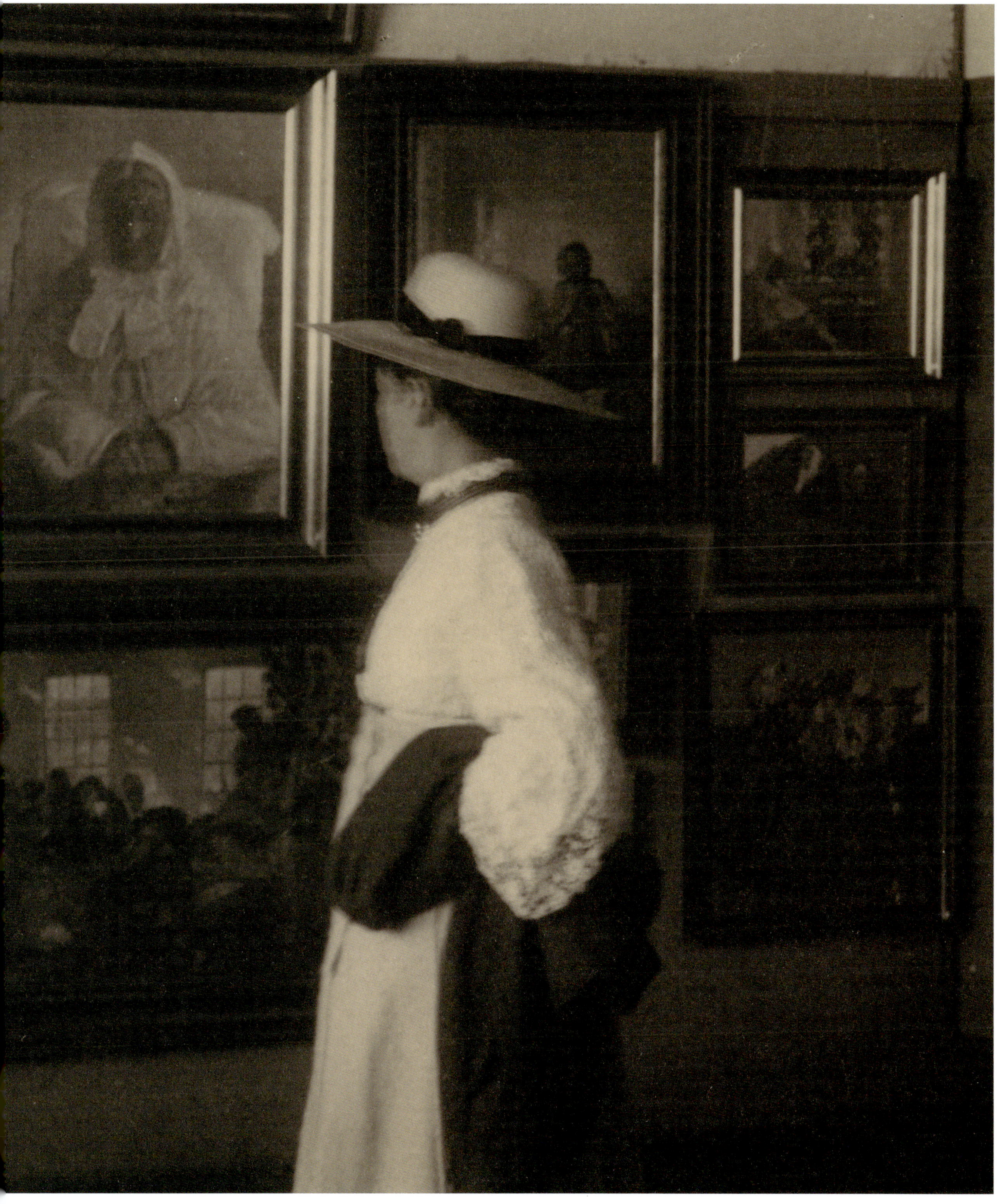

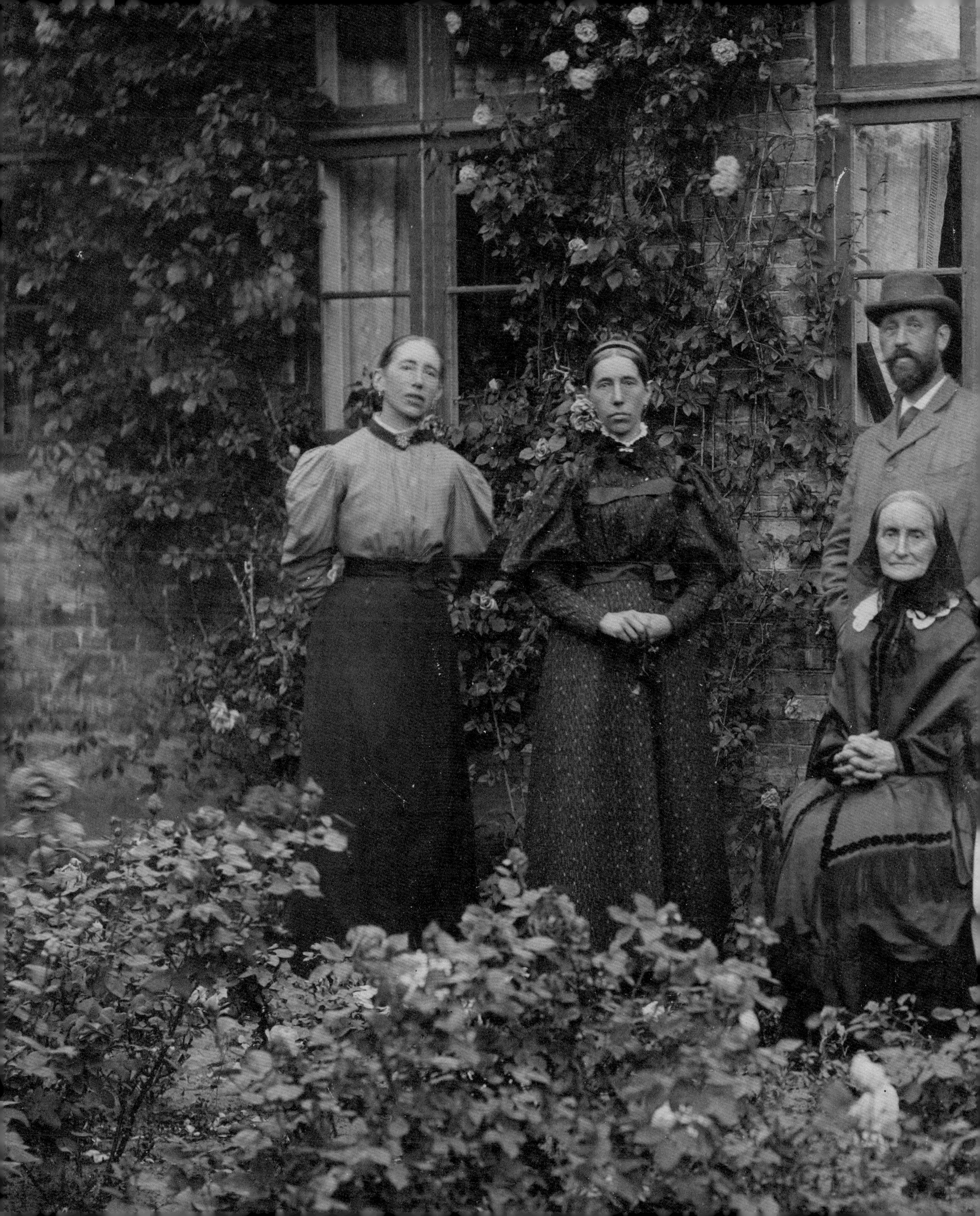

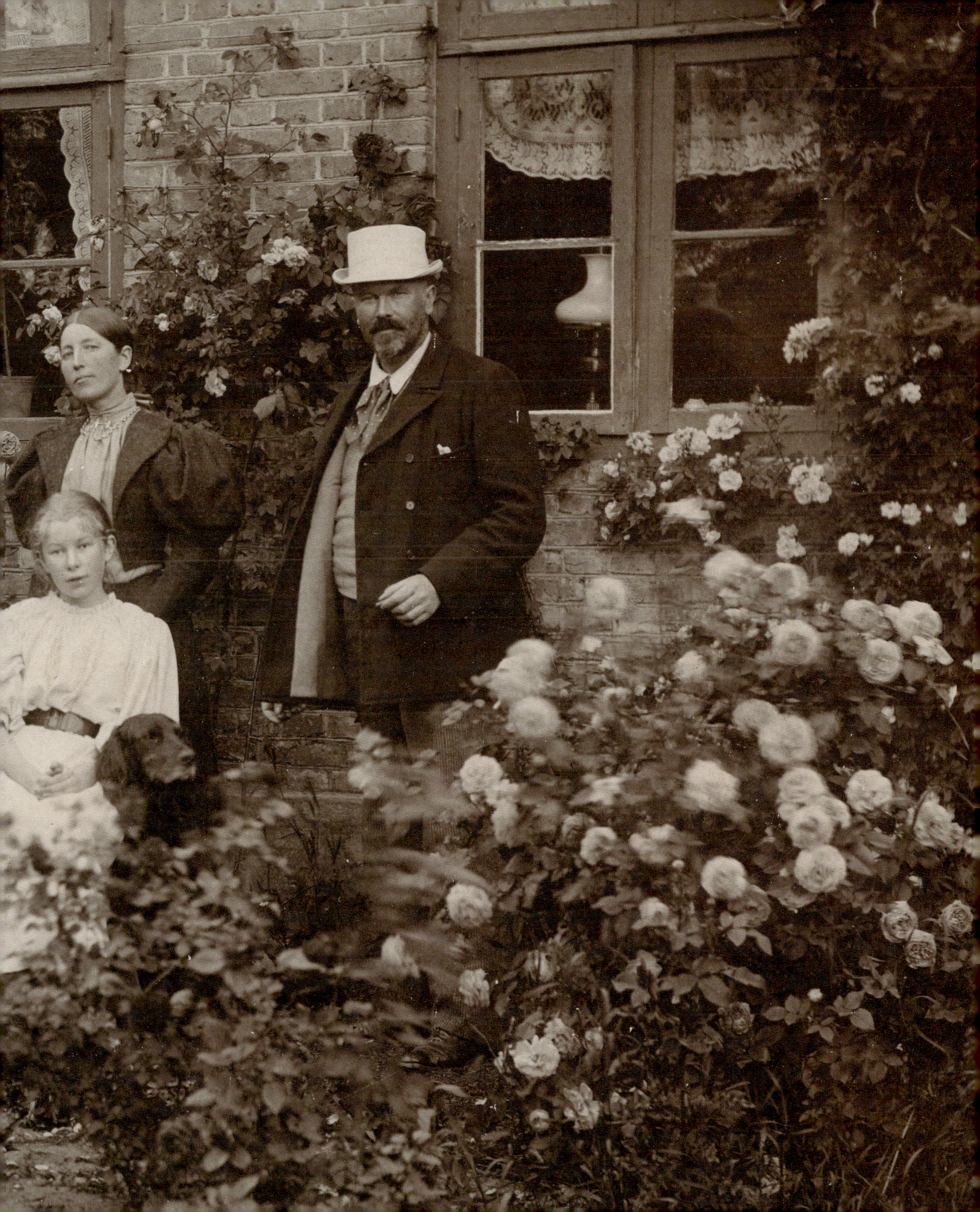

List of Exhibition Works

Listed in Chronological Order:

Anna Ancher, *Self-Portrait*, c. 1879, oil on canvas, 18.8 × 11.6 cm, Skagens Museum, HAF3003 [Cat. 1]

Anna Ancher, *Stine Bollerhus Counts the Money Earned Selling Bread*, 1879, oil on canvas, 52.7 × 35.5 cm, Skagens Museum, SKM1632 [Cat. 3]

Anna Ancher, *Old Man Whittling Sticks*, 1880, oil on panel, 21.4 × 27 cm, Skagens Museum, SKM1029 [Cat. 2]

Anna Ancher, *At the Meal*, 1880s, oil on panel, 39 × 29.2 cm, Skagens Museum, SKM737 [Cat. 28]

Anna Ancher, *Fisherman with Red Scarf*, 1880s, oil on canvas, 31.1 × 25.8 cm, Skagens Museum, SKM1203 [Cat. 31]

Anna Ancher, *Boats at Sønderstrand, Moonlight*, c. 1883, oil on canvas, 25.2 × 19.5 cm, Skagens Museum, HAF1019 [Cat. 21]

Anna Ancher, *The Maid in the Kitchen*, 1883–86, oil on canvas, 87.7 × 68.5 cm, The Hirschsprung Collection [Cat. 4]

Anna Ancher, *Old Lene Plucking a Goose*, 1885/90, oil on canvas, 70.5 × 54 cm, Skagens Museum, SKM868 [Cat. 23]

Anna Ancher, *Young Mother with her Child*, 1887, oil on canvas, 41 × 32 cm, Skagens Museum, SKM1870 [Cat. 26]

Anna Ancher, *Sunlight in the Blue Room*, 1891, oil on canvas, 65.2 × 58.8 cm, Skagens Museum, SKM222 [Cat. 8]

Anna Ancher, *An Old Couple with their Rabbits*, 1891/93, oil on card, 23.5 × 19.5 cm, Skagens Museum, SKM775 [Cat. 24]

Anna Ancher, *Helga Ancher and Ane Torup on the Garden Bench*, before 1892, oil on card, 23.8 × 32.8 cm, Skagens Museum, HAF2002 [Cat. 18]

Anna Ancher, *A Vaccination. Study*, 1898/99, oil on canvas on card, 26.9 × 34.9 cm, Skagens Museum, SKM1224 [Cat. 11]

Anna Ancher, *Study of a Seamstress in Blue*, c. 1899, oil on canvas, glued on card, 21 × 29 cm, Skagens Museum, HAF206 [Cat. 9]

Anna Ancher, *A Young Girl from Skagen*, c. 1900, oil on canvas, 32.2 × 23.5 cm, Skagens Museum, SKM1204 [Cat. 29]

Anna Ancher, *Grief*, 1902, oil on canvas, 86.5 × 73.8 cm, Skagens Museum, SKM1468 [Cat. 34]

Anna Ancher, *Grief. Study*, c. 1902, oil on canvas, 41.6 × 28.8 cm, Skagens Museum, HAF65 [Cat. 35]

Anna Ancher, *Women Plucking Chickens*, 1902, oil on canvas, 32.3 × 50.4 cm, Skagens Museum, SKM424 [Cat. 38]

Anna Ancher, *A Field Sermon*, 1903, oil on canvas, 100.5 × 145 cm, Skagens Museum, SKM302 [Cat. 37]

Anna Ancher, *Lunch Before the Hunt*, 1903, oil on canvas, 48.2 × 56.8 cm, Skagens Museum, SKM1246 [Cat. 5]

Anna Ancher, *Plucking the Geese*, 1904, oil on canvas, 55 × 67 cm, SMK, National Gallery of Denmark [Cat. 39]

Anna Ancher, *Harvesters*, 1905, oil on canvas, 56.2 × 65 cm, Skagens Museum, SKM358 [Cat. 15]

Anna Ancher, *Interior with Red Poppies*, 1905, oil on canvas, 43.4 × 56.2 cm, Skagens Museum, SKM1465 [Cat. 42]

Anna Ancher, *Children Playing on Skagen Beach*, c. 1905, oil on card, glued on wood, 24.7 × 31 cm, Skagens Museum, SKM1604 [Cat. 22]

Anna Ancher, *Profile Portrait of a Woman from Skagen*, c. 1905, oil on panel, 39 × 29.2 cm, Skagens Museum, SKM1266 [Cat. 30]

Anna Ancher, *Two Little Girls Being Taught How to Sew*, c. 1907, oil on canvas, 26.9 × 21.8 cm, Skagens Museum, SKM868 [Cat. 10]

Anna Ancher, *Three Old Seamstresses*, 1910, oil on canvas, 54.8 × 68.7 cm, Skagens Museum, SKM734 [Cat. 25]

Anna Ancher, *Mrs Brøndum at the Bed of her Daughter Agnes*, 1910, oil on canvas, 42.3 × 52.4 cm, Skagens Museum, HAF1003 [Cat. 33]

Anna Ancher, *Mrs Brøndum in the Red Room*, c. 1910, oil on canvas, 23.6 × 31.8 cm, Skagens Museum, HAF2013 [Cat. 40]

Anna Ancher, *At the Grave*, 1913, oil on canvas, 79.5 × 61.4 cm, Skagens Museum, SKM1342 [Cat. 14]

Anna Ancher, *Mrs Ane Brøndum in the Blue Room*, 1913, oil on canvas, 55.8 × 42.7 cm, Skagens Museum, SKM1097 [Cat. 6]

Anna Ancher, *Evening Sun in the Artist's Studio at Markvej*, after 1913, oil on canvas, 52.6 × 39.2 cm, Skagens Museum, HAF5078 [Cat. 7]

Anna Ancher, *A Girl in the Garden in Summertime. Skagen*, 1914, oil on card, 35 × 28 cm, Skagens Museum, SKM1922 [Cat. 19]

Anna Ancher, *The Old Window*, 1914, oil on canvas, 44 × 40.4 cm, Skagens Museum, SKM1693 [Cat. 43]

Anna Ancher, *Daphnesvej*, c. 1915, oil on plywood, 36.5 × 47 cm, Skagens Museum, SKM1165 [Cat. 16]

Anna Ancher, *Østerbyvej*, c. 1915, oil on canvas glued on card, 34 × 41.5 cm, Skagens Museum, SKM1269 [Cat. 17]

Anna Ancher, *The Artist's Dead Mother*, 1916, oil on card, 24.7 × 39.7 cm, Skagens Museum, HAF5106 [Cat. 32]

Anna Ancher, *Interior. Brøndum's Annex*, c. 1916, oil on panel, 44.4 × 37.9 cm, Skagens Museum, SKM1210 [Cat. 12]

Anna Ancher, *After the Labours of the Day*, 1917, oil on canvas, 52 × 64 cm, Skagens Museum, SKM2008 [Cat. 41]

Anna Ancher, *A Woman Knitting. Evening Light*, 1919, oil on canvas, 82.5 × 64.5 cm, Skagens Museum, SKM1590 [Cat. 27]

Anna Ancher, *Blue Sunset*, undated, oil on canvas, 43.3 × 68.5 cm, Skagens Museum, HAF5246 [Cat. 20]

Anna Ancher, *Fireworks on Fyrbakken*, undated, oil on canvas, 38.8 × 57.5 cm, Skagens Museum, HAF3262 [Cat. 36]

Anna Ancher, *Moorland*, undated, oil on canvas, 22.7 × 27.8 cm, Skagens Museum, HAF3079 [Cat. 13]

Anna Ancher's Contemporaries:

Marie Luplau, *Landscape from Vallerød with a Rye Field*, 1903, oil on canvas, 42 × 29 cm, Collection of Sandi Toksvig [Cat. 44]

Louise Bonfils, *Evening Light from Stavanger Fjord*, 1910, oil on canvas, 35 × 55 cm, Collection of Sandi Toksvig [Cat. 46]

Emilie Mundt, *Woman Reading by a Window*, 1914, oil on canvas, 61 × 52 cm, Collection of Sandi Toksvig [Cat. 45]

Marie Sandholdt, *A View from Gothersgade Towards the Botanical Gardens of Copenhagen*, undated, oil on canvas, 87 × 90 cm, Collection of Sandi Toksvig [Cat. 47]

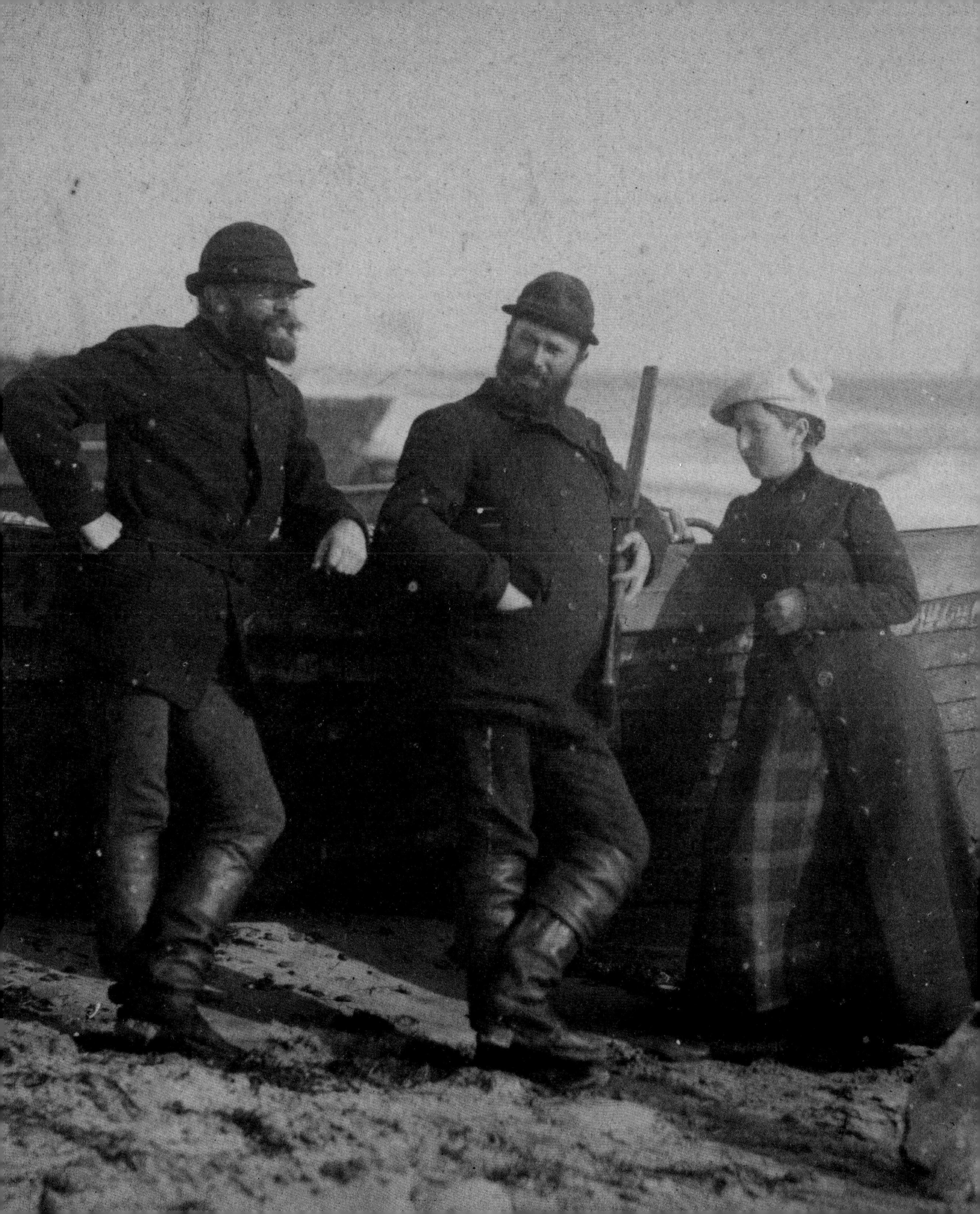

Bibliography

Alfort 2025
Sara Alfort, 'She Would Never Settle for Anything Less: The Life Choices of Women Artists during the Modern Breakthrough' in Copenhagen/Randers 2025, pp. 258–77.

Amsterdam 2023
Pieter Roelofs and Gregor J.M Weber (eds.) in *Vermeer*, exh. cat., Amsterdam (Rijksmuseum), 2023.

Bøgh Jensen 2011
Mette Bøgh Jensen (ed.), *Brøndum's dining room – in gratitude for happy days*, Skagens Museum, 2011.

Boime 1986
Albert Boime, *The Academy and French Painting in the Nineteenth Century*, New Haven, 1986.

Copenhagen/Helsinki/Oslo 2015
Gabriel Weisberg, Anna-Maria von Bonsdorff, Hanne Selkokari (eds.), *Japanomania in the Nordic Countries: 1875–1918*, exh. cat., Copenhagen (SMK), Helsinki (Ateneum) and Oslo (Nasjonalmuseet) 2015.

Copenhagen/Randers 2025
Lise Mogensen Bech and Lene Bøgh Rønberg (eds.), *Women Artists in Denmark 1880–1910*, exh. cat., Copenhagen (The Hirschsprung Collection) and Randers (Randers Kunstmuseum), 2025.

Copenhagen/Skagen/Lillehammer 2020
Peter Nørgaard Larsen (ed.), *Anna Ancher*, exh. cat., Copenhagen (SMK), Skagen (Skagens Museum) and Lillehammer (Lillehammer Kunstmuseum), 2020.

Fabritius 2007
Elisabeth Fabritius, *Danish Artists' Colonies*, Faaborg, 2007.

Fabritius 2008
Elisabeth Fabritius, Anna Ancher: The Pastels, Copenhagen, 2008

Fabritius 2013
Elisabeth Fabritius, 'An Unusual Fate', in Washington 2013, pp. 13–31.

Fabritius 2018
Elisabeth Fabritius, *Skagensmalerne Anna og Michael Ancher og deres kreds: breve og fotografier 1866–1935*, 5 vols., Copenhagen, 2018.

Fabritius 2020
Elisabeth Fabritius, 'Ancher and the Men of the Modern Breakthrough', in Copenhagen/Skagen/Lillehammer 2020, pp. 163–75.

Groningen/Munich 2012–13
David Jackson (ed.), *Nordic Art: The Modern Breakthrough 1860–1910*, exh. cat., Groningen (Groninger Museum) Munich (Hypo-Kulturstiftung), 2012.

Harbo Lehmann 2022a
Mette Harbo Lehmann, 'Krøyer in France', in Paris/Skagen 2021–22, pp. 35–57.

Harbo Lehmann 2022b
Mette Harbo Lehmann, 'Krøyer and the Scandinavian Artists in Paris', in Paris/Skagen 2021–22, pp. 59–71.

Høgsbro Østergaard 2020
Cecilie Høgsbro Østergaard, 'The Woman Question' in Copenhagen/Skagen/Lillehammer 2020, pp. 179–93.

Houlberg Rung 2020
Mette Houlberg Rung, 'Skagen as Studio' in Copenhagen/Skagen/Lillehammer 2020, pp. 69–93.

Kolle Martinsen 2025
Lone Kolle Martinsen, 'The Overlooked Faith: Feminism, Religion and Emancipation' in Copenhagen/Randers 2025, pp. 190–209

London 2019
Jennifer Scott and Helen Hillyard (eds.), *Rembrandt's Light*, exh. cat., London (Dulwich Picture Gallery), 2019.

London/The Hague 2019
Ariane van Suchtelen (ed.), *Nicolaes Maes: Dutch Master of the Golden Age*, exh. cat., London (National Gallery) and The Hague (Mauritshuis), 2019.

London 2023
MaryAnne Stevens (ed.) *After Impressionism: Inventing Modern Art*, exh. cat., London (National Gallery), 2023.

London 2024
Karen Serres (ed.), *Monet and London: Views of the Thames*, exh. cat., London (Courtauld), 2024.

Madsen 1929
Karl Madsen, *Skagens Malere og Skagens Museum*, Copenhagen, 1929.

Mejer Antonsen 2017
Inge Mejer Antonsen, *Et Kunstner Hjem: Michael og Anna Anchers Hus i Skagen og familiens boliger gennem årene*, Skagens Museum, 2017.

Norgaard Larsen 2012
Peter Norgaard Larsen, 'With and Against the Modern: Nordic counter-images to Modernity', in Groningen/Munich 2012–13.

Ohlsen 2020
Nils Ohlsen 'Notes from Paris', in Copenhagen/Skagen/Lillehammer 2020, pp. 140–59.

Paris/Skagen 2021–22
Mette Harbo Lehmann and Dominique Lobstein (ed.), *Krøyer and Paris. French Connections and Nordic Light*, exh. cat., Paris (Musée Marmottan Monet) and Skagen (Skagens Museum), 2022.

Rudy Price 2016
Alice Rudy Price, 'Loss, the Female Nude, and Anna Ancher's Song: A Woman's Own Modernism', in *Scandinavian Studies*, vol. 88, no. 2 (Summer 2016).

Skagen 2025
Øjeblikke fra Skagen, exh.cat., Skagen (Skagens Museum), 2025.

Svanholm 2003
Lise Svanholm (ed.), *Skagen leksikon. Malerne, modellerne, værkerne og stederne*, Copenhagen, 2003.

Svanholm 2005
Lise Svanholm (ed.), *Breve fra Anna Ancher*, Copenhagen, 2005.

Uhlenbeclk, Van Tilborgh and Oikawa 2018
Chris Uhlenbeck, Louis van Tilborgh, Shigeru Oikawa (eds.), *Japanese Prints: The Collection of Vincent van Gogh*, London, 2018.

Washington 2013
Elizabeth Lynch (ed.), *A World Apart: Anna Ancher and the Skagen Art Colony*, exh. cat., Washington, D.C (National Museum of Women in the Arts), 2013.

NEWSPAPERS AND MAGAZINES

Christian Andersen 1860
Hans Christian Andersen, 'Skagen', *Folkekalender for Danmark*. 1860, December 1859.

'Kunstudstillingen paa Charlottenborg. III', *Berlingske Politiske og Avertissementstidende*, 25 May 1880.

'Kunstudstillingen på Charlottenborg IV', *Fyens Stiftstidende* and *Slagelse-Posten*, 4 May, 1880.

Müller 1881
Sigurd Müller, 'Fra Kunstudstillingen paa Charlottenborg', *Dagbladet*, Copenhagen, 6 May, 1881.

H 1883 H., 'Genremaleriet paa Kunstudstillingen ved Charlottenborg', *Nationaltidende*, Copenhagen, 20 May, 1883.

C.H 1892 C.H., 'Kunstudstillingen ved Charlottenborg IV', *Nationaltidende*, Copenhagen, 7 May, 1892.

'Amatør': 'Gennem Salene', Politiken, Copenhagen, 1 April, 1892.

'Kunstudstillingen ved Charlottenborg II', *Berlingske Tidende*, Copenhagen, 26 April, 1892

'I Forbigaaende' in *Nationaltidende* 16 April, 1907.

Unknown author, 'Malerinden Anna Ancher fylder 70 Aar. Et Interview med Fru Ancher. – Nogle Data af en stor Kunstnerindes Liv', *Fyns Venstreblad*, 14 August, 1928.

Unknown author, 'Malerinden Anna Ancher fylder 70 Aar. Et Interview med Fru Ancher. – Nogle Data af en stor Kunstnerindes Liv', *Fyns Venstreblad*, 14 August, 1929.

Schwarz 1939
Walter Schwarz, 'Skagens Datter', *Politiken*, 17 August 1939.

ARCHIVES

The Van Gogh Letters Project

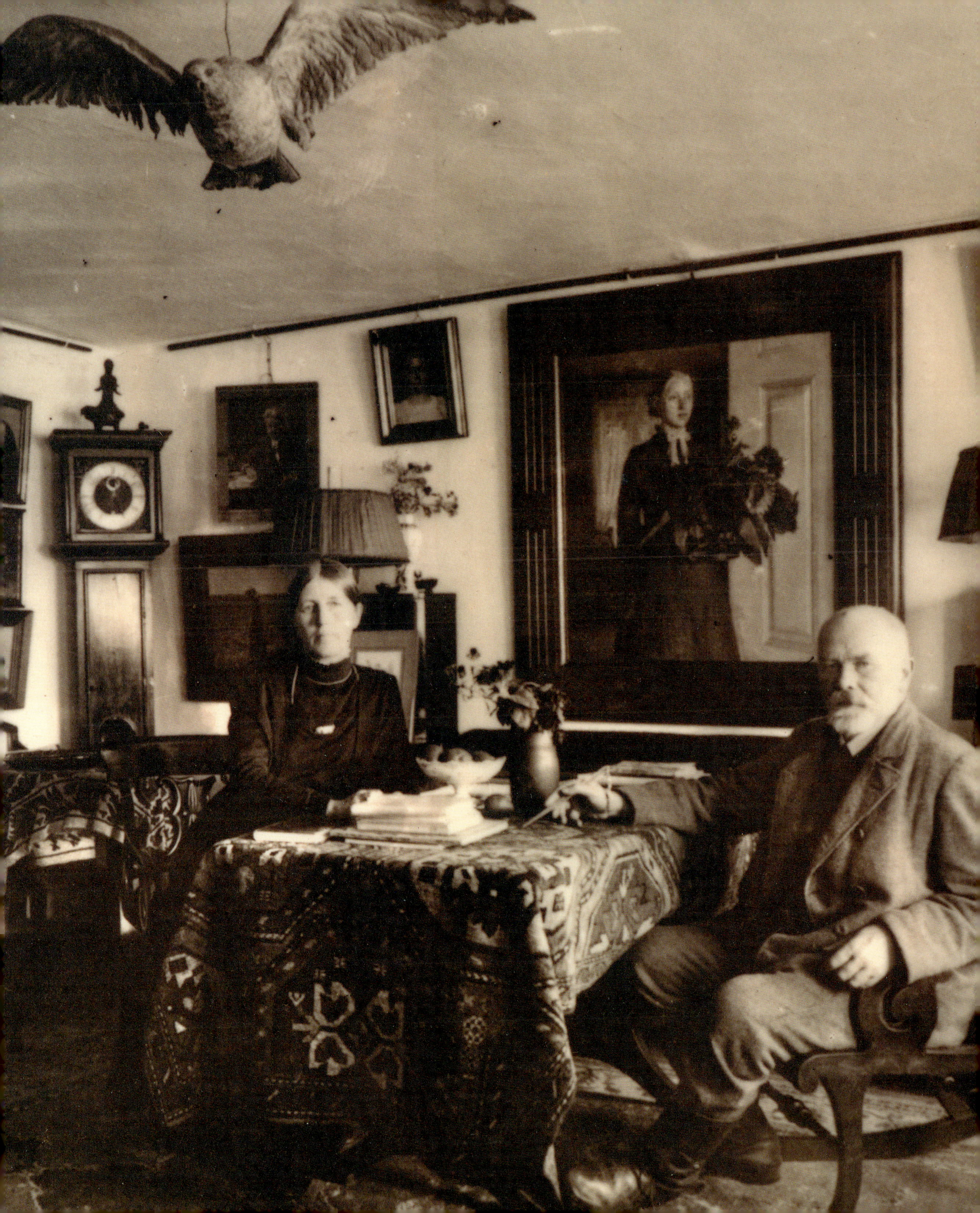

Notes

AN ARTIST IN HER OWN RIGHT
Mette Harbo Lehmann

1 Madsen 1929, p.45.
2 Anonymous, 'Malerinden Anna Ancher fylder 70 Aar. Et Interview med Fru Ancher. – Nogle Data af en stor Kunstnerindes Liv', in *Fyns Venstreblad*, 14 August 1929.
3 Fabritius 2018, vol. 1, p. 36.
4 Letter from Michael Ancher to Anna Brøndum, Copenhagen, 17 January 1875, in Fabritius 2018, vol. 1, p. 85.
5 Svanholm 2003, pp. 34–35.
6 Letter from Ane Hedvig Brøndum to Anna Brøndum, Skagen, October 5, 1875, in Fabritius 2018, vol. 1, p. 105.
7 The exhibition catalogues are found at The Royal Library in Copenhagen.
8 Anonymous, 'Kunstudstillingen paa Charlottenborg. III', in *Berlingske Politiske og Avertissementstidende*, 25 May 1880, p. 1 and the local newspapers; Anonymous, Kunstudstillingen på Charlottenborg IV' in *Fyens Stiftstidende* and *Slagelse-Posten*, 4 May 1880.
9 The artists noted in Brøndum's Hotel's guest books are cited in Bøgh Jensen 2011, p. 292.
10 Elisabeth Fabritius, 'Ancher and the Modern Breakthrough', in Copenhagen/Skagen/Lillehammer 2020, p. 164.
11 There is one rare exception from this rule in Danish art history. A married female painter with an active career before the 1870s was Polish born, Danish married Elisabeth Jerichau Baumann (1818–1881).
12 Letter from Henrik Pontoppidan to Michael Ancher, Jørlunde, 24 February 1884, in Fabritius 2018, vol. 1, p. 601.
13 Letter from Peder Severin Krøyer to Michael Ancher, København, 5 April 1884, in Fabritius 2018, vol. 1, p. 611.
14 Letter from Michael Ancher to Georg Brandes, Skagen, 19 October 1883, in Fabritius 2018, vol. 1, pp. 568-70.
15 Harbo Lehmann 2022a, p. 57.
16 Anonymous, 'Malerinden Anna Ancher fylder 70 Aar. Et Interview med Fru Ancher. – Nogle Data af en stor Kunstnerindes Liv', in *Fyns Venstreblad*, 14 August 1928.
17 Anonymous, "I Forbigaaende" in *Nationaltidende*, 16 April 1907.
18 Letter from Ane Brøndum to Michael Ancher, Skagen, 9 April 1907, in Fabritius 2018, vol. 4, pp. 36–37.
19 From 1895 she could exhibit without censure at the spring exhibition, as she then had her fifteenth anniversary and was automatically granted the right to do so.

LIFE IN A SUNBEAM
Mette Harbo Lehmann

1 Madsen 1929, p.48.
2 Boime 1986, Chapter 4: 'The Academic Sketch'.
3 Houlberg Rung, 2020, p.79.
4 Letter from Michael Ancher to H. Boesgaard-Rasmussen, 12 May 1906, in Fabritius 2018, vol. 3, pp. 714–15. *A Blind Woman in her Room. Evening Sun*, The Hirschsprung Collection. *The Maid in the Kitchen*, The Hirschsprung Collection. *Two Old People Plucking Gulls*, The Hirschsprung Collection. *Portrait of an Old Woman*, Unidentified, was exhibited at Kunstforeningen Gl. Strand. *A Funeral*, The National Gallery of Denmark. *A Field Sermon*, Gift from the artist 1928 to Skagens Museum. *Kyhn in his Studio*, Gift from the artist 1928 to Skagens Museum.
5 Müller 1881.
6 *Old Couple Plucking Gulls*, 1883, The Hirschsprung Collection, inventory number 6.
7 H 1883, p. 2.
8 Anonymous, 'Kunstudstillingen ved Charlottenborg II', *Berlingske Tidende*, Copenhagen, 26 April 1892.
9 C.H 1892
10 'Amatør': 'Gennem Salene', *Politiken*, Copenhagen, 1 April 1892.
11 She may also have changed the colour of a room based on an artistic consideration, which seems to be the case for *A Funeral*, where sketches indicate that the room has been tested in yellow and then painted over with a red background colour.
12 Svanholm 2003, p. 28.
13 The painting is presumed wrongly dated by Anna Ancher herself according to the museum registrations.
14 *Portrait of the Norwegian Painter Kitty Kielland*, 1889, oil on canvas, 28.5 × 24 cm, Skagens Museum, HAF7.
15 *Valdemar Schønheyder Møller*, 1893, oil on canvas, 35 × 32 cm, Skagens Museum, SKM630.

LOOKING BACK, LOOKING FORWARDS: ANNA ANCHER'S ARTISTIC INFLUENCES
Helen Hillyard

1 Vincent van Gogh to Theo van Gogh, on or about 10 October 1885 (no. 534). 'Letter 534. To Theo van Gogh. on or about Saturday, 10 October 1885.' *The Van Gogh Letters Project*, accessed 20 January 2025, https://vangoghletters.org/vg/letters/let534/letter.html.
2 Anna Ancher to Martha Johansen, 11 June 1891, in Fabritius 2018, vol. 2, no. 850.
3 Walter Schwarz was among the first, describing Anna Ancher as 'the first modern colourist in Denmark'. Schwarz 1939.
4 Anna Ancher, *Female Model with Headdress in the style of Rembrandt*, c. 1875/77, oil on canvas, 31.9/31.8 × 24/23.4 cm, HAF3057. Anna Ancher, *A Lumpfish*, unknown date, oil on canvas, HAF243; Anna Ancher, *A Copper Kettle*, c. 1875/77, oil on canvas, 25.6/25.5 × 26.3 cm, HAF3053; Anna Ancher, *A brass dish, mortar and ceramic bowl*, c. 1875/77, oil on canvas, 25.7 × 34 cm, HAF3054. All Skagens Museum.
5 The Academy did not formally admit women until 1888 and, even then, the women's school was located on a different site. The women's school was not fully incorporated into the Royal Academy until 1908.
6 Anna Ancher to Viggo Johansen in Svanholm 2005, p. 90.
7 Alfort 2025, p. 260.
8 Anna Ancher to the Brøndum family and Helga Ancher, 1885 in Fabritius 2018, vol. 2, no. 513.
9 It is unclear when these photographs were acquired or who acquired them, however, it is possible that they acted as a sort of reference collection for the artist couple. The photographs were recently catalogued as part of the research project *Tilstedeværelsesbeviser. Fotografiet og dets betydning i kunstnerkolonien i Skagen* led by Mette Bøgh Jensen at Skagens Museum.
10 See Gregor J.M Weber, 'Windows Between Outer and Inner Worlds', in Amsterdam 2023, p. 162.
11 See Ariane van Suchtelen, 'Genre: Picturing Everyday Life', in London/The Hague 2019, p. 65.
12 Anna Ancher to Martha Johanson, 25 November 1888, in Fabritius 2018, vol. 2, no. 637.
13 Laurits Tuxen, *En gammel ven, Rembrandt*, undated, pencil and watercolour on paper, 163 × 138 mm, HAF1082, Skagens Museum. The author thanks Mette Harbo Lehmann for bringing this object to her attention.
14 Fabritius 2013, pp. 19–21.
15 Helen Hillyard, 'Manipulating Light', in London 2019, p. 67.
16 Another interesting point of comparison might be Rembrandt's *Hundred Guilder Print*, a reproduction of which has also been catalogued within the Anchers' photographic collection.
17 Helen Hillyard, 'Lighting the Figure', in London 2019, p. 67.
18 There are numerous reproductions of drawings by both Da Vinci and Raphael catalogued in the Anchers' photographic collection, as well as portraits of Rembrandt at different ages.
19 The Danish Golden Age (c. 1815–50) focused on painting landscapes and real life, albeit in a manner that appears highly idealised when compared to the work of the Skagen painters. Key figures of the movement included Christoffer Wilhelm Eckersberg (1783–1853), Christen Købke (1810–1848), Martinus Rørbye (1803–1848) and the sculptor Bertel Thorvaldsen (1770–1844).
20 Anna Ancher to Karl and Thora Madsen, 17 April 1916, in Svanholm 2005, p. 153.
21 See MaryAnne Stevens, 'Paris', in London 2023, p. 62.
22 Ohlsen 2020, p. 140.
23 It is likely Anna Ancher and her husband attended shows of French art in Copenhagen organised by the brewer and art collector Carl Jacobsen (1842–1914) in 1879 and the artist and art historian Karl Madsen (1855–1938) in 1889. The latter exhibition included Paul Gauguin's collection of impressionist art, which had been left to his Danish wife, Mette (1850–1920).
24 Norgaard Larsen 2012, p. 208.
25 See Karren Serres, 'Catalogue: Waterloo Bridge, Effect of Sunlight in the Fog', in London 2024, p. 122.
26 See MaryAnne Stevens, 'After Impressionism: Inventing Modern Art', in London 2023, p. 11.

27 Fabritius 2020, p. 174.
28 See also Anna Ancher, *Study of the Head of a Sewing Girl*, 1890, pastel on canvas, 39.5 × 30 cm, Skagens Museum.
29 Another example of Anna Ancher's rare symbolist works is her painting *Yellow Irises*, also in the collection of Skagens Museum (SKM1915).
30 Anna Ancher to Helga Ancher, 22 October 1901, in Fabritius 2018, vol. 3, no. 1484.
31 Paul Gauguin, *Study of a Nude (Suzanne sewing)*, 1880, oil on canvas, 114.5 cm × 79.5 cm, Ny Carlsberg Glyptotek, Copenhagen.
32 Høgsbro Østergaard 2020, p. 188.
33 Ibid., p. 192.
34 Uhlenbeclk, Van Tilborgh and Oikawa 2018, p. 13.
35 Anna and Michael Ancher, *Mrs Ancher by the Desk*, 1892, oil on canvas, 37 × 46 cm, Skagens Museum.
36 See Nils Ohlsen, 'From Prop to Total Work of Art: A Japanese Perspective on Nordic Interior Painting', in Copenhagen/Helsinki/Oslo 2015, pp. 176–77.
37 Ohlsen 2020, pp. 149–52.
38 See 'Anna Ancher 1859–1935', in Copenhagen/Randers 2025, p. 315.
39 From Anna Ancher's letters we can understand that Michael found it more difficult to absorb the techniques coming out of France; see Svanholm 2005, pp. 54–55.
40 Michael Ancher, *The Red Room*, 1914, oil on canvas, Ribe Kunstmuseum, RKMm0815.

'THE DESERT BETWEEN TWO ROARING SEAS': ANNA ANCHER AND SKAGEN
Helen Hillyard

1 Christian Andersen 1860, pp. 46–58.
2 Danish Golden Age painter Martinus Rørbye (1803–1848) had been the first painter to 'discover' Skagen when he visited in 1833, travelling there again for two summers in 1847 and 1848.
3 Brøndum's was the only hotel until 1884. Alternatively, artists could find private lodgings; Bøgh Jensen 2011, pp. 21, 24.
4 See Fabritius 2007.
5 Fabritius 2008.
6 In Paris, she took classes in a private academy for women, alongside Marie Triepke (1867–1940). While in Paris she also painted a portrait of Norwegian artist Kitty Kielland (1843–1914). See also Harbo Lehmann 2022b.
7 See Skagen 2025.
8 Holger Drachmann chose not to be buried in a church graveyard, and the artist's grave is instead located in the dunes close to Grenen.
9 This same subject was later depicted in Peder Severin Krøyer's large-scale work of 1906: Peder Severin Krøyer, *Midsummer Eve Bonfire on Skagen Beach*, 1906, oil on canvas, 149.5 × 257 cm, Skagens Museum.
10 From Anna Ancher, *Barndomsminder fra Skagen*, i: *Mit Hjem*, 1911, in Svanholm 2005, p. 13.
11 Anna Ancher to Martha Johansen, 1 February 1909, Svanholm 2005, pp. 146–47.
12 Michael Ancher, *The Drowned Fisherman*, 1896, oil on canvas, 212.5 × 289 cm, SMK, National Gallery of Denmark.
13 Høgsbro Østergaard 2020, pp. 183–88.
14 Rudy Price 2016, p. 100.
15 Anna Ancher's husband Michael depicted religious themes on occasion. The most monumental of these is his painting depicting the baptism of the couple's daughter Helga: Michael Ancher, *A Christening*, 1883–88, oil on canvas, 186 × 250 cm, Ribe Kunstmuseum (RKMm0006).
16 See Kolle Martinsen 2025.
17 See Houlberg Rung 2020.
18 Ibid, p. 69.
19 London 2024, pp. 34, 41–44.
20 Edgar Degas, *Combing the Hair (La Coiffure)*, c. 1896, oil on canvas, 114.3 × 146.7 cm, National Gallery, London.
21 Anna Ancher, *Portrait of Ane Hedvig Brøndum*, c. 1898, oil on canvas, 67.8 × 59.8 cm, Skagens Museum.
22 At the death of her mother, Helga Ancher locked the family home and moved to Brøndum's Hotel. At Helga Ancher's death 30 years later, the Helga Ancher foundation was established and the house was opened to the public.
23 Mejer Antonsen 2017, pp. 39–43.
24 See Skagen 2025.
25 'A woman must have money and a room of her own if she is to write fiction'; Virginia Woolf, 'A Room of One's Own', 1929.
26 'Med Hensyn til Kvindevrøvlet da har jeg netop ogsaa tænkt paa det samme som Du, at melde mig ud, jeg gjorde det forresten en Gang, saa bad Fru Gauguin om Navnet maatte blive staaende, og det var jeg fjollet nok til at sige ja til; men nu skriver jeg igjen og udmelder mig, for naar man bor heroppe saa langt borte, kan man ingen Nytte gjøre alligevel, og det er jo kedeligt at have Ansvar fra Frk. Krebs og alle de andre finder paa at gjøre.' Anna Ancher to Martha Johansen, 1892; Svanholm 2005, p. 113.
27 Høgsbro Østergaard 2020, p. 179.
28 A painting by Emilie Mundt in the collection of Skagens Museum depicts a young Anna Ancher at work. It suggests that the artists knew each other early on, possibly with Mundt acting in the capacity of a teaching assistant. According to Mette Harbo Lehmann (personal communication, 24 March 2025). Emilie Mundt, *Anna Brøndum at Kyhn's art school for women*, c. 1876, oil on canvas, Skagens Museum.
29 'Marie Luplau 1848–1925' in Copenhagen/Randers 2025, p. 293.
30 Martha Johansen to Anna Ancher, 15 February 1891, in Fabritius 2018, vol. 2, no. 821.
31 Høgsbro Østergaard 2020, p. 180.

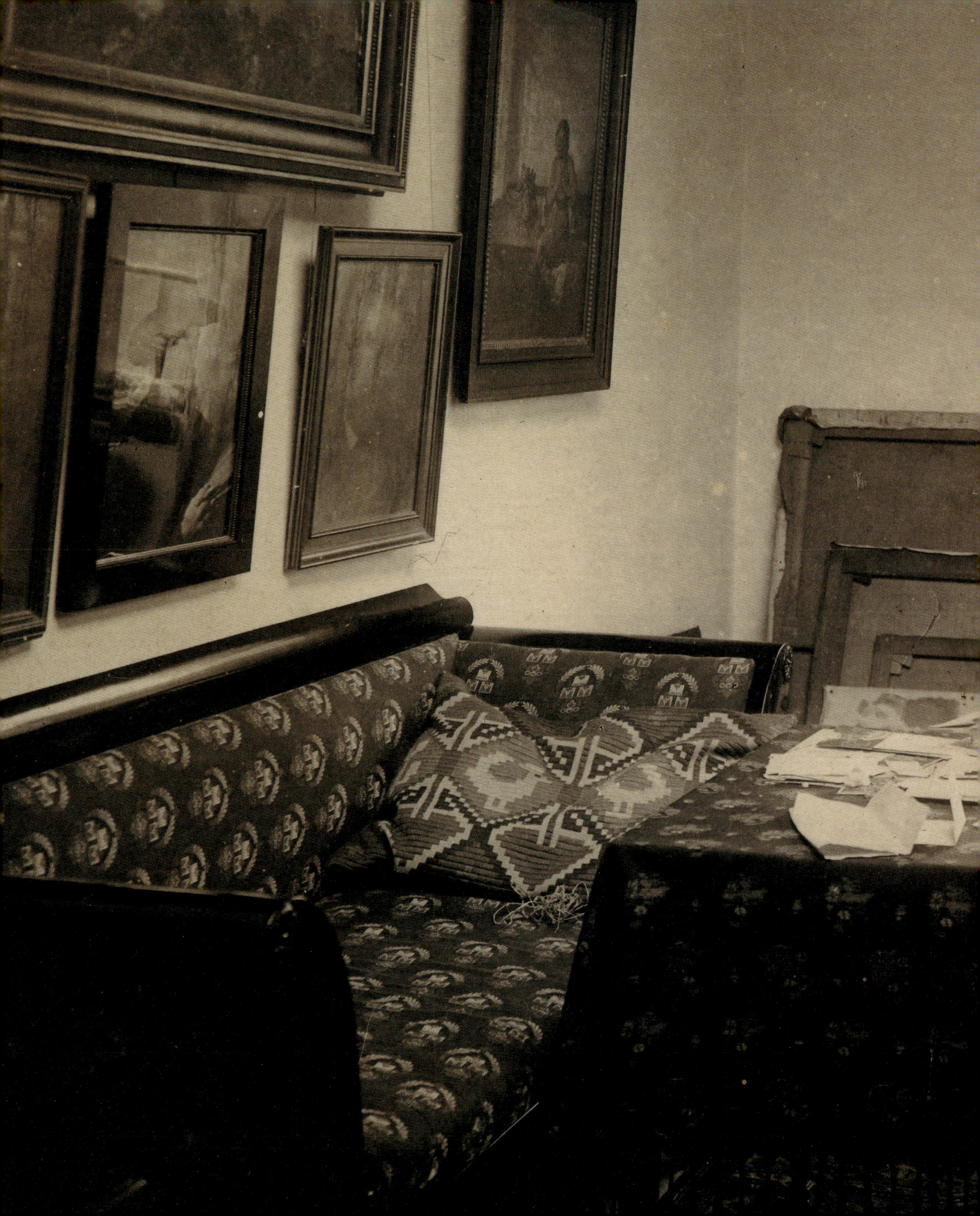

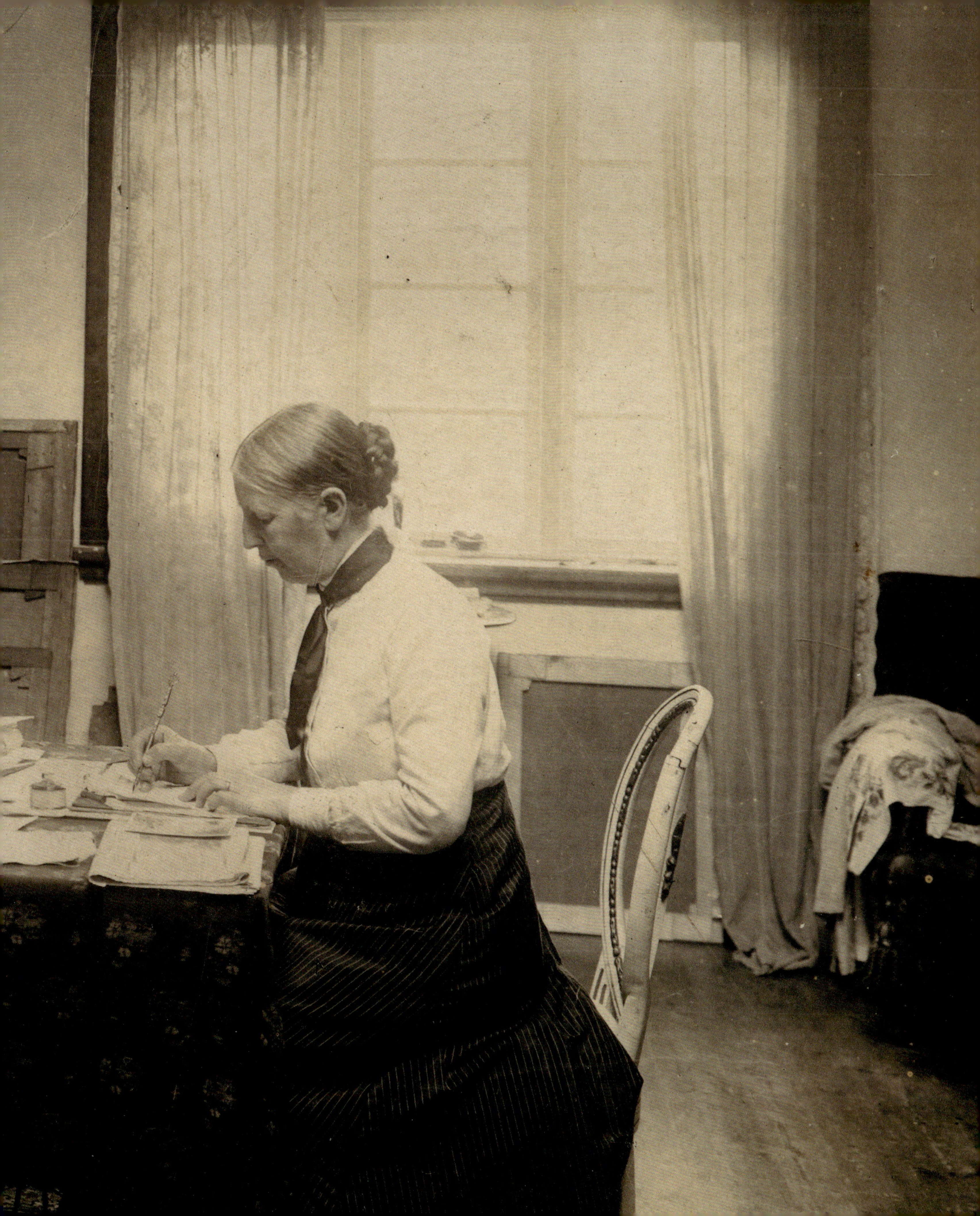

Index

Page numbers in *italics* refer to illustrations.
Artworks are by Anna Ancher unless otherwise stated

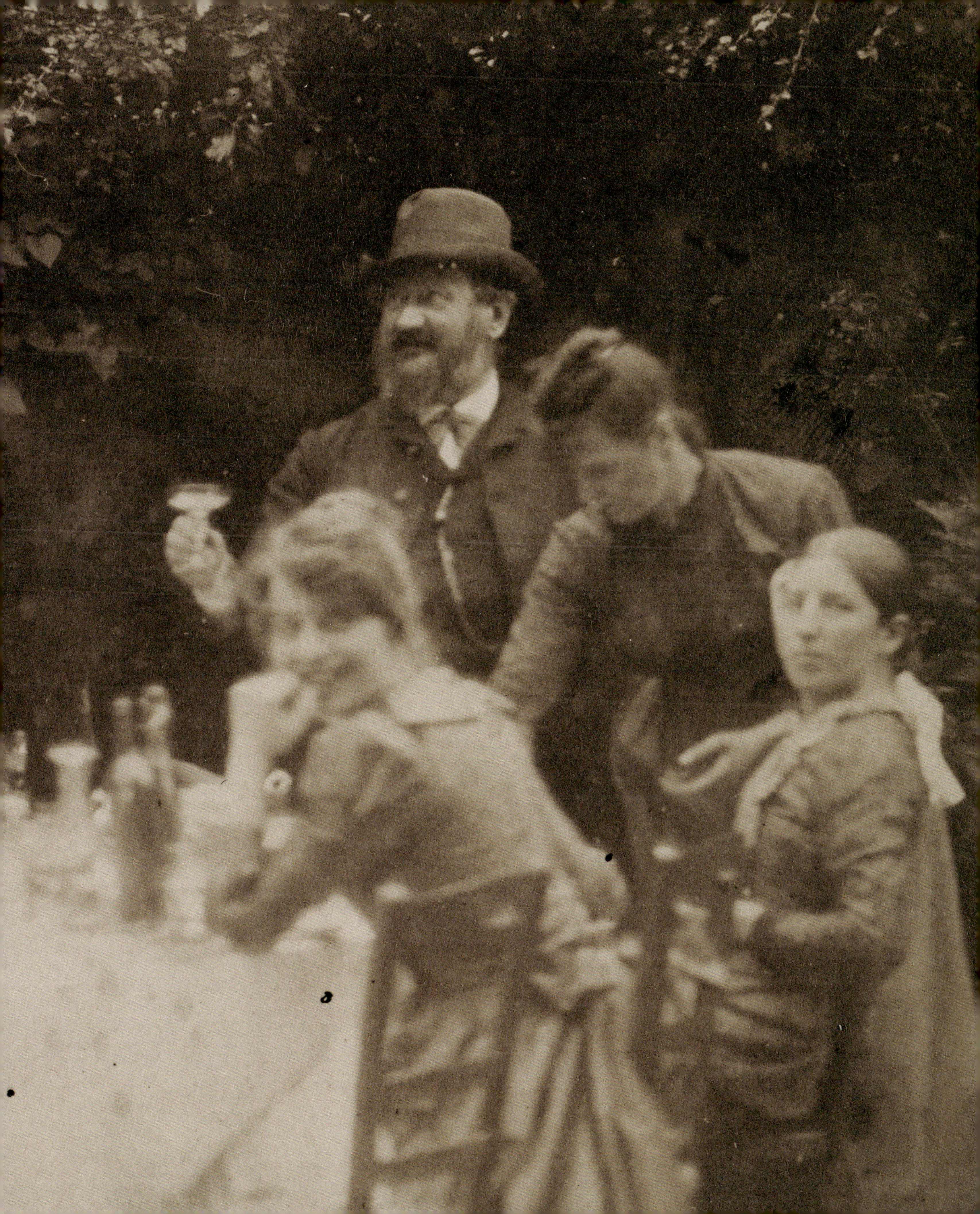

Image Credits

CATALOGUE WORKS
Cat. 1–3, 5–38, 40–43 Skagens Museum
Cat. 4 © The Hirschsprung Collection
Cat. 39 SMK Photo/Jakob Skou-Hansen
Cat. 44–47 Matthew Hollow

ESSAY FIGURES
Fig. 1 Depositum at Skagens Museum from the National Gallery of Denmark. SMK Photo/Jakob Skou-Hansen
Fig. 2–6, 8, 11, 16–21, 24 Skagens Museum
Fig. 7, 9 Rijksmuseum, Amsterdam
Fig. 10 Mauritshuis, The Hague
Fig. 12 Musée Jacquemart-André, Paris
Fig. 13 Dulwich Picture Gallery, London
Fig. 14 Musée Marmottan Monet, Paris
Fig. 15 Van Gogh Museum, Amsterdam
Fig. 22 Roberta Fortuna/Skagens Museum
Fig. 23 Gothenburg Museum of Art

THE EXPERT CONTRIBUTORS
Exhibition Design: Annabel Dalziel
Exhibition Lighting: Luminance
Art Handling: Patina Art Collection Care Ltd.
Transport and Logistics: Constantine Ltd.
Conservation: Nicole Ryder
Catalogue Design: Sandra Zellmer
Catalogue Copy Editor: Susannah Worth

THE DULWICH PICTURE GALLERY TEAM
OF STAFF AND TRUSTEES
Curator: Helen Hillyard
Curatorial Advisor: Mette Harbo Lehmann
Head of Programme and Engagement: Jane Findlay
Senior Exhibitions Manager: Imogen Lyons
Collection & Programme Committee: Helen Macintyre,
Dame Janet Vitmayer, Benedict Brogan, Adeola Gay
Publication Management: Alexander Moore,
Sophie James and Bryony Haffner

First published in Great Britain in 2025 by
Dulwich Picture Gallery on the occasion
of the exhibition *Anna Ancher: Painting Light*,
4 November 2025 – 8 March 2026.

Edited by Alexander Moore
Design and creative direction by Sandra Zellmer
Printed in the UK by &Printed

Front cover:
Anna Ancher, *Evening Sun in the Artist's Studio at Markvej*, after 1913

ISBN: 978-1-898519-54-6

FSC www.fsc.org
MIX
Paper | Supporting responsible forestry
FSC® C114687